The Presentation Secrets of Steve Jobs

How to Be
Insanely Great
in Front of Any Audience

Carmine Gallo

Mc
Graw
Hill
Education

New York   Chicago   San Francisco   Athens   London
Madrid   Mexico City   Milan   New Delhi
Singapore   Sydney   Toronto

To my father, Franco, an insanely great man
who has lived an extraordinary life

———————————

1 2 3 4 5 6 7 8 9   QFR   21 20 19 18 17 16

ISBN   978-1-259-83588-9
MHID   1-259-83588-X

e-ISBN   978-0-07-163675-9
e-MHID   0-07-163675-7

The Presentation Secrets of Steve Jobs is in no way authorized, prepared, approved, or endorsed by the Steve Jobs estate and is not affiliated with or endorsed by any of his organizations.

Interior design by Think Design LLC

CONTENTS

ACKNOWLEDGMENTS

ACKNOWLEDGMENTS

This book is a collaborative effort. The content took shape with the help of family, colleagues, and the amazing staff at McGraw-Hill. Big thanks to my editor, John Aherne, for his enthusiasm and counsel, and to Kenya Henderson, for making it all happen! McGraw-Hill design, marketing, and public relations staff are among the best in the book publishing industry. I'm honored they share my excitement about the subject.

My wife, Vanessa, manages our business at Gallo Communications Group. She worked tirelessly to prepare the manuscript. How she found the time between juggling our business and caring for our two children is beyond the scope of "mere mortals."

Many thanks to my former editor at BusinessWeek.com, Nick Leiber, who always seemed to find a way to improve my columns. As always, thank you, Ed Knappman, my encouraging agent at New England Publishing Associates. Ed's knowledge and insight are second to none.

I owe thanks to my parents, Franco and Giuseppina, for their unwavering support. Thank you, Tino, Donna, Francesco, Nick, Patty, Ken, and many other close friends and family members who understood why I couldn't be around or why I had to skip golf on weekends. Back to the course!

My girls, Josephine and Lela. You are Daddy's inspiration. All your patience during Daddy's absence will be rewarded with an insanely great visit to Chuck E. Cheese.

PREFACE

Steve Jobs transformed business presentations into an art form, and he continues to do so years after his death. Ask business professionals anywhere in the world to describe the "Steve Jobs style" of presentations, and most will have an answer. They may not be able to break it down like this book does, but they'll recognize the style as using more pictures than words and clean, minimalistic slides. The Steve Jobs style is another way of saying that a presentation is irresistible, entertaining, and engaging.

Leaders who mesmerize their audiences are often practitioners of the Jobs method. When Mark Zuckerberg takes the stage today, his presentations are nearly identical to Jobs's keynotes. Facebook is one of many companies instructing its senior managers to adopt elements of the Steve Jobs style, too. The *Wall Street Journal* once suggested that Chinese billionaire and entrepreneur Jack Ma might be the next Steve Jobs because of his charisma and theatrical flair on stage.

On the topic of communication, "I was never in his league," Bill Gates once said fondly as he remembered Steve Jobs. "I mean, it was just amazing to see how precisely he would rehearse . . . he's even a bit nervous because it's a big performance. But then he's on, and quite an amazing thing," Gates recalled in the book *Becoming Steve Jobs*. Bill Gates has transformed himself into a compelling speaker. I don't doubt that he was inspired by Jobs's performances.

In the pages that follow, you will learn the presentation secrets of the greatest business storyteller of our time. Whether you're giving the presentation of a lifetime, pitching an idea, or trying to grow in your career, these principles will work for you. They might make you a fortune. I've seen it happen many times to many people in many countries.

Thousands of leaders have learned to communicate more successfully, thanks to reading this book. I don't have the space here to discuss all of the success stories I've received since the first edition of this book became an international bestseller. Those stories would fill another book.

Here's just one.

In 2008 a recession rocked the global economy. Like many companies, a small construction company in Canada felt the shock. Sales plummeted and employees were let go. For the next year the company struggled to generate new business. One day in 2009, the head of marketing for the company picked up a copy of *The Presentation Secrets of Steve Jobs*. He couldn't put it down. He finished reading it at 2:00 a.m. The next day he walked into the office and asked his boss for a budget for six lunch-and-learns, where they would deliver a presentation to prospects based on each of the principles in the book. The manager's boss was skeptical. "It'll never work," he flatly stated. "What's the alternative? We're heading toward bankruptcy," the manager replied. The budget was approved.

Using the principles in the book, the manager took a bloated 72-slide PowerPoint and reduced it to 30 slides. A presentation that previously took two hours to deliver could now be completed in 30 minutes. It also included video clips, compelling visuals, and, most important, made the company's data relatable and compelling.

The response to the presentation shocked nearly everyone in the company, but not the marketing manager. By the third lunch-and-learn, "we were rock stars in the industry," he said. Each presentation attracted bigger audiences. The world changed for this small company after the fourth presentation. An executive at a large energy corporation asked the company to submit a bid for an upcoming project. The company won the business—an $875-million construction project.

"Why did you choose our company?" the marketing manager asked the executive after they had won the bid.

"It started with your presentation. You showed us that you think differently."

I sincerely hope that this book will help you think differently, too, and win the business that will grow your company, sell your products and services, build your career, or trigger your movement. I know it will. I've interviewed CEOs, billionaires, and business legends. They all credit communication skills as the key to success, and they all hold Steve Jobs up as the gold standard in public presentations.

The success stories come from far and wide. LinkedIn's marketing department used the principles in this book to completely reimagine the company's presentation prior to its hugely successful IPO. Go to YouTube and watch Intel's CES presentations in 2015 and 2016. Intel's keynotes are designed according to this book's guidelines. In fact, hundreds of managers at Intel have been trained to deliver their presentations using the Steve Jobs method. Former Ford CEO Alan Mulally has read and applied the lessons in this the book, as have leaders at Google, Microsoft, Facebook, Medtronic, Pfizer, Coca-Cola, Accenture, and countless companies around the world. Yes, even Apple.

The Presentation Secrets of Steve Jobs sparked an unplanned spinoff—*The Apple Experience,* the first book to pull back the curtain on the Apple Store customer service model. I remember the day I came up with the idea. I was standing in line at the airport when I received a call from an Apple Store manager who simply wanted to thank me for writing *Presentation Secrets.* He made the book required reading for new employees.

"That's great, but since it's primarily a presentation book, how are you applying it?"

"What do you think we're doing every day?" he responded. "The sales floor is our stage, and we need to inspire our customers. Your book teaches us how to communicate the Steve Jobs way. It's like having Apple's cofounder mentor us through the sales process."

The conversation reminded me that presentation skills go well beyond delivering a PowerPoint. When you pitch an idea, you're giving a presentation. When you're speaking to a client or customer, you're making a presentation. When you're answering questions in a job interview, you're delivering a presentation. You're presenting yourself constantly, and those who present themselves better will stand out in a sea of competition.

This book is the closest you'll ever get to learning exactly how Steve Jobs created mesmerizing presentations. The template Jobs developed and detailed in this book still serves as the foundation for Apple's awe-inspiring keynotes delivered today. Since Apple is one of the most secretive companies on the planet, I never expected a public endorsement from its senior leaders. One day, however, I received a short e-mail from one of its top executives, a man who was very close to Steve Jobs and whose name you might recognize. I never asked him if I could use his comments publicly, and I won't mention his name now. I simply filed the e-mail away as a private acknowledgment that I had successfully accomplished what I had set out to do. The e-mail simply said,

I've read your book about SJ's presentation secrets. Well done.

I once spoke to an economist who gave a TED talk that became a viral sensation. When we signed off he said, "I don't wish anyone 'good luck' because it implicitly accepts society's belief that most of the time success is a matter of luck. Success is a matter of passion, effort, focus, and creativity. I don't wish you luck with your book; I wish you success."

Wishing you success,

Carmine Gallo
March 2016

How to Be Insanely Great in Front of Any Audience

A person can have the greatest idea in the world— completely different and novel—but if that person can't convince enough other people, it doesn't matter.

—GREGORY BERNS

The concepts in this book will help you win over an audience in ways that you've never imagined. I've seen it happen. I've watched business professionals around the world adopt these techniques to win multi-million dollar accounts. I've met Apple Store employees who use the book to learn to pitch new products on the showroom floor. Thousands of readers in North America, Asia, Europe, and South America have reinvented their presentations with these techniques. If you read this book and study its examples, your presentations will never be the same. And that's the point. Your customers, employees, investors, and partners are bored to death with the same old lackluster style of presentation design and delivery. But a Steve Jobs presentation was unlike anything you'd ever seen. It informed, educated, and entertained. It illuminated and inspired. Best of all, because Steve Jobs did presentations "by the book," you can adopt his template to rock the house in your very next presentation!

Since *The Presentation Secrets of Steve Jobs* was first published, many individuals and businesses have used this book to change the way they tell their own stories. Those case studies alone can, well, fill an entire book. There's the story of a major medical device manufacturer whose marketing team has completely overhauled its presentations based on this book. There's the story of a global energy company whose leaders are using the book to change the way they pitch foreign governments. There's the story of the law firm managing partner who bought the book for every one of the firm's attorneys. There's the story of the CEO for a major European media conglomerate who read the book and admonished his sales staff, "No more bullet points!" There's the story of the sales team at a popular social networking site who used the book to pitch their company prior to launching a hugely successful IPO. There's also the story of the prominent technology analyst who called Steve Jobs's business rival and urged him to read the book. (The CEO wasn't pleased to get the tip so the analyst added the caveat, "I think every CEO should read it.") There are the stories of MBA students at Stanford, Berkeley, UCLA, and other universities who are learning ideas that are not taught in school. This book has touched professionals in every industry and in nearly every part of the world. It will touch you and transform the way you tell your brand story.

Why study Steve Jobs? The Apple cofounder was the most captivating communicator on the world stage. No one else came close. A Jobs presentation unleashed a rush of dopamine into the brains of his audience. Some people went to great lengths to get this hit, even spending the night in freezing temperatures to ensure the best seat at one of his speeches. When they didn't get that buzz, they went through withdrawal. How else do you explain the fact that some fans threatened to protest Jobs's absence from a conference he had keynoted for years? That's what happened when Apple announced that Jobs would not deliver his traditional keynote presentation at Macworld Expo in 2009. (Apple also announced that it would be the last year in which the company would participate in this annual trade show produced by Boston-based IDG World Expo.)

As Jobs's health declined, he performed fewer presentations than he had in the past, but he still managed to make appearances for major announcements like the release of the iPad2 in March 2011 and for the unveiling of Apple's "cloud" strategy in June 2011. Even so, there were fewer and fewer Steve Jobs keynotes. As reporter Jon Fortt wrote at the time: "The sun is setting on the first generation of rebellious whiz kids who invented the PC, commercialized the Internet, and grew their companies into powerhouses."[1]

A Steve Jobs keynote presentation was an extraordinary experience. I wrote this book to capture the best of Jobs's presentations and to reveal, for the first time, the exact techniques he used to inspire his audience. Best of all, you can learn his skills and adopt his techniques to blow away your audience, giving people a high they will crave again and again.

Watch a Macworld keynote—"Stevenotes," as they are known among the Mac faithful—and you will begin to reconsider everything about your current presentations: what you say, how you say it, and what your audience sees when you say it. I wrote a column about Steve Jobs and his presentation skills for BusinessWeek.com. It quickly became hugely popular around the world (Daniel Lyons, aka "Fake Steve Jobs," even featured it). It appealed to Mac and PC owners alike who wanted to improve the way they sell themselves and their ideas. A select few readers had seen Jobs in person, while others had watched video of Jobs online, but the vast majority of readers had never seen him give a keynote. What they learned was eye-opening and forced many of them to go back to the proverbial drawing board.

For educational purposes, use YouTube as a complement to the techniques revealed in the pages to follow. In this case, YouTube offers a rare opportunity to read about a particular individual, learn about specific techniques that made him successful, and see those techniques in action.

What you'll learn is that Jobs was a magnetic pitchman who sold his ideas with a flair that turned prospects into customers and customers into evangelists. He had charisma, defined by the German sociologist Max Weber as "a certain quality of an individual personality, by virtue of which he is set apart from ordinary people and treated as endowed with supernatural, superhuman, or at least specifically exceptional powers or qualities."[2] Jobs became superhuman among his most loyal fans. But Weber got one thing wrong. Weber believed that charisma was not "accessible to the ordinary person." Once you learn *exactly* how Jobs crafted and delivered one of his famous presentations, you will realize that these exceptional powers are available to you as well. If you adopt just *some* of his techniques, yours will stand out from the legions of mediocre presentations delivered on any given day. Your competitors and colleagues will look like amateurs in comparison.

"Presentations have become the de facto business communication tool," writes presentation design guru Nancy Duarte in *Slide:ology*. "Companies are started, products are launched, climate systems are saved—possibly based on the quality of presentations. Likewise, ideas, endeavors, and even careers can be cut short due to ineffective communication. Out of the millions of presentations delivered each day, only a small percentage are delivered well."[3]

Duarte transformed Al Gore's 35 mm slides into the award-winning documentary *An Inconvenient Truth*. As with Al Gore, who sits on Apple's board, Steve Jobs used presentations as a transformative experience. Both men revolutionized business communications and have something to teach us, but where Gore has *one* famous presentation repeated a thousand times, Jobs gave awe-inspiring presentations since the launch of the Macintosh in 1984. In fact, the Macintosh launch, which you will read about in the pages to follow, is still one of the most dramatic presentations in the history of corporate America. I find it amazing that Jobs actually improved his presentation style over the twenty-five years after the launch. The 1984 presentation was tough to beat—one of the greatest presentations of our time. Still, Jobs's keynotes at the Macworld

Expo in 2007 and 2008 were his best ever. Jobs's introduction of the iPad in 2010 and the iPad2 in 2011 also rivaled almost any presentation he delivered. Both presentations are discussed and dissected in a "Postscript" at the end of this book. Everything that he had learned about connecting with audiences came together to create truly magnificent moments.

Now the bad news. Your presentations are being compared with those of Steve Jobs. He transformed the typical, dull, technical, plodding slide show into a theatrical event complete with heroes, villains, a supporting cast, and stunning backdrops. People who witnessed a Steve Jobs presentation for the first time would describe it as an extraordinary experience. In a *Los Angeles Times* article about Jobs's 2009 medical leave, Michael Hiltzik wrote: "No American CEO is more intimately identified with his company's success . . . Jobs is Apple's visionary and carnival barker. If you want a taste of the latter persona, watch the video of the original iPod launch event in October 2001. Jobs's dramatic command is astonishing. Viewing the event recently on YouTube, I was on the edge of my seat, even though I knew how the story came out."[4] Jobs was the Tiger Woods of business, who raised the bar for the rest of us.

Now the good news. You can identify and adopt each of Jobs's techniques to keep your audience members at the edge of their seats. Tapping into his qualities will help you create your own magnificent presentations and give you the tools to sell your ideas far more persuasively than you have ever imagined.

Consider *The Presentation Secrets of Steve Jobs* your road map to presentation success. It's as close as you will ever get to having Jobs speak directly in your ear as you present the value behind your service, product, company, or cause. Whether you are a CEO launching a new product, an entrepreneur pitching investors, a sales professional closing a deal, or an educator trying to inspire a class, you have something to learn from Jobs's presentation techniques. Most business professionals give presentations to deliver information. Not Jobs. A Steve Jobs presentation was intended to create an experience—"a reality distortion field"—that left his audience awed, inspired, and wildly excited.

Moving On Up

> As soon as you move one step up from the bottom, your effectiveness depends on your ability to reach others through the spoken and written word. [5]
>
> —PETER DRUCKER

Some of the most common terms used to describe Steve Jobs are "seductive," "magnetic," "captivating," and "charismatic." Other terms, typically related to his interpersonal traits, are less flattering. Jobs was a complicated man who created extraordinary products, cultivated intense loyalty, and also scared the shit out of people. He was a passionate perfectionist and a visionary, two qualities that created a combustible combination when the way things were did not match the way Jobs believed they should have been. This book is not intended to tackle everything about Steve Jobs. It is neither a biography of the man nor a history of Apple. This book is not about Jobs the boss, but about Jobs the communicator. One prominent industry analyst recomends that the book should be in every executive's library. It offers the most thorough breakdown of exactly how Jobs crafted and delivered the story behind the Apple brand. You will learn how Jobs did all of the following:

» Crafted messages
» Presented ideas
» Generated excitement for a product or feature
» Delivered a memorable experience
» Created customer evangelists

The techniques will help you create your own "insanely great" presentations. The lessons are remarkably simple to learn, but applying them is up to you. Speaking the way Steve spoke requires work, but the benefit to your career, company, and personal success will be well worth your commitment.

Why Not Me?

When I appeared on CNBC's "The Big Idea with Donny Deutsch," I was struck by the host's infectious energy. Deutsch offered his viewers this piece of advice: "When you see someone who has turned his passion into a profit, ask yourself, 'Why not me?'"[6] I urge you to do the same. When you read about Jobs in the pages to follow, ask yourself, "Why not me? Why can't I energize my listeners like Jobs?" The answer is, "You can." As you'll learn, Jobs was not a natural. He worked at it. Although he always had a theatrical flair, his style evolved and improved over the years. Jobs was relentlessly focused on improvement, laboring over every slide, every demo, and every detail of a presentation. Each presentation told a story, and every slide revealed a scene. Jobs was a showman and, as with all great actors, he rehearsed until he got it right. "Be a yardstick of quality," Jobs once said. "Some people aren't used to an environment where excellence is expected."[7] There are no shortcuts to excellence. Presenting like Jobs will require planning and practice, but if you are committed to reaching the top, there is no better teacher than Apple's master showman. (See Figure 1.)

Performance in Three Acts

The Presentation Secrets of Steve Jobs is structured like one of Jobs's favorite presentation metaphors: a three-act play. In fact, a Steve Jobs presentation was very much like a dramatic play— a finely crafted and well-rehearsed performance that informed, entertained, and inspired. When Jobs introduced the video iPod on October 12, 2005, he chose the California Theatre in San Jose as his stage. It was an appropriate setting as Steve divided the product introductions into three acts, "like every classic story." In act 1, he introduced the new iMac G5 with built-in video camera. Act 2 kicked off the release of the fifth-generation iPod, which played video content for the first time. In act 3, he talked about iTunes 6, with the news that ABC would make television shows available for iTunes and the new video

Figure 1 Apple's master showman turned presentations into theatrical experiences.

Photo by Justin Sullivan/Getty Images

iPod. Jobs even introduced jazz legend Wynton Marsalis as an encore.

In keeping with Jobs's metaphor of a presentation as a classic story, *The Presentation Secrets of Steve Jobs* is divided into three acts:

» **Act 1: Create the Story.** The seven chapters—or scenes—in this section will give you practical tools to craft an exciting story behind your brand. A strong story will give you the confidence and ability to win over your audience.

» **Act 2: Deliver the Experience.** In these six scenes, you will learn practical tips to turn your presentations into visually appealing and "must-have" experiences.

» **Act 3: Refine and Rehearse.** The remaining five scenes will tackle topics such as body language, verbal delivery, and making "scripted" presentations sound natural and conversational. Even your choice of wardrobe will be addressed. You will learn why mock turtlenecks, jeans, and running shoes were suitable for Jobs but could mean the end of your career.

Short intermissions divide the acts. These intermissions contain nuggets of great information culled from the latest findings in cognitive research and presentation design. These findings will help you take your presentations to an entirely new level.

What Are You Really Selling?

Jobs was "the master at taking something that might be considered boring—a hunk of electronic hardware—and enveloping it in a story that made it compellingly dramatic," writes Alan Deutschman in *The Second Coming of Steve Jobs*.[8] Only a handful of leaders whom I have had the pleasure of meeting have this skill, the ability to turn seemingly boring items into exciting brand stories. Cisco executive chairman and former CEO John Chambers is one of them. Chambers does not sell routers and switches that make up the backbone of the Internet. What Chambers *does* sell is human connections that change the way we live, work, play, and learn.

The most inspiring communicators share this quality—the ability to create something meaningful out of esoteric or everyday products. Starbucks CEO Howard Schultz does not sell coffee. He sells a "third place" between work and home. Financial guru Suze Orman does not sell trusts and mutual funds. She sells the dream of financial freedom. In the same way, Jobs did not sell computers. He sold tools to unleash human potential. Throughout this book, ask yourself, "What am I really selling?" Remember, your widget doesn't inspire. Show me how your widget improves my life, and you've won me over. Do it in a way that entertains me, and you'll have created a true evangelist.

Along the way, you'll also discover that Steve Jobs was motivated by a messianic zeal to change the world, to put a "dent in the universe." In order for these techniques to work, you must cultivate a profound sense of mission. If you are passionate about your topic, you're 80 percent closer to developing the magnetism that Jobs had. At the age of twenty-one when Jobs cofounded Apple with his friend Steve Wozniak, Jobs fell in love with the vision of how personal computing would change society, education, and entertainment. His passion was contagious, infecting everyone in his presence. That passion came across in every presentation.

We all have passions that drive us. The purpose of this book is to help you capture that passion and turn it into a story so mesmerizing that people will want to help you achieve your vision. You see, it's quite possible that your ideas or products vastly improve the lives of your customers—from computers, to automobiles, to financial services, to products that create a cleaner environment—but the greatest product in the world will be useless without a strong brand evangelist to promote it. If you cannot get people to care, your product will never stand a chance of success. Your audience will not care, they will not understand, nor will they be interested. People do not pay attention to boring things. Do not let your ideas die because you failed to present them in a way that sparked the imagination of your listeners. Use Jobs's techniques to reach the hearts and the minds of everyone you hope to influence.

As Jobs often said to kick off a presentation, "Now let's get started."

ACT I

Create the Story

Creating the story, the plot, is the first step to selling your ideas with power, persuasion, and charisma. Succeeding at this step separates mediocre communicators from extraordinary ones. Most people fail to think through their story. Effective communicators plan effectively, develop compelling messages and headlines, make it easy for their listeners to follow the narrative, and introduce a common enemy to build the drama. The seven chapters—or scenes—in Act 1 will help set the foundation for presentation success. Each scene will be followed by a short summary of specific and tangible lessons you can easily apply today. Let's review the scenes here:

» **SCENE 1: "Plan in Analog."** In this chapter, you will learn how truly great presenters like Steve Jobs visualize, plan, and create ideas well before they open the presentation software.

» **SCENE 2: "Answer the One Question That Matters Most."** Your listeners are asking themselves one question and one question only: "Why should I care?" Disregard this question, and your audience will dismiss you.

» **SCENE 3: "Develop a Messianic Sense of Purpose."** Steve Jobs was worth more than $100 million by the time he was twenty-five, and it didn't matter to him. Understanding this one fact will help you unlock the secret behind Jobs's extraordinary charisma.

» **SCENE 4: "Create Twitter-Like Headlines."** The social networking site has changed the way we communicate. Developing headlines that fit into 140-character sentences will help you sell your ideas more persuasively.

» **SCENE 5: "Draw a Road Map."** Steve Jobs made his argument easy to follow by adopting one of the most powerful principles of persuasion: the rule of three.

» **SCENE 6: "Introduce the Antagonist."** Every great Steve Jobs presentation introduced a common villain that the audience can turn against. Once he introduced an enemy, the stage was set for the next scene.

» **SCENE 7: "Reveal the Conquering Hero."** Every great Steve Jobs presentation introduced a hero the audience could rally around. The hero offers a better way of doing something, breaks from the status quo, and inspires people to embrace innovation.

Plan in Analog

**Marketing is really theater.
It's like staging a performance.**

—JOHN SCULLEY

S teve Jobs has built a reputation in the digital world of bits and bytes, but he created stories in the very old-world tradition of pen and paper. His presentations were theatrical events intended to generate maximum publicity, buzz, and awe. They contained all of the elements of great plays or movies: conflict, resolution, villains, and heroes. And, in line with all great movie directors, Jobs storyboarded the plot before picking up a "camera" (i.e., opening the presentation software). It was marketing theater unlike any other.

Jobs was closely involved in every detail of a presentation: writing descriptive taglines, creating slides, practicing demos, and making sure the lighting was just right. Jobs took nothing for granted. He did what most top presentation designers recommend: he started on paper. "There's just something about paper and pen and sketching out rough ideas in the 'analog world' in the early stages that seems to lead to more clarity and better, more creative results when we finally get down to representing our ideas digitally," writes Garr Reynolds in *Presentation Zen*.[1]

Design experts, including those who create presentations for Apple, recommend that presenters spend the majority of their time thinking, sketching, and scripting. Nancy Duarte is the genius behind Al Gore's *An Inconvenient Truth*. Duarte suggests that a presenter spend up to ninety hours to create an hour-long presentation that contains thirty slides. However, only one-third of that time should be dedicated to *building* the slides, says Duarte.[2] The first twenty-seven hours are dedicated to researching the topic, collecting input from experts, organizing ideas, collaborating with colleagues, and sketching the structure of the story.

Bullets Kill

Think about what happens when you open PowerPoint. A blank-format slide appears that contains space for words—a title and subtitle. This presents a problem. There were very few words in a Steve Jobs presentation. Now think about the first thing you see in the drop-down menu under Format: Bullets & Numbering. This leads to the second problem. There were no bullet points in a Steve Jobs presentation. The software itself forces you to create a template that represents the exact opposite of what you need to speak like Steve did! In fact, as you will learn in later scenes, texts and bullets are the *least* effective way to deliver information intended to be recalled and acted upon. Save your bullet points for grocery lists.

Visually engaging presentations will inspire your audience. And yes, they require a bit of work, especially in the planning phase. As a communications coach, I work with CEOs and other top executives on their media, presentation, and public speaking skills. One of my clients, a start-up entrepreneur, had spent sixty straight days in Bentonville, Arkansas, to score an appointment with Wal-Mart. His technology intrigued company executives, who agreed to a beta test, or trial run. Wal-Mart asked him to present the information to a group of advertisers and top executives. I met with my client over a period of days at the offices of the Silicon Valley venture capital firm that invested in his company. For the first day, we did nothing but sketch the story. No computer and no PowerPoint—just pen and paper (whiteboard, in this case). Eventually we turned the sketches into slide ideas. We needed only five slides for a fifteen-minute presentation. Creating the slides did not take as much time as developing the story. Once we wrote the narrative, designing the slides was easy. Remember, it's the story, *not the slides*, that will capture the imagination of your audience.

The Napkin Test

A picture is the most powerful method for conveying an idea. Instead of booting up your computer, take out a napkin. Some of the most successful business ideas have been sketched on the back of a napkin. One could argue that the napkin has been more important to the world of business ideas than PowerPoint. I used to think that "napkin stories" were just that—stories, from the imagination of journalists. That is until I met Richard Tait, the founder of Cranium. I prepared him for an interview on CNBC. He told me that during a cross-country flight from New York to Seattle, he took out a small cocktail napkin and sketched the idea of a board game in which everyone had a chance to excel in at least one category, a game that would give everyone a chance to shine. Cranium became a worldwide sensation and was later purchased by Hasbro. The original concept was simple enough to write on a tiny airline napkin.

One of the most famous corporate napkin stories involves Southwest Airlines. A lawyer at the time, Herb Kelleher met with one of his clients, Rollin King, at the St. Anthony's Club, in San Antonio. King owned a small charter airline. He wanted to start a low-cost commuter airline that avoided the major hubs and instead served Dallas, Houston, and San Antonio. King sketched three circles, wrote the names of the cities inside, and connected the three—a strikingly simple vision. Kelleher understood immediately. Kelleher signed on as legal counsel (he later became CEO), and the two men founded Southwest Airlines in 1967. King and Kelleher would go on to reinvent airline travel in the United States and build a corporate culture that would earn Southwest's place among the most admired companies in the world. Never underestimate the power of a vision so simple that it can fit on a napkin!

The Story Takes Center Stage

In *Beyond Bullet Points*, Cliff Atkinson stresses, "The single most important thing you can do to dramatically improve your presentations is to have a story to tell *before* you work on your PowerPoint file."[3] Atkinson advocates a three-step storyboard approach to creating presentations:

Writing → Sketching → Producing

Only after writing—scripting—the scenes does he advocate thinking visually about how the slides will look. "To write a script, you need to momentarily set aside PowerPoint design issues like fonts, colors, backgrounds, and slide transitions. Although it might sound counterintuitive, when you write a script first, you actually expand your visual possibilities, because writing defines your purpose before you start designing. A script unlocks the undiscovered power of PowerPoint as a visual story-telling tool in ways that might surprise and delight you and your audiences."[4] With a completed script in hand, you'll be ready to sketch and "produce" the experience. The script, however, must come first.

Nine Elements of Great Presentations

Persuasive presentation scripts contain nine common elements. Think about incorporating each of these components before you open the presentation program, whether you work in PowerPoint, Keynote, or any other design software. Some of these concepts will be explored in more detail later, but for now keep them in mind as you develop your ideas.

HEADLINE

What is the one big idea you want to leave with your audience? It should be short (140 characters or less), memorable, and written in the subject-verb-object sequence. When Steve Jobs unveiled the iPhone, he exclaimed, "Today Apple reinvents the phone!"[5] That's a headline. Headlines grab the attention of your audience and give people a reason to listen. Read *USA Today* for ideas. Here are some examples from America's most popular daily newspaper:

» "Apple's Skinny MacBook Is Fat with Features"
» "Apple Unleashes Leopard Operating System"
» "Apple Shrinks iPod"

PASSION STATEMENT

Aristotle, the father of public speaking, believed that successful speakers must have "pathos," or passion for their subject. Very few communicators express a sense of excitement about their topic. Steve Jobs exuded an almost giddy enthusiasm every time he presented. Former employees and even some journalists have claimed that they found his energy and enthusiasm completely mesmerizing. Spend a few minutes developing a passion statement by filling in the following sentence: "I'm excited about this product [company, initiative, feature, etc.] because it _____." Once you have identified the passion statement, don't be bashful—share it.

THREE KEY MESSAGES

Now that you have decided on your headline and passion statement, write out the three messages you want your audience to receive. They should be easily recalled without the necessity of looking at notes. Although Scene 5 is dedicated to this subject, for now keep in mind that your listeners can recall only three or four points in short-term memory. Each of the key messages will be followed by supporting points.

METAPHORS AND ANALOGIES

As you develop key messages and supporting points, decide on which rhetorical devices will make your narrative more engaging. According to Aristotle, metaphor is "the most important thing by far." A metaphor—a word or phrase that denotes one thing and is used to designate another for purposes of comparison—is a persuasive tool in the best marketing, advertising, and public relations campaigns. Jobs used metaphors in conversations and presentations. In one famous interview, Jobs said, "What a computer is to me is the most remarkable tool that we have ever come up with. It's the equivalent of a bicycle for our minds."[6]

Sales professionals are fond of sports metaphors: "We're all playing for the same team"; "This isn't a scrimmage; it's for real"; or "We're batting a thousand; let's keep it up." While sports metaphors work fine, challenge yourself to break away from what your audience expects. I came across an interesting metaphor for a new antivirus suite of applications from Kaspersky. The company ran full-page ads (the one I saw was in *USA Today*) that showed a dejected medieval soldier in a full suit of armor walking away, with his back toward the reader. The headline read, "Don't be so sad. You were very good once upon a time." The metaphor compared today's Internet security technologies (Kaspersky's competitors) to slow, cumbersome medieval armor, which of course is no match for today's military technology. The company extended the metaphor to the website with an image of a suit of armor and the same tagline. The metaphor was consistent throughout the company's marketing material.

Analogies are close cousins of metaphors and also are very effective. An analogy is a comparison between two different things in order to highlight some area of similarity. Analogies help us understand concepts that might be foreign to us. "The microprocessor is the brain of your computer" is an analogy that works well for companies such as Intel. In many ways, the chip serves the same function in the computer as a brain serves in a human. The chip and the brain are two different things with like features. This particular analogy is so useful that it is widely picked up by the media. When you find a strong analogy that works, stick with it and make it consistent across your presentations, website, and marketing material. Jobs liked to have fun with analogies, especially if they could be applied to Microsoft. During an interview with the *Wall Street Journal*'s

Walt Mossberg, Jobs pointed out that many people say iTunes is their favorite application for Windows. "It's like giving a glass of ice water to someone in hell!"[7]

DEMONSTRATIONS

Jobs shared the spotlight with employees, partners, and products. Demos made up a large part of his presentations. In June 2007, when Jobs unveiled a new version of the OS X operating system, code-named Leopard, at Apple's Worldwide Developers Conference (WWDC)—an annual Apple event showcasing new software and technologies—he said Leopard had three hundred new features. He chose ten to discuss and demonstrate, including Time Machine (automated backup), Boot Camp (runs Windows XP and Vista on Mac), and Stacks (file organization). Instead of simply listing the features on a slide and explaining them, he sat down and showed the audience how they worked. He also chose the features *he* wanted the press to highlight. Why leave it to the media to decide which of three hundred new features were the most compelling? He would tell them.

Does your product lend itself to a demonstration? If so, script it into the presentation. Your audience wants to see, touch, and experience your product or service. Bring it to life.

I worked with Goldman Sachs investors to prepare the CEO of a Silicon Valley semiconductor start-up that was about to go public. The company shrinks chips that create audio sound for mobile computers. As we were planning the investor presentation, the CEO pulled out a chip the size of a fingernail and said, "You wouldn't believe the sound that this generates. Listen to this." He turned up the volume on his laptop and played music that impressed those of us who were in the room. It was a no-brainer to use the same demonstration (with a more dramatic buildup) when the executive pitched the company to investors. The IPO went on to become a huge success. An investor who had underwritten the company later called me and said, "I don't know what you did, but the CEO was a hit." I didn't have the heart to say that I stole the idea from the Steve Jobs playbook.

PARTNERS

Jobs shared the stage with key partners as well as his products. In September 2005, Jobs announced that all of Madonna's albums would be available on iTunes. The pop star herself suddenly appeared via webcam and joked with Jobs that she had tried to hold out as long as possible but got tired of not being able to download her own songs. Whether it was an artist or an industry partner like the CEOs of Intel, Fox, or Sony, Jobs often shared the stage with people who contributed to Apple's success.

CUSTOMER EVIDENCE AND THIRD-PARTY ENDORSEMENTS

Offering "customer evidence" or testimonials is an important part of the selling cycle. Few customers want to be pioneers, especially when budgets are tight. Just as recruiters ask for references, your customers want to hear success stories. This is especially critical for small companies. Your sales and marketing collateral might look great in that glossy four-color brochure, but it will be met with a healthy degree of skepticism. The number one influencer is word of mouth. Successful product launches usually have several customers who were involved in the beta and who can vouch for the product. Incorporate customer evidence into your pitch. Including a quote is simple enough, but try going one step further by recording a short testimonial and embedding the video on your site and in your presentation. Even better, invite a customer to join you in person (or via webcam) at a presentation or an important sales meeting.

Do you have third-party reviews of your product? Always use third-party endorsements when available. Word of mouth is one of the most effective marketing tools available, and when your customers see an endorsement from a publication or an individual they respect, it will make them feel more comfortable about their purchasing decisions.

VIDEO CLIPS

Very few presenters incorporate video into their presentations. Jobs played video clips very often. Sometimes he showed video of employees talking about how much they enjoyed working on a product. Jobs was also fond of showing Apple's most recent television ads. He did so in nearly every major new product announcement and had been doing so since the launch of the famous Macintosh 1984 Super Bowl ad. He had been known to enjoy some ads so much that he showed them twice. Near the end of his presentation at Apple's WWDC in June 2008, Jobs announced the new iPhone 3G, which connected to higher-speed data networks and cost less than the iPhone that was then on the market. He showed a television ad with the tagline "It's finally here. The first phone to beat the iPhone." When the thirty-second spot ended, a beaming Jobs said, "Isn't that nice? Want to see it again? Let's roll that again. I love this ad."[8]

Including video clips in your presentation will help you stand out. You can show ads, employee testimonials, scenes of the product or of people using the product, and even customer endorsements. What could be more persuasive than hearing directly from a satisfied customer—if not in person, then through a short video clip embedded in your presentation? You can easily encode video into digital formats such as MPEG 1, Windows Media, or Quicktime files, all of which will work for most presentations. Keep in mind that the average viewed clip on YouTube is 2.5 minutes. Our attention spans are shrinking, and video, while providing a great way to keep the audience engaged, can be overused if left to run too long. Use video clips in your presentations, but avoid clips that run much longer than two to three minutes.

Video is a terrific tool for even the most nontechnical of presentations. I was helping the California Strawberry Commission prepare for a series of presentations set to take place on the East Coast. Commission members showed me a short video of strawberry growers expressing their love of the land and the fruit. The images of strawberry fields were gorgeous, and I suggested they create a digital file of the video clip and embed it in the presentation. In the presentation itself, they introduced the video by saying something like this: "We realize that you probably have never visited a California strawberry field, so we decided to bring the farmers to you." The video clip was the most memorable part of the presentation, and the East Coast editors loved it.

FLIP CHARTS, PROPS, AND SHOW-AND-TELL

There are three types of learners: visual (the majority of people fall into this category), auditory (listeners), and kinesthetic (people who like to feel and touch). Find ways to appeal to everyone. A presentation should comprise more than just slides. Use whiteboards, flip charts, or the high-tech flip chart—a tablet PC. Bring "props" such as physical products for people to see, use, and touch. In Scene 12, you'll learn much more about reaching the three types of learners.

Most communicators get so caught up in the slides: Which font should I use? Should I use bullets or dashes? Should I include a graph here? How about a picture there? These are the wrong questions to be asking in the planning stage. If you have a tangible product, find other ways outside of the slide deck to show it off. On October 14, 2008, Steve introduced a new line of MacBooks carved out of one piece of aluminum, a "unibody enclosure." After Jobs discussed the manufacturing process, Apple employees handed out examples of the new frame so audience members could see it and touch it for themselves.

Incorporating all of these elements in a presentation will help you tell a story worth listening to. Slides don't tell stories; you do. Slides complement the story. This book is software agnostic; it avoids a direct comparison between PowerPoint and Keynote because the software is not the main character in an effective presentation—the speaker is. Jobs himself started using Apple's Keynote software in 2002, so what are we to make of the extraordinary presentations Jobs gave dating back to 1984? The software is not the answer. The fact that Steve Jobs used Keynote instead of PowerPoint does not mean your presentation will look more like his did if you make the switch. You will, however, win over your audience by spending more time creating the plot than producing the slides.

Use a notepad or whiteboard to script your ideas. It will help you visualize the story and simplify its components. When Jobs returned to Apple in 1996, taking over for ousted Gil Amelio,

Aristotle's Outline for Persuasive Arguments

A Steve Jobs presentation followed Aristotle's classic five-point plan to create a persuasive argument:

1. Deliver a story or statement that arouses the audience's interest.
2. Pose a problem or question that has to be solved or answered.
3. Offer a solution to the problem you raised.
4. Describe specific benefits for adopting the course of action set forth in your solution.
5. State a call to action. For Steve, it was as simple as saying, "Now go out and buy one!"

he found a company with more than forty different products, which confused the customer. In a bold move, he radically simplified the product pipeline. In *Inside Steve's Brain*, Leander Kahney writes that Jobs called senior management into his office. "Jobs drew a very simple two-by-two grid on the whiteboard. Across the top he wrote 'Consumer' and 'Professional,' and down the side, 'Portable' and 'Desktop.' "[9] Under Jobs, Apple would offer just four computers—two notebooks and two desktops—aimed at consumer and professional users. This is one of many stories in which we learn that Jobs did his best thinking when he was thinking visually. Whether you plan best on a whiteboard, a yellow legal pad, or Post-it notes, spend time in analog before jumping to digital. Your ultimate presentation will be far more interesting, engaging, and relevant.

DIRECTOR'S NOTES

» Start planning before you open the presentation software. Sketch ideas on paper or whiteboards.

» Incorporate some, if not all, of the following nine elements to make your presentation come alive: headline, passion statement, three key messages, analogies, demonstrations, partner showcase, customer evidence, video clips, and props.

» Speaking like Jobs has little to do with the type of presentation software you use (PowerPoint, Keynote, etc.) and everything to do with how you craft and deliver the story.

Answer the One Question That Matters Most

You've got to start with the customer experience and work back toward the technology—not the other way around.

—STEVE JOBS, MAY 25, 1997, WORLDWIDE DEVELOPERS CONFERENCE

In May 1998, Apple launched a splashy new product aimed at shoring up its dwindling share of the computer market, which had sunk to under 4 percent. When Jobs unveiled the new translucent iMac, he described the reason for building the computer, the target market, and the benefit customers would see from buying the new system:

> Even though this is a full-blown Macintosh, we are targeting this for the number one use consumers tell us they want a computer for, which is to get on the Internet simply and fast. We're also targeting this for education. They want to buy these. It's perfect for most of the things they do in instruction . . . We went out and looked at all of the consumer products out there. We noticed some things about them pretty much universally. The first is they are very slow. They are all using last year's processor. Secondly, they all have pretty crummy displays on them . . . likely no networking on them . . . old-generation I/O devices, and what that means is they are

lower performance and harder to use . . . and these things are uuugly! So, let me tell you about iMac.[1]

After describing the weaknesses of current products in the preceding excerpt, Jobs drew a verbal road map for his audience, listing the features he would explain in more detail. (Learn more about drawing a road map in Scene 5.) The audience learned that the new iMac was fast ("it screams") and that it had a "gorgeous" fifteen-inch display, a large amount of built-in memory, and components that would make accessing a network easier for students and home users. In one of his typical surprise moments, Jobs then walked to the center of the stage and pulled the cover off the new computer.

Your audience wants to be informed, educated, and entertained: informed about your product, educated on how it works, and entertained while learning about it. Above all, people want to know the answer to one question: Why should I care? Let's take a closer look at that iMac excerpt. Jobs told the audience, "what that means is . . ." Jobs connects the dots for his listeners. Although he might leave the industry in the dark about future Apple releases, he never leaves his audience guessing when the product is finally introduced. Why should you care about Apple's new computer, MP3 player, phone, or gadget? Don't worry. Jobs will tell you.

The Rumors Are True

For years, Apple had a rivalry with Intel—even setting fire to an Intel bunny man in a 1996 TV spot. One decade later, Apple put its rivalry to rest and announced that Intel processors would power its new Macintosh systems, replacing IBM's PowerPC chips. On June 6, 2005, Jobs announced the switch at Apple's Worldwide Developers Conference in San Francisco.

Rumors of the switch had been floating around for months, and many observers expressed concern about the transition. Reporters for *eWeek* magazine found it difficult to believe Apple would swap the PowerPC for Intel, since the PowerPC had worked well for the brand. Developers were grumbling. Jobs had to convince the audience that the switch was the right thing to do. His presentation was enormously persuasive in changing people's opinions because, using plain and direct language, he answered the one question that mattered most: Why should Apple's customers and developers care?

> Yes, it's true. We are going to begin the transition from PowerPC to Intel processors. Now, why are we going to do this? Didn't we just get through going from OS 9 to OS X? Isn't the business great right now? Because we want to make the best computers for our customers looking forward. Now, I stood up here two years ago and promised you this [slide shows desktop computer with 3 GHz], and we haven't been able to deliver it to you. I think a lot of you would like a G5 in your PowerBook, and we haven't been able to deliver it. But these aren't even the most important reasons. As we look ahead, though we have some great products now, we can envision some amazing products we want to build for you, and we don't know how to build them with the future PowerPC road map. That's why we're going to do this.[2]

Jobs articulated the argument so convincingly that few people in the audience that day left without a high degree of confidence that the transition had been the right thing for Apple, its developers, and its customers.

Why Should I Care?

During the planning phase of your presentation, always remember that it's not about you. It's about them. The listeners in your audience are asking themselves one question: "Why should I care?" Answering that one question right out of the gate will grab people's attention and keep them engaged.

I was preparing a CEO for a major analyst presentation and asked how he planned to kick it off. He offered this dry, boring, and confusing introduction: "Our company is a premier developer of intelligent semiconductor intellectual property solutions that dramatically accelerate complex system-on-a-chip designs

Channel Your Best Steve Jobs Impression

In the summer of 2006, Intel released a processor branded Core 2 Duo. The "duo" stood for dual-core, meaning there were two cores, or brains, on each microprocessor. That may not sound exciting, but if you answer the *one* question that matters—Why should I care?—it becomes very interesting.

Take two scenarios: in both scenarios, a customer walks into a computer store and asks the salesperson for information about notebook computers. The sales professional in the first scenario has not read this book and fails to answer the one question that matters. The salesperson in the second scenario is more likely to win the sale, by virtue of channeling his or her inner Steve Jobs and answering the one question on the mind of the customer: Why should I care?

Scenario One

CUSTOMER: Hi, I'm looking for a notebook computer that is light and fast and includes a DVD.

SALESPERSON: You should look for an Intel Core 2 Duo.

CUSTOMER: OK. I didn't know Intel makes computers.

SALESPERSON: They don't.

CUSTOMER: Can you tell me more?

SALESPERSON: An Intel dual-core processor has two performance engines that simultaneously process data at a faster rate.

CUSTOMER: Oh. Maybe I should look somewhere else.

Of course the customer in this scenario will look somewhere else. Although the salesperson was technically accurate, the customer had to work far too hard to figure out how the new system would make the person's life better. It took too much brainpower, and as you'll learn, the brain is a lazy piece of meat that tries to preserve energy. Make the brain work too hard, and you'll lose your audience. The customer had one question in mind and one question only. The salesperson failed to answer it and seemed indifferent, even arrogant. Let's try it again. This time, the salesperson will do a stellar Steve Jobs impression.

Scenario Two

SALESPERSON: Hi, can I help you find something?

CUSTOMER: Sure. I'm looking for a notebook computer. One that is light and fast and includes a DVD.

SALESPERSON: You've come to the right place. We have a huge selection of small notebooks that are blazingly fast. Have you considered a system with an Intel Core 2 Duo?

CUSTOMER: Not really. What's that?

SALESPERSON: Think of the microprocessor as the brain of your computer. Now, with these Intel chips, you get two brains in one computer. *What that means to you* is that you can do a lot of fun and productive stuff at the same time. For example, you can download music while your computer is running a full virus scan in the background, and it won't slow down the system at all. Your productivity applications will load much faster, you can work on multiple documents at the same time, your DVDs will play much better, and you get much longer battery life on top of it! And that's not all: the displays are gorgeous.

CUSTOMER: Great. Please show me those computers!

In this scenario, the salesperson spoke in plain English, used tangible examples to make the product relevant, and answered the only question that really mattered to the customer: Why should I care about the processor? Retailers who train their sales staffs to describe products in this way will stand out from the competition. Come to think of it, there is a retailer that does exactly that—Apple. Walk into most any Apple store, and you will be greeted by enthusiastic men and women who are eager to explain how Apple products will make your life better.

while minimizing risk." I was dumbfounded and suggested he take a page from the Steve Jobs playbook, eliminating all of the buzzwords such as *intelligent* and *solutions* and simply answering one question: Why should your customers care about your product?

The CEO revised his introduction. He decided to walk onstage and ask everyone to take out his or her cell phone. He said, "Our company creates software that is used to build the chips inside many of the phones you're holding up. As those chips get smaller and cheaper, your phones will get smaller, last longer on a single charge, and play music and video, all thanks to our technology working behind the scenes."

Which introduction would be more effective in grabbing your attention? The second one, of course. It is free of jargon and, by answering the *one* question that matters, gives the audience a reason to listen.

Reporters are skilled at answering the one question for their readers. Pay attention to product descriptions in the *New York Times* or *USA Today*. Articles are written to be followed and understood. For example, on January 20, 2009, Cisco Systems announced that it planned a big push into the server market, a category dominated by IBM, HP, and Dell. The product would be a server with virtualization software. Now, virtualization is one of the most complicated concepts to explain. Wikipedia defines server virtualization as "a method of partitioning a physical server computer into multiple servers such that each has the appearance and capabilities of running on its own dedicated machine."[3] Got it? Didn't think so. The *New York Times'* Ashlee Vance took a different approach: "Virtualization products let companies run numerous business applications, rather than just one, on each physical server, allowing them to save electricity and get more out of their hardware purchases."[4]

The difference, of course, is that Vance answered the one question on the minds of his readers: What does "virtualization" mean to me? In this case, he identified his audience as investors, IT decision makers, and business leaders who would care about such things.

Your listeners are asking themselves, "Why should I care?" If your product will help your customers make money, tell them. If it helps them save money, tell them. If it makes it easier or more enjoyable for them to perform a particular task, tell them. Tell them early, often, and clearly. Jobs didn't leave people guessing. Well before he explained the technology behind a new product or feature, he explained how it would improve the experience people have with their computers, music players, or gadgets.

Table 2.1 offers a review of some other examples of how Jobs sold the benefit behind a new product or feature.

Nobody has time to listen to a pitch or presentation that holds no benefit. If you pay close attention to Jobs's

TABLE 2.1 JOBS SELLING THE BENEFIT

DATE/PRODUCT	BENEFIT
January 7, 2003 Keynote presentation software	"Using Keynote is like having a professional graphics department to create your slides. This is the application to use when your presentation really counts."[5]
September 12, 2006 iPod nano	"The all-new iPod nano gives music fans more of what they love in their iPods—twice the storage capacity at the same price, an incredible twenty-four-hour battery life, and a gorgeous aluminum design in five brilliant colors."[6]
January 15, 2008 Time Capsule backup service for Macs running Leopard OS	"With Time Capsule, all your irreplaceable photos, movies, and documents are automatically protected and incredibly easy to retrieve if they are ever lost."[7]
June 9, 2008 iPhone 3G	"Just one year after launching the iPhone, we're launching the new iPhone 3G. It's twice as fast at half the price."[8]
September 9, 2008 Genius feature for iTunes	"Genius lets you automatically create playlists from songs in your music library that go great together, with just one click."[9]

Avoid Self-Indulgent, Buzzword-Filled Wastes of Time

Answer the one question in all of your marketing materials: website, presentation slides, and press releases. The people who should know better—public relations professionals—are often the worst violators of this rule. The majority of press releases are usually self-indulgent, buzzword-filled wastes of time. Few members of the press even read press releases, because the documents fail to answer the *one* question that matters most to a reporter: Why should my readers care? As a journalist, I've seen thousands of press releases and rarely, if ever, covered a story based on one. Most other journalists would concur. Far too many press releases focus on corporate changes (management appointments, new logos, new offices, etc.) that nobody cares about, and if people should happen to care, the information is far from clear. Read press releases issued on any given day, and you will go numb trying to figure out why anyone would care about the information.

For fun, I took a few samples from press releases issued within hours of one another. The date does not matter. The majority of all press releases violate the same fundamental principles of persuasion:

"_____ Industries announced today that it has signed an exclusive distribution agreement with _____ . Under terms of the agreement, _____ will be the exclusive national distributor of _____ 's diesel exhaust fluid." Now, seriously, who cares? I wish I could tell you how the new distribution agreement benefits anyone, even shareholders. I can't, because the rest of the press release never answers the question directly.

"_____ has been named 2008 Pizza Chain of the Year by *Pizza Marketplace*." The press release said this honor comes after the chain delivered consistent profits, six quarters of same-store sales increases, and a new management team. Now, if the chain offered its customers a special discount to celebrate this honor, it would be newsworthy, but the press release mentions nothing that distinguishes this pizza chain from the thousands of other pizza parlors. This type of release falls under the "look at us" category—announcements that are largely meaningless to anyone outside the executive suites.

"_____ has announced the addition of the 'Annual Report on China's Steel Market in 2008 and the Outlook for 2009' report to their offering." Really? I'm sure millions of people around the world were waiting for this new report! Just kidding. This is another example of a wasted opportunity. If this release had started with one new, eye-opening piece of information from the new report, I might have been slightly more interested. However, that would have meant putting the reader first, and, sadly, most PR pros who write press releases intended for journalists have never been trained as journalists themselves.

Here's another gem, courtesy of an electric company in Hawaii:

"_____ today announced that _____ has been named president and CEO, effective January 1, 2009. _____ replaces _____ , who stepped down as president and CEO in August of this year." We also learned that the new CEO has thirty-two years of experience in the utilities industry and has lived on the big island for twenty years. Isn't that wonderful? Doesn't it give you a warm feeling? Again, this press release represents a lost opportunity to connect with the company's investors and customers. If the release had started with one thing that the new CEO planned to do immediately to improve service, it would have been far more interesting and newsworthy.

For the most part, press releases fail miserably at generating interest because they don't answer the one question that matters most to the reader. Do not make the same mistake in your presentation, publicity, and marketing material.

presentations, you will see that he didn't "sell" products; he sold the dream of a better future. When Apple launched the iPhone in early 2007, then CNBC reporter Jim Goldman asked Jobs, "Why is the iPhone so important to Apple?" Jobs avoided a discussion of shareholder value or market share; instead, he offered the vision of a better experience: "I think the iPhone may change the whole phone industry and give us something that is vastly more powerful in terms of making phone calls and keeping your contacts. We have the best iPod we've ever made fully integrated into it. And it has the Internet in your pocket with a real browser, real e-mail, and the best implementation of Google Maps on the planet. iPhone brings all this stuff in your pocket, and it's ten times easier to use."[10] Jobs explained the "why" before the "how."

Your audience doesn't care about your product. People care about themselves. According to former Apple employee and Mac evangelist Guy Kawasaki, "The essence of evangelism is to passionately show people how you can make history together. Evangelism has little to do with cash flow, the bottom line, or co-marketing. It is the purest and most passionate form of sales because you are selling a dream, not a tangible object."[11] Sell dreams, not products.

DIRECTOR'S NOTES

» Ask yourself, "Why should my listener care about this idea/information/product/service?" If there is only one thing that you want your listener to take away from the conversation, what would it be? Focus on selling the benefit behind the product.

» Make the *one thing* as clear as possible, repeating it at least twice in the conversation or presentation. Eliminate buzzwords and jargon to enhance the clarity of your message.

» Make sure the *one thing* is consistent across all of your marketing collateral, including press releases, website pages, and presentations.

SCENE 3

SCENE 3

Develop a Messianic Sense of Purpose

We're here to put a dent in the universe.

—STEVE JOBS

New York's luxury, Upper West Side apartment building, the San Remo, is located on Seventy-Fifth Street with commanding views of Central Park. Its most famous residents read like a who's who of contemporary culture: Tiger Woods, Demi Moore, Dustin Hoffman, Bono, and, at one time, a young man on a mission—Steve Jobs.

In 1983, Jobs was aggressively courting then PepsiCo president John Sculley. Apple desperately wanted to bring in someone with Sculley's marketing and managing experience, but despite Steve's charm, Sculley failed to budge. The position would require that Sculley relocate his family to the West Coast, and it paid less than he wanted. One sentence would change everything, transforming Apple, shifting the trajectory of Sculley's career, and beginning Jobs's amazing path from whiz kid, to failure, to hero, and, finally, to legend. In his book *Odyssey*, Sculley recounts the conversation that would lead to his decision to take the job. The conversation also provided one of the most famous quotes in the history of corporate America.

According to Sculley, "We were on the balcony's west side, facing the Hudson River, when he [Jobs] finally asked me directly: 'Are you going to come to Apple?' 'Steve,' I said, 'I really love what you're doing. I'm excited by it; how could anyone not be captivated? But it just doesn't make sense. Steve, I'd love to be an adviser to you, to help you in any way. But I don't think I can come to Apple.'"

Sculley said Jobs's head dropped; he paused and stared at the ground. Jobs then looked up and issued a challenge to Sculley that would "haunt" him. Jobs said, "Do you want to spend the rest of your life selling sugared water or do you want a chance to change the world?"[1] Sculley said it was as if someone delivered a stiff blow to his stomach.

The Reality Distortion Field

Sculley had witnessed what Apple's vice president Bud Tribble once described as Jobs's "reality distortion field": an ability to convince anyone of practically anything. Many people could not resist this magnetic pull and were willing to follow Jobs to the promised land (or at least to the next cool iPod).

Few people could escape the Jobs charisma, a magnetism steeped in passion for his products. Observers have said that there was something about the way Jobs talked, the enthusiasm that he conveyed, that grabbed everyone in the room and didn't let go. Even journalists who should have built up an immunity to such gravitational forces could not escape the influence. Former Wired .com editor Leander Kahney interviewed Jobs biographer Alan Deutschman, who described a meeting with Jobs: "He uses your first name very often. He looks directly in your eyes with that laser-like stare. He has these movie-star eyes that are very hypnotic. But what really gets you is the way he talks—there's something about the rhythm of his speech and the incredible enthusiasm he conveys for whatever it is he's talking about that is just infectious."[2]

Do What You Love

Deutschman said the Steve Jobs "X" factor was the way he talked. But what exactly was it about the way he talked that pulled you in? Jobs spoke with passion, enthusiasm, and energy. Jobs himself told us where his passion came from: "You've got to find what you love. Your work is going to fill a large part of your life, and the only way to be truly satisfied is to do what you believe is great work. And the only way to do great work is to love what you do. If you haven't found it yet, keep looking. Don't settle."[3]

We all have a unique purpose. Some people, such as Jobs, identify that purpose from an early age; others never do, because they are caught up in catching up with the Joneses. One sure way to lose sight of your purpose is to chase money for the sake of chasing money. Jobs was a billionaire and an extraordinary communicator precisely because he followed his heart, his passion. The money, he most certainly knew, would come.

FINDING YOUR CORE PURPOSE

What is your core purpose? Once you find it, express it enthusiastically. One of the most profound experiences of my journalism career happened during an interview with Chris Gardner. Actor

In That Craziness, We See Genius

I think you always had to be a little different to buy an Apple computer. I think the people who do buy them are the creative spirits in this world. They are the people who are not out just to get a job done; they're out to change the world. We make tools for those kinds of people . . . We are going to serve the people who have been buying our products since the beginning. A lot of times, people think they're crazy. But in that craziness, we see genius. And those are the people we're making tools for.[4]

—STEVE JOBS

Will Smith played Gardner in the movie *The Pursuit of Happyness*. In the eighties, the real-life Gardner pursued an unpaid internship to become a stockbroker. He was homeless at the time, spending nights in the bathroom of an Oakland, California, subway station. To make the situation even harder, Gardner took care of his two-year-old son. The two slept together on the bathroom floor. Every morning, Gardner would put on the one suit he had, drop his son off at a very questionable day care, and take his classes. Gardner finished top of his class, became a stockbroker, and earned many millions of dollars. For a *BusinessWeek* column, I asked him, "Mr. Gardner, how did you find the strength to keep going?" His answer was so profound that I remember it to this day: "Find something you love to do so much, you can't wait for the sun to rise to do it all over again."[5]

In *Built to Last: Successful Habits of Visionary Companies*, authors Jim Collins and Jerry Porras studied eighteen leading companies. Their conclusion: individuals are inspired by "core values and a sense of purpose beyond just making money."[6] From his earliest interviews, it becomes clear that Jobs was more motivated by creating great products than by calculating how much money he would make at building those products.

In a PBS documentary, *Triumph of the Nerds*, Jobs said, "I was worth over a million dollars when I was twenty-three, and over ten million dollars when I was twenty-four, and over a hundred million dollars when I was twenty-five, and it wasn't that important, because I never did it for the money."[7] *I never did it for the money.* This phrase holds the secret between becoming an extraordinary presenter and one mired in mediocrity for the rest of your life. Jobs once said that being "the richest man in the cemetery" didn't matter to him; rather, "going to bed at night saying we've done something wonderful, that's what matters to me."[8] Great presenters are passionate, because they follow their hearts. Their conversations become platforms to share that passion.

Malcolm Gladwell shares a fascinating observation in *Outliers*. He argues that most of the leaders who are responsible for the personal computing revolution were born in 1955. That's the magic year, he says. According to Gladwell, the chronology makes sense because the first "minicomputer," the Altair, was introduced in 1975, marking one of the most important developments in the history of personal computers. He states: "If you were more than a few years out of college in 1975, then you belonged to the old paradigm. You had just bought a house. You're married. A baby is on the way. You're in no position to give up a good job and pension for some pie-in-the-sky $397 computer kit."[9] Likewise, if you were too young, you would not be mature enough to participate in the revolution.

Gladwell speculates that the ideal age of tech industry titans was around twenty or twenty-one, those born in 1954 or 1955. Steve Jobs was born on February 24, 1955. He was born at the right time and in the right neighborhood to take advantage of the moment. Gladwell points out that Jobs was one of an amazing number of technology leaders born in 1954 and 1955 (including Bill Gates, Paul Allen, Steve Ballmer, Eric Schmidt, Scott McNealy, and others). Gladwell's conclusion is that these men became successful precisely because computers were not big moneymakers at the time. They were cool, and these men loved to tinker. The message, claims Gladwell, is: to achieve success, do what you find interesting. Do what you love, and follow your core purpose. As Jobs said, your heart knows where it wants to be.

THE LUCKIEST GUYS ON THE PLANET

On May 30, 2007, Steve Jobs and Bill Gates shared the stage in a rare joint appearance at the technology conference D: All

Lust for It

In a *New York Times* article after the launch of the MacBook Air, John Markoff wrote about witnessing Steve's enthusiasm in person. Markoff spent thirty minutes with Jobs after the conference and noted that Jobs's passion for personal computing came across even more so than it did when he was performing onstage. Jobs excitedly told Markoff, "I'm going to be the first one in line to buy one of these. I've been lusting after this."[10]

Things Digital. *Wall Street Journal* columnists Walt Mossberg and Kara Swisher covered a variety of topics with the two tech titans. In response to a question about Bill Gates's "second act" as a philanthropist, Jobs credited Gates for making the world a better place because Gates's goal wasn't to be the richest guy in the cemetery.

> You know, I'm sure Bill was like me in this way. I mean, I grew up fairly middle-class, lower middle-class, and I never really cared much about money. And Apple was so successful early on in life that I was very lucky that I didn't have to care about money then. And so I've been able to focus on work and then later on, my family. And I sort of look at us as two of the luckiest guys on the planet because we found what we loved to do, we were at the right place at the right time, and we've gotten to go to work every day with superbright people for thirty years and do what we love doing. And so it's hard to be happier than that. And so I don't think about legacy much. I just think about being able to get up every day and go in and hang around these great people and hopefully create something that other people will love as much as we do. And if we can do that, that's great.[11]

Nowhere in that quote do you hear Jobs speak of wealth, stock options, or private planes. Those things are nice, but they didn't motivate Jobs. His drive came from doing what he loved—designing great products that people enjoy.

Rally People to a Better Future

It all starts with passion. Passion stirs the emotions of your listeners when you use it to paint a picture of a more meaningful world, a world that your customers or employees can play a part in creating.

Marcus Buckingham interviewed thousands of employees who excelled at their jobs during his seventeen years at the

Oprah Shares Jobs's Secret to Success

> *Follow your passion. Do what you love, and the money will follow. Most people don't believe it, but it's true.*[12]
>
> —OPRAH WINFREY

Gallup organization. After interviewing thousands of peak performers, he arrived at what he considers the single best definition of leadership: "Great leaders rally people to a better future," he writes in *The One Thing You Need to Know.*[13]

According to Buckingham, a leader carries a vivid image in his or her head of what a future could be. "Leaders are fascinated by the future. You are a leader if, and only if, you are restless for change, impatient for progress, and deeply dissatisfied with the status quo." He explains, "As a leader, you are never satisfied with the present, because in your head you can see a better future, and the friction between 'what is' and 'what could be' burns you, stirs you up, propels you forward. This is leadership."[14] Jobs's vision must have certainly burned him, stirred him, and propelled him forward. Jobs once told John Sculley he dreamed that every person in the world would own an Apple computer. But Jobs did not stop there. He shared that dream with all who would listen.

True evangelists are driven by a messianic zeal to create new experiences. "It was characteristic of Steve to speak in both vivid and sweeping language," writes Sculley. " 'What we want to do,' he [Steve Jobs] explained, 'is to change the way people use computers in the world. We've got some incredible ideas that will revolutionize the way people use computers. Apple is going to be the most important computer company in the world, far more important than IBM.' "[15] Jobs was never motivated to build computers. Instead, he had a burning desire to create tools to unleash human potential. Once you understand the difference, you'll understand what sparked his famous reality distortion field.

An Incredible Journey

> *Apple was this incredible journey. I mean, we did some amazing things there. The thing that bound us together at Apple was the ability to make things that were going to change the world. That was very important. We were all pretty young. The average age in the company was mid to late twenties. Hardly anybody had families at the beginning, and we all worked like maniacs, and the greatest joy was that we felt we were fashioning collective works of art much like twentieth-century physics. Something important that would last, that people contributed to and then could give to more people; the amplification factor was very large.*[16]
>
> —STEVE JOBS

What Computers and Coffee Have in Common

Lee Clow, chairman of TBWA/Chiat/Day, the agency behind some of Apple's most notable ad campaigns, once said of Jobs, "From the time he was a kid, Steve thought his products could change the world."[17] That's the key to understanding Jobs. His charisma was a result of a grand but strikingly simple vision—to make the world a better place.

Jobs convinced his programmers that they were changing the world together, making a moral choice against Microsoft and making people's lives better. For example, Jobs gave an interview to *Rolling Stone* in 2003 in which he talked about the iPod. The MP3 player was not simply a music gadget, but much more. According to Jobs, "Music is really being reinvented in this digital age, and that is bringing it back into people's lives. It's a wonderful thing. And in our own small way, that's how we're going to make the world a better place."[18] Where some people see an iPod as a music player, Jobs saw a world in which people could easily access their favorite songs and carry the music along with them wherever they went, enriching their lives.

Jobs reminded me of another business leader whom I had the pleasure of meeting, Starbucks CEO Howard Schultz. Prior to our interview, I read his book, *Pour Your Heart into It*. Schultz is passionate about what he does; in fact, the word *passion* appears on nearly every page. But it soon became clear that he is not as passionate about coffee as he is about the people, the baristas who make the Starbucks experience what it is. You see, Schultz's core vision was not to make a great cup of coffee. It was much bigger. Schultz would create an experience; a third place between work and home where people would feel comfortable gathering. He would build a company that treats people with dignity and respect. Those happy employees would, in turn, provide a level of customer service that would be seen as a gold standard in the industry. When I reviewed the transcripts from my time with Schultz, I was struck by the fact that the word *coffee* rarely appeared. Schultz's vision had little to do with coffee and everything to do with the experience Starbucks offers.

"Some managers are uncomfortable with expressing emotion about their dreams, but it's the passion and emotion that will attract and motivate others," write Collins and Porras.[19] Communicators like Steve Jobs and Howard Schultz are passionate about how their products improve the lives of their customers. They're not afraid to express it. Coffee, computers, iPods—it doesn't matter. What matters is that they are motivated by a vision to change the world, to "leave a dent in the universe."

This book is filled with techniques to help you sell your ideas more successfully, but no technique can make up for a lack of passion for your service, product, company, or cause. The secret is to identify what it is you're truly passionate about. More often than not, it's not "the widget," but how the widget will improve the lives of your customers. Here is an excerpt from an interview Jobs gave *Wired* magazine in 1996: "Design is a funny word. Some people think design means how it looks. But of course, if you dig deeper, it's really how it works. The design of the Mac wasn't what it looked like, although that was part of it. Primarily, it was how it worked. To design something really well, you have to get it. You have to really grok what it's all about. It

The Charismatic Leader

> *When I wasn't sure what the word charisma meant, I met Steve Jobs and then I knew.*[20]
>
> —FORMER APPLE CHIEF SCIENTIST LARRY TESLER

takes a passionate commitment to really thoroughly understand something, chew it up, not just quickly swallow it. Most people don't take the time to do that."[21] Yes, *grok* is the word Jobs used. Just as Howard Schultz isn't passionate about the product itself, coffee, Jobs wasn't passionate about hardware. He was passionate about how design enabled something to work more beautifully.

Think Different

Los Angeles ad agency TBWA/Chiat/Day created an Apple television and print advertising campaign that turned into one of the most famous campaigns in corporate history. "Think Different" debuted on September 28, 1997, and became an instant classic. As black-and-white images of famous iconoclasts filled the screen (Albert Einstein, Martin Luther King, Jr., Richard Branson, John Lennon, Amelia Earhart, Muhammad Ali, Lucille Ball, Bob Dylan, and others), actor Richard Dreyfuss voiced the narration:

> Here's to the crazy ones. The misfits. The rebels. The troublemakers. The round pegs in the square hole. The ones who see things differently. They're not fond of rules. And they have no respect for the status quo. You can quote them, disagree with them, glorify or vilify them. About the only thing you can't do is ignore them. Because they change things. They push the human race forward. And while some may see them as the crazy ones, we see genius. Because the people who are crazy enough to think they can change the world are the ones who do.[22]

The campaign won a ton of awards, became a cult favorite, and lasted five years, which is an eternity in the life cycle of ad campaigns. The campaign reinvigorated the public's appetite for all things Apple, including an interest in one of the most influential iconoclasts in the computer world, Steve Jobs himself.

In *The Second Coming of Steve Jobs*, Alan Deutschman, who, as mentioned earlier, was pulled into Jobs's reality distortion field, describes a meeting between Jobs and *Newsweek*'s Katie Hafner, the first outsider to see the new "Think Different" ads. According to Deutschman, Hafner arrived at Apple's headquarters on a Friday morning and waited a long time for Jobs to show up. "Finally he emerged. His chin was covered by stubble. He was exhausted from having stayed up all night editing footage for the 'Think Different' television spot. The creative directors at Chiat/Day would send him video clips over a satellite connection, and he would say yes or no. Now the montage was finally complete. Steve sat with Katie and they watched the commercial. Steve was crying. 'That's what I love about him,' Katie recalls. 'It wasn't trumped up. Steve was genuinely moved by that stupid ad.'"[23]

Those ads touched Jobs deeply because they reflected everything that pushed Jobs to innovate, excel, and succeed. He saw himself in the faces of those famous people who advanced the human race and changed the world.

As a journalist, I learned that everyone has a story to tell. I realize we are not all creating computers that will change the way people live, work, play, and learn. Notwithstanding, the fact is that most of us are selling a product or working on a project that has some benefit to the lives of our customers. Whether you work in agriculture, automobiles, technology, finance, or any number of other industries, you have a magnificent story to tell. Dig deep to identify that which you are most passionate about. Once you do, share that enthusiasm with your listeners. People want to be moved and inspired, and they want to believe in something. Make them believe in you.

"There's an old Wayne Gretzky quote that I love," Steve Jobs once said: " 'I skate to where the puck is going to be, not where it has been.' We've always tried to do that at Apple. Since the very, very beginning. And we always will."[24]

DIRECTOR'S NOTES

» Dig deep to identify your true passion. Ask yourself, "What am I really selling?" Here's a hint: it's not the widget, but what the widget can do to improve the lives of your customers. What you're selling is the dream of a better life. Once you identify your true passion, share it with gusto.

» Develop a personal "passion statement." In one sentence, tell your prospects why you are genuinely excited about working with them. Your passion statement will be remembered long after your company's mission statement is forgotten.

» If you want to be an inspiring speaker but you are not doing what you love, consider a change. After interviewing thousands of successful leaders, I can tell you that, while it's possible to be financially successful in a job you hate, you will never be considered an inspiring communicator. Passion—a messianic zeal to make the world a better place—makes all the difference.

Create Twitter-Like Headlines

Today Apple reinvents the phone!

—STEVE JOBS, MACWORLD 2007

"Welcome to Macworld 2008. There is something clearly in the air today."[1] With that opening line, Steve Jobs set the theme for what would ultimately be the big announcement of his keynote presentation—the introduction of an ultrathin notebook computer. No other portable computer could compare to this three-pound, 0.16-inch-thin "dreambook," as some observers called it. Steve Jobs knew that everyone would be searching for just the right words to describe it, so he did it for them: "MacBook Air. The world's thinnest notebook."

The MacBook Air is Apple's ultrathin notebook computer. The best way to describe it is as, well, the world's thinnest notebook. Search for "world's thinnest notebook" on Google, and the search engine will return about four hundred thousand citations, most of which were written after the announcement. Jobs took the guesswork out of a new product by creating a one-line description or headline that best reflected the product. The headlines worked so well that the media would often run with them word for word. You see, reporters (and your audience) are looking for a category in which to place your product and a way of describing the product in one sentence. Take the work out of it and write the headline yourself.

140 Characters or Less

Jobs created headlines that were specific, were memorable, and, best of all, could fit in a Twitter post. Twitter has changed the nature of business communication in a fundamental way—it forces people to write concisely. The maximum post—or tweet—is 140 characters. Characters include letters, spaces, and punctuation. For example, Jobs's description of the MacBook Air took thirty characters, including the period: "The world's thinnest notebook."

Jobs had a one-line description for nearly every product, and it was carefully created in the planning stage well before the presentation, press releases, and marketing material were finished. Most important, the headline was consistent. On January 15, 2008, the day of the MacBook Air announcement, the headline was repeated in every channel of communication: presentations, website, interviews, advertisements, billboards, and posters.

In Table 4.1, you see how Apple and Jobs consistently delivered the vision behind MacBook Air.

Most presenters cannot describe their company, product, or service in one sentence. Understandably, it becomes nearly impossible to create consistent messaging without a prepared headline developed early in the planning stage. The rest of the presentation should be built around it.

Setting the Stage for the Marketing Blitz

The minute Jobs delivered a headline onstage, the Apple publicity and marketing teams kicked into full gear. Posters were dropped down inside the Macworld Expo, billboards went up, the front page of the Apple website revealed the product and headline, and ads reflected the headline in newspapers and magazines, as well as on television and radio. Whether it was "1,000 songs in your pocket" or "The world's thinnest notebook," the headline was repeated consistently in all of Apple's marketing channels.

TABLE 4.1 JOBS'S CONSISTENT HEADLINES FOR MACBOOK AIR

HEADLINE	SOURCE
"What is MacBook Air? In a sentence, it's the world's thinnest notebook."[2]	Keynote presentation
"The world's thinnest notebook."[3]	Words on Jobs's slide
"This is the MacBook Air. It's the thinnest notebook in the world."[4]	Promoting the new notebook in a CNBC interview immediately after his keynote presentation
"We decided to build the world's thinnest notebook."[5]	A second reference to MacBook Air in the same CNBC interview
"MacBook Air. The world's thinnest notebook."	Tagline that accompanied the full-screen photograph of the new product on Apple's home page
"Apple Introduces MacBook Air—The World's Thinnest Notebook."[6]	Apple press release
"We've built the world's thinnest notebook."[7]	Steve Jobs quote in the Apple press release

Today Apple Reinvents the Phone

On January 9, 2007, *PC World* ran an article that announced Apple would "Reinvent the Phone" with a new device that combined three products: a mobile phone, an iPod, and an Internet communicator. That product, of course, was the iPhone. The iPhone did, indeed, revolutionize the industry and was recognized by *Time* magazine as the invention of the year. (Just two years after its release, by the end of 2008, the iPhone had grabbed 13 percent of the smartphone market.) The editors at *PC World* did not create the headline themselves. Apple provided it in its press release, and Steve Jobs reinforced it in his keynote presentation at Macworld. Apple's headline was specific, memorable, and consistent: "Apple Reinvents the Phone."

During the keynote presentation in which Jobs unveiled the iPhone, he used the phrase "reinvent the phone" five times. After walking the audience through the phone's features, he hammered it home once again: "I think when you have a chance to get your hands on it, you'll agree, we have reinvented the phone."[8]

Jobs did not wait for the media to create a headline. He wrote it himself and repeated it several times in his presentation. Jobs delivered the headline before explaining the details of the product. He then described the product, typically with a demo, and repeated the headline immediately upon ending the explanation.

For example, here is how Jobs introduced GarageBand for the first time: "Today we're announcing something so cool: a fifth app that will be part of the iLife family. Its name is GarageBand. What is GarageBand? GarageBand is a major new pro music tool. But it's for everyone."[9] Jobs's slide mirrored the headline. When he announced the headline for GarageBand, the slide on the screen read: "GarageBand. A major new pro music tool." Jobs followed the headline with a longer, one-sentence description of the product. "What it does is turn your Mac into a pro-quality musical instrument and complete recording studio," Jobs told the audience. This was typical Jobs method for introducing a product. He revealed the headline, expanded on it, and hammered it home again and again.

The Excitement of the Internet, the Simplicity of Macintosh

The original iMac (the "i" stood for Internet) made getting on the Web easier than ever. The customer had to go through only two steps to connect to the Internet. ("There's no step three," actor Jeff Goldblum declared in one popular ad.) The introduction captured the imagination of the computer industry in 1998 and was one of the most influential computer announcements of the decade. According to Macworld.com, the iMac redeemed

Steve Jobs, who had returned to Apple in 1997, and it saved Apple itself at a time when the media had pronounced the company all but dead. Jobs had to create excitement about a product that threw some common assumptions out the window—the iMac shipped with no floppy drive, a bold move at the time and a decision met with considerable skepticism.

"iMac combines the excitement of the Internet with the simplicity of Macintosh," Jobs said as he introduced the computer. The slide on the screen behind Jobs read simply: "iMac. The excitement of the Internet. The simplicity of Macintosh." Jobs then explained whom the computer was created to attract: consumers and students who wanted to get on the Internet "simply and fast."[10]

The headlines Steve Jobs created worked effectively because they were written from the perspective of the user. They answered the question: Why should I care? (See Scene 2.) Why should you care about the iMac? Because it lets you experience "the excitement of the Internet with the simplicity of Macintosh."

One Thousand Songs in Your Pocket

Apple is responsible for one of the greatest product headlines of all time. According to author Leander Kahney, Jobs himself settled on the description for the original iPod. On October 23, 2001, Jobs could have said, "Today we're introducing a new, ultraportable MP3 player with a 6.5-ounce design and a 5 GB hard drive, complete with Apple's legendary ease of use." Of course, Jobs did not say it quite that way. He simply said, "iPod. One thousand songs in your pocket."[11] No one could describe it better in more concise language. One thousand songs that could fit in your pocket. What else is there to say? One sentence tells the story and also answers the question, Why should I care?

Many reporters covering the event used the description in the headline to their articles. Matthew Fordahl's headline in the Associated Press on the day of the announcement read,

"Apple's New iPod Player Puts '1,000 Songs in Your Pocket.'"[12] Apple's headline was memorable because it meets three criteria: it is *concise* (twenty-seven characters), it is *specific* (one thousand songs), and it offers a *personal benefit* (*you* can carry the songs in your pocket).

Following are some other examples of Apple headlines that meet all three criteria. Although some of these are slightly longer than ten words, they can fit in a Twitter post:

» "The new iTunes store. All songs are DRM-free." (Changes to iTunes music store, January 2009)

» "The industry's greenest notebooks." (New MacBook family of computers, introduced in October 2008)

» "The world's most popular music player made even better." (Introduction of the fourth-generation iPod nano, September 2008)

» "iPhone 3G. Twice as fast at half the price." (Introduction of iPhone 3G, July 2008)

» "It gives Mac users more reasons to love their Mac and PC users more reasons to switch." (Introduction of iLife '08, announced July 2007)

» "Apple reinvents the phone." (Introduction of iPhone, January 2007)

» "The speed and screen of a professional desktop system in the world's best notebook design." (Introduction of the seventeen-inch MacBook Pro, April 2006)

» "The fastest browser on the Mac and many will feel it's the best browser ever created." (Unveiling of Safari, January 2003)

Keynote Beats PowerPoint in the Battle of the Headlines

Microsoft's PowerPoint has one big advantage over Apple's Keynote presentation software—it's everywhere. Microsoft commands 90 percent of the computing market, and among the 10 percent of computer users on a Macintosh, many still use

Headlines That Changed the World

When the "Google guys," Sergey Brin and Larry Page, walked into Sequoia Capital to seek funding for their new search-engine technology, they described their company in one sentence: "Google provides access to the world's information in one click." That's sixty-three characters, ten words. An early investor in Google told me that with those ten words, the investors immediately understood the implications of Google's technology. Since that day, entrepreneurs who walk into Sequoia Capital have been asked for their "one-liner," a headline that describes the product in a single sentence. As one investor told me, "If you cannot describe what you do in ten words or less, I'm not investing, I'm not buying, I'm not interested. Period." Following are some more examples of world-changing headlines that are ten words or less:

» "Cisco changes the way we live, work, play, and learn."—Cisco executive chairman and former CEO John Chambers, who repeats this line in interviews and presentations

» "Starbucks creates a third place between work and home." —Starbucks CEO Howard Schultz, describing his idea to early investors

» "We see a PC on every desk, in every home."—Microsoft co-founder Bill Gates, expressing his vision to Steve Ballmer, who, shortly after joining the company, was second-guessing his decision. Ballmer, Microsoft's CEO from 2000 to 2014, said Gates's vision convinced him to stick it out. With a personal net worth of $15 billion, Ballmer is glad he did.

PowerPoint software designed for Macs. While the actual numbers of presentations conducted on PowerPoint versus Keynote are not publicly available, it's safe to say that the number of Keynote presentations given daily is minuscule in comparison with PowerPoint. Although most presentation designers who are familiar with both formats prefer to work in the more elegant Keynote system, those same designers will tell you that the majority of their client work is done in PowerPoint.

As I mentioned in Scene 1, this book is software agnostic because all of the techniques apply equally to PowerPoint or Keynote. That said, Keynote was still the application that Steve Jobs preferred, and the Twitter-like headline he created to introduce the software was certainly an attention grabber. "This is another brand-new application that we are announcing here today, and it is called Keynote," Jobs told the audience at Macworld 2003. Then:

> Keynote is a presentation app for when your presentation really counts [slide reads: "When your presentation really counts"]. And Keynote was built for me [slide reads: "Built for me"]. I needed an application to build the kind of slide show that I wanted to show you at these Macworld keynotes: very graphics intensive. We built this for me; now I want to share it with you. We hired a low-paid beta tester to beta test this app for an entire year, and here he is [audience laughs as screen shows photo of Jobs]. Rather than a bunch of slides about slides, let me just show you [walks to stage right to demo the new software].[13]

Again, we see a remarkable consistency in all of Apple's marketing material surrounding the new product launch. The Apple press release for Keynote described it as "The application to use when your presentation really counts."[14] This headline can easily fit in a Twitter post and, without revealing the details, tells a story in one sentence. A customer who wanted more details could read the press release, watch Jobs's demonstration, or view the online demo on Apple's website. Still, the headline itself offered plenty of information. We learned that it was a new application specifically for presentations and made for those times when presentations can make or break your career. As a bonus, it was built for Jobs. For many people who give frequent presentations, that headline was enough to pique their interest and give the software a try.

Journalists learn to write headlines on the first day of J-school. Headlines are what persuade you to read particular stories in newspapers, magazines, or blogs. Headlines matter. As individuals become their own copywriters for blogs, presentations, Twitter posts, and marketing material, learning to write catchy, descriptive headlines becomes even more important to professional success.

DIRECTOR'S NOTES

» Create your headline, a one-sentence vision statement for your company, product, or service. The most effective headlines are concise (140 characters maximum), are specific, and offer a personal benefit.
» Consistently repeat the headline in your conversations and marketing material: presentations, slides, brochures, collateral, press releases, and website.
» Remember, your headline is a statement that offers your audience a vision of a better future. It's not about you. It's about them.

Draw a Road Map

Today we are introducing three revolutionary products.

—STEVE JOBS, REVEALING THE iPHONE

O n January 9, 2007, thousands of Mac faithful watched as Steve Jobs delivered an electrifying announcement. "Today Apple reinvents the phone," Jobs said as he revealed the iPhone for the first time to the public.[1]

Before delivering that headline, however, Jobs added to the drama and suspense when he told the audience that Apple would introduce not one, but three revolutionary products. He identified the first one as a wide-screen iPod with touch controls. This met with a smattering of applause. Jobs said the second product would be a revolutionary mobile phone. The audience cheered that announcement. And the third, said Jobs, was a breakthrough Internet communications device. At this point, the audience members sat back and waited for what they thought would be further product descriptions and perhaps some demos of the three new devices—but the real thrill was yet to come. Jobs continued, "So, three things: a wide-screen iPod with touch controls, a revolutionary mobile phone, and a breakthrough Internet communications device. An iPod, a phone, and an Internet communicator. An iPod, a phone—are you getting it? These are not three separate devices. This is one device, and we are calling it iPhone." The audience went wild, and Jobs basked in the glow of nailing yet another product launch that would solidify Apple's role as one of the world's most innovative companies.

Jobs drew a verbal road map for his audience, a preview of coming attractions. Typically these road maps were outlined in groups of three—a presentation might be broken into "three acts," a product description into "three features," a demo into "three parts." Jobs's love of threes could be traced back at least as early as the original Macintosh introduction on January 24, 1984. Appearing at the Flint Center, in Cupertino, California, Jobs told the audience, "There have only been two milestone products in our industry: the Apple II in 1977 and the IBM PC in 1981. Today we are introducing the third industry milestone product, the Macintosh. And it has turned out insanely great!"[2]

Verbal guideposts serve as road maps, helping your listeners follow the story. When coaching clients to appear in the media, I always instruct them to create an easy-to-follow story by clearly outlining three or, at the most, four main points before filling in the details. When this technique is followed, reporters will often take extensive notes. If the spokesperson misses a point, reporters will ask, "Didn't you say you had three points? I heard only two." A verbal road map of three things will help your listeners keep their place. See Figure 5.1.

Figure 5.1 Jobs stuck to the rule of three in his presentations.
ROBYN BECK/AFP/Getty Images

It is well established that we can hold only small amounts of information in short-term, or "active," memory. In 1956, Bell Labs research scientist George Miller published a classic paper titled "The Magical Number Seven, Plus or Minus Two." Miller cited studies that showed we have a hard time retaining more than seven to nine digits in short-term memory. Contemporary scientists have put the number of items we can easily recall closer to three or four. So, it should not be surprising that Jobs rarely offered more than three or four key message points. As for that, in a Steve Jobs presentation, the number three was much more common than four. Steve understood that the "rule of three" was one of the most powerful concepts in communication theory.

Why Goldilocks Didn't Encounter Four Bears

Listeners like lists. But how many points should you include in the list?

Three is the magic number.

Comedians know that three is funnier than two. Writers know that three is more dramatic than four. Jobs knew that three was more persuasive than five. Every great movie, book, play, or presentation has a three-act structure. There were three musketeers, not five. Goldilocks encountered three bears, not four. There were three stooges, not two. Legendary NFL coach Vince Lombardi told his players there were three important things in life: family, religion, and the Green Bay Packers. And the U.S. Declaration of Independence states that Americans have a right to "life, liberty, and the pursuit of happiness," not simply life and liberty. The rule of three is a fundamental principle in writing and in humor, just as it was in a Steve Jobs presentation.

The U.S. Marine Corps has conducted extensive research into this subject and has concluded that three is more effective than two or four. Divisions within the marines are divided into three: a corporal commands a team of three; a sergeant commands three rifle teams in a squad; a captain has three platoons; and so on. If the marines were kind enough to study this stuff, why should we reinvent the wheel? Go ahead and use it. So few communicators incorporate the rule of three in their presentations that you will stand apart simply by doing so. The rule of three—it works for the marines, it worked for Jobs, and it will work for you.

At the Apple Worldwide Developers Conference on June 6, 2005, Jobs announced the switch from IBM's PowerPC chips to Intel microprocessors. "Let's talk about transitions," Jobs said.

The Mac in its history has had two major transitions so far [begins to outline three points]. The *first* one, 68K to PowerPC. That transition happened about ten years ago in the midnineties. The PowerPC set Apple up for the next decade. It was a good move. The *second* major transition has been

How the Rule of Three Can Improve Your Golf Game

During a break from writing this chapter, I took a golf lesson from a local coach. Any golfer will tell you that the toughest part of the game is remembering the dozens of small moves that ultimately result in a fluid swing: posture, grip, takeaway, balance, hinging, weight shift, follow-through, and other variables. Problems occur when you think about too many things at the same time. The marines have found that giving directions in groups of three makes it easier for soldiers to follow the directions. So, I asked my instructor to give me three directives, and three only, to improve my swing. "Fine," he said. "Today you're going to focus on closing your hips, shifting your weight to the right side on the backswing, and making a full follow-through. So, think hips, shift, follow-through." *Hips, shift, follow.* That's it. The instruction worked wonders, and since that day, my golf game has improved considerably. The rule of three—good for presentations and good for golf, too!

even bigger. And that's the transition from OS 9 to OS X that we just finished a few years ago. This was a brain transplant. And although these operating systems vary in name by just one [digit], they are worlds apart in technology. OS X is the most advanced operating system on the planet, and it has set Apple up for the next twenty years. Today it's time to begin a *third* transition. We want to constantly be making the best computers for you and the rest of our users. It's time for a third transition. And yes, it's true. We are going to begin the transition from PowerPC to Intel processors [emphasis added].[3]

Revealing the narrative in groups of three provides direction for your audience. It shows people where you've been and where you're going. In the preceding excerpt, Jobs set the theme of "transitions," and we assume there will be at least a third transition because, as Jobs explained, the Mac had already had two of them. He also built the drama with each point. The first transition was a "good move." The second was "even bigger." By extension, the third must be bigger still.

Apple's Three-Legged Stool

At the Apple Worldwide Developers Conference in September 2008, Jobs displayed a slide of a stool with three legs. "As you know, there's three parts to Apple now," he said. "The first part, of course, is the Mac. The second part is our music businesses, the iPod and iTunes. And the third part is now the iPhone." Jobs introduced the executives who would speak about the Mac and the iPod business. Jobs would take the iPhone portion himself.

As he launched into the iPhone discussion, Jobs once again provided a road map for his listeners—this time, a road map in *four* parts: "In a few weeks, it's going to be the iPhone's first birthday. We shipped our first iPhone on June 29. It was an amazing introduction, the most amazing one we've ever had. iPhone has had tremendous critical acclaim. It's the phone that has changed phones forever. But we have mountains to climb

The *USA Today* Method

Journalists are trained to distill complex ideas into specific points, or takeaways. Read *USA Today*, America's most popular newspaper, and you will find that most articles condense main points into groups of three. When Intel rolled out a faster chip called Centrino 2, Michelle Kessler covered it for the newspaper. Kessler outlined three specific benefits and explained why each was important—why they matter:

» **Battery life.** "The best laptop in the world isn't worth much when its battery dies. Intel's new chip features an ultra low power processor and other energy-saving tools."

» **Graphics.** "Laptops traditionally use low-end graphics chips. But now 26 percent have powerful stand-alone graphics chips and more people watch movies, play games, and use graphics-intensive programs."

» **Wireless Internet.** "Intel's new chip line features the latest version of Wi-Fi, known as 802.11n. Later this year it plans to roll out chips using a new wireless Internet standard, WiMax, which can send a signal over several miles."[4]

Kessler proves that you can take the most complex technology —or idea—and describe it in three concise points.

Ed Baig also writes for *USA Today*, reviewing some of the latest technology products. After testing Microsoft's new operating system (Windows 7) in its beta, or test mode, Baig focused on three highlights:

» **Getting around.** "Icons on the task bar are bigger and you can arrange them in any way you choose."

» **Security.** "Windows 7 won't constantly bog you down with annoying security messages every time you try to load programs or change settings."

» **Compatibility.** "Even as a beta, Windows 7 recognized my printer and digital camera."[5]

Baig, Kessler, and other top reporters write their material in manageable chunks to make it easier to read. So did Jobs. He wriote the content of his presentation just as a *USA Today* reporter would review a product: headline, introduction, three points, conclusion.

to reach the next level. What are these challenges? The first, 3G networking—faster networking. Second, enterprise support. Third, third-party application support. And fourth, we need to sell iPhone in more countries."

After providing that verbal preview of the four points he would discuss in more detail, Jobs returned to the first point. "So, as we arrive at iPhone's first birthday, we're going to take it to the next level, and today we're introducing the iPhone 3G."[6] This was a remarkably consistent technique in Jobs's presentations. He outlined three or four points, returned to the first point, explained each one in more depth, and then summarized each point. This is a simple recipe for ensuring your audience will retain the information you are sharing.

Jobs and Ballmer Share a Love of Threes

In January 2009, then Microsoft CEO Steve Ballmer opened the Consumer Electronics Show in Las Vegas. It was his first keynote speech at the conference, replacing Bill Gates, who had moved on to his philanthropic pursuits. Over fifteen years, it had become a tradition for Microsoft to open the conference, and Gates had delivered nearly every keynote. As a presenter, Ballmer was much different from Gates. He exuded passion, energy, and excitement. He stripped his talk of esoteric jargon and technical buzzwords. Ballmer also understood the value of the rule of three in providing a verbal road map for his listeners.

How the Rule of Three Helped DuPont Face an Economic Meltdown

In his book *Leadership in the Era of Economic Uncertainty*, management guru Ram Charan wrote about the global giant DuPont and how it aggressively responded to the economic meltdown in 2008. Chief executive Chad Holliday met with the company's top leaders and economists, formulating a crisis plan that was implemented within ten days. DuPont had sixty thousand employees at the time. Every employee met with a manager who explained in plain English what the company had to accomplish. Employees were then asked to identify three things that they could do immediately to conserve cash and reduce costs. The company had decided that if employees felt overwhelmed, they wouldn't take any action. Three, however, was a manageable and meaningful number that would spark employees to take action.

The groups of three just kept coming. Here are a few examples from his keynote:

» "I want to spend time with you talking about the economy, our industry, and the work that we are doing at Microsoft."
» "When I think about opportunities, in my mind I frame it in three key areas. The first is the convergence of the three screens people use every day: the PC, the phone, and the TV . . . The second major area is how you will interact with your computer and other devices in a more natural way . . . and the last area of opportunity is what I call connected experiences."
» "Looking back, there were three things that made Windows and the PC successful. First, the PC enabled the best applications and let them work together. Second, the PC enabled more choice in hardware. And, third, the Windows experience helped us all work together."

» "We're on track to deliver the best version of Windows ever. We're putting in all the right ingredients—simplicity, reliability, and speed."[7]

Ballmer used groups of three no fewer than five times in one presentation, making his speech much easier to follow than any of Gates's keynotes. Although there was no love lost between Apple and Microsoft, both Ballmer and Jobs understood that explaining complex technology in language that was easy to follow was the first step to creating excitement among their existing and future customers.

The Road Map as an Agenda

Jobs kicked off Macworld 2008 with the verbal equivalent of an agenda (there were no agenda slides in a Steve Jobs presentation, just verbal road maps). "I've got four things I'd like to talk to you about today, so let's get started," he said.

The *first* one is Leopard. I'm thrilled to report that we have delivered over five million copies of Leopard in the first ninety days. Unbelievable. It's the most successful release of Mac OS X ever . . . Number *two* is about the iPhone. Today happens to be the two hundredth day that the iPhone went on sale. I'm extraordinarily pleased that we have sold four million iPhones to date . . . OK, number *three*. This is a good one, too. Number three is about iTunes. I'm really pleased to report that last week we sold our four billionth song. Isn't that great? On Christmas Day we set a new record, twenty million songs in one day. Isn't that amazing? That's our new one-day record . . . So, that brings us to number *four*. There is something in the air. What is it? Well, as you know, Apple makes the best notebooks in the business: the MacBook and the MacBook Pro. Well, today we're introducing a third kind of notebook. It's called the MacBook Air . . ."[8]

What the World's Greatest Speechwriters Know

Ted Sorensen, John F. Kennedy's speechwriter, believed that speeches should be written for the ear and not for the eye. His speeches would list goals and accomplishments in a numbered sequence to make it easier for listeners. Kennedy's speech to a joint session of Congress on May 25, 1961, offers a perfect example of Sorensen's technique. In calling for a major commitment to explore space, Kennedy said:

> First, I believe that this nation should commit itself to achieving the goal, before this decade is out, of landing a man on the moon and returning him safely to earth. No single space project in this period will be more impressive to mankind, or more important for the long-range exploration of space . . . Secondly, an additional twenty-three million dollars, together with the seven million already available, will accelerate development of the Rover nuclear rocket . . . Third, an additional fifty million dollars will make the most of our present leadership, by accelerating the use of space satellites for worldwide communications. Fourth, an additional seventy-five million dollars will help give us at the earliest possible time a satellite system for worldwide weather observation. Let it be clear that I am asking the Congress and the country to accept a firm commitment to a new course of action, a course which will last for many years and carry heavy costs . . . If we are to go only halfway, or reduce our sights in the face of difficulty, in my judgment it would be better not to go at all.[9]

U.S. president Barack Obama, a fan of Kennedy's speeches, adopted some of Sorensen's rules to make his own speeches more impactful. Here are some samples from Obama's speeches that follow the rule of three, beginning with the speech that put him on the map, his keynote address at the 2004 Democratic National Convention:

> I believe that we can give our middle class relief and
> provide working families with a road to opportunity . . .
> I believe we can provide jobs to the jobless, homes to
> the homeless, and reclaim young people in cities across
> America from violence and despair . . . I believe that we
> have a righteous wind at our backs and that as we stand
> on the crossroads of history, we can make the right
> choices and meet the challenges that face us.[10]

As illustrated in this excerpt, Obama not only breaks up his speeches into paragraphs of three sentences but also often delivers three points within sentences.

When Obama took the oath of office to become America's forty-fourth president on Tuesday, January 20, 2009, he delivered a historical address to some two million people who gathered to watch the speech in person and millions more on television around the world. Obama made frequent use of threes in the speech:

> » "I stand here today humbled by the task before us, grateful for the trust you have bestowed, mindful of the sacrifices born by our ancestors."
> » "Homes have been lost, jobs shed, businesses shuttered."
> » "Our health care is too costly, our schools fail too many, and each day brings further evidence that the ways we use energy strengthen our adversaries and threaten our planet."
> » "Today I say to you that the challenges we face are real, they are serious, and they are many."
> » "Our workers are no less productive than when this crisis began, our minds no less inventive, our goods and services no less needed than they were last month or last year."[11]

Every time Jobs announced a numeral, his slide contained just one image—the number itself (1, 2, 3, and 4). We will explore the simplicity of Jobs's slide design more thoroughly in Scene 8, but for now keep in mind that your slides should mirror your narrative. There is no need to make the slides complicated.

Jobs not only broke up his presentations into groups but also described features in lists of three or four items. "There are *three* major breakthroughs in iPod," Jobs said in 2005. "The *first* one is, it's ultraportable" [5 GB, one thousand songs in your pocket]. "*Second*, we've built in Firewire" [Jobs explained how Firewire enabled a download of an entire CD in five to ten seconds, versus five to ten minutes via a USB connection]. "*Third*, it has extraordinary battery life," Jobs said.[12] He then described how the iPod provided ten hours of battery life, ten hours of continuous music.

This chapter could easily have become the longest in the book, because every Steve Jobs presentation contained verbal road maps with the rule of three playing a prominent role. Even when he was not using slides in a traditional keynote presentation, Jobs was speaking in threes. Jobs kicked off his now famous Stanford commencement address by saying, "Today I want to tell you *three* stories from my life."[13] His speech followed the outline. He told three personal stories from his life, explained what they taught him, and turned those stories into lessons for the graduates.

Applying the Rule of Three

As we've learned, business leaders often prepare for major television interviews or keynote presentations by structuring their message around three or four key points. I know, because I train them to do so! Here is how I would apply the advice from Scenes 4 and 5 to prepare for an interview on the topic of this book. First, I would create a headline of no more than 140 characters: "Deliver a presentation like Steve Jobs." Next, I would write three big ideas: (1) Create the story, (2) Deliver the experience, and (3) Package the material. Under each of the three ideas, I would include rhetorical devices to enhance the narrative: stories, examples, and facts. Following is an example of how an abbreviated interview might unfold:

REPORTER: Carmine, tell us more about this book.

CARMINE: *The Presentation Secrets of Steve Jobs* reveals, for the first time, how to do deliver a presentation like Steve Jobs. The Apple CEO was considered one of the most electrifying speakers in the world. This book walks you through the very steps he used to sell his ideas. Best of all, anyone can learn these techniques to improve his or her very next presentation.

REPORTER: OK, so where would we start?

CARMINE: You can deliver a presentation like Steve Jobs [repeat the headline at least twice in a conversation] if you follow these three steps: First, create the story. Second, deliver the experience. And third, package the material. Let's talk about the first step, creating the story . . .

Jimmy V's Famous Speech

On March 4, 1993, college basketball coach Jimmy Valvano gave one of the most emotional speeches in recent sports history. Valvano had led North Carolina State to the NCAA championship in 1983. Ten years later, dying of cancer, Valvano accepted the Arthur Ashe Courage & Humanitarian Award. Valvano's use of the rule of three provided the two most poignant moments of the speech (emphasis added):

> To me, there are *three* things we all should do every day. We should do this every day of our lives. *Number one* is laugh. You should laugh every day. *Number two* is think. You should spend some time in thought. And *number three* is, you should have your emotions moved to tears—could be happiness or joy. But think about it. If you laugh, you think, and you cry, that's a full day . . . Cancer can take away all my physical ability. It cannot touch my mind; it cannot touch my heart; and it cannot touch my soul. And those three things are going to carry on forever. I thank you and God bless all of you.[14]

As you can tell in this example, providing a road map of three parts creates an outline for a short interview, a much longer interview, or an entire presentation.

Your listeners' brains are working overtime. They're consuming words, images, and sensory experiences, not to mention conducting their own internal dialogues. Make it easy for them to follow your narrative.

DIRECTOR'S NOTES

» Create a list of all the key points you want your audience to know about your product, service, company, or initiative.

» Categorize the list until you are left with only three major message points. This group of three will provide the verbal road map for your pitch or presentation.

» Under each of your three key messages, add rhetorical devices to enhance the narrative. These could include some or all of the following: personal stories, facts, examples, analogies, metaphors, and third-party endorsements.

SCENE 6

Introduce the Antagonist

**Will Big Blue dominate the entire computer
industry? Was George Orwell right?**

—STEVE JOBS

n every classic story, the hero fights the villain. The same storytelling outline applies to world-class presentations. Steve Jobs established the foundation of a persuasive story by introducing his audience to an antagonist, an enemy, and a problem in need of a solution. In 1984, the enemy was "Big Blue."

Apple is behind one of the most influential television ads in history and one in which we begin to see the hero-villain scenario playing out in Jobs's approach to messaging. The television ad, "1984," introduced Macintosh to the world. It ran only once, during the January 22 Super Bowl that same year. The Los Angeles Raiders were crushing the Washington Redskins, but more people remember the spot than the score.

Ridley Scott, of *Alien* fame, directed the Apple ad, which begins with shaven-headed drones listening to their leader (Big Brother) on a giant screen. An athletic blonde woman, dressed in skimpy eighties-style workout clothes, is running with a sledgehammer. Chased by helmeted storm troopers, she throws the hammer into the screen, which explodes in a blinding light as the drones sit with their mouths wide open. The spot ends with a somber announcer saying, "On January 24, Apple Computer will introduce Macintosh and you'll see why 1984 won't be like *1984*."[1]

Apple's board members had unanimously disliked the commercial and were reluctant to run it. Jobs, of course, supported it, because he understood the emotional power behind the classic story structure of the hero and villain. He realized every protagonist needs an enemy. In the case of the historic 1984 television ad, IBM represented the villain. IBM, a mainframe computer maker at the time, had made the decision to build a competitor to the world's first mass-market home computer, the Apple II. Jobs explained the ad in a 1983 keynote presentation to a select group of Apple salespeople who previewed the sixty-second television spot.

"It is now 1984," said Jobs. "It appears IBM wants it all. Apple is perceived to be the only hope to offer IBM a run for its money . . . IBM wants it all and is aiming its guns on its last obstacle to industry control: Apple. Will Big Blue dominate the entire computer industry? The entire information age? Was George Orwell right?"[2]

With that introduction, Jobs stepped aside as the assembled salespeople became the first public audience to see the commercial. The audience erupted into a thunderous cheer. For another sixty seconds, Steve remained onstage basking in the adulation, his smile a mile wide. His posture, body language, and facial expression said it all—*I nailed it!*

Problem + Solution = Classic Jobs

Introducing the antagonist (the problem) rallies the audience around the hero (the solution). Jobs structured his most exciting presentations around this classic storytelling device. For example, thirty minutes into one of his most triumphant presentations, the launch of the iPhone at Macworld 2007, he spent three minutes explaining why the iPhone was a product whose time had come. The villains in this case included all the current smartphones on the market, which, Jobs argued, weren't very smart.

Listed in the left column of Table 6.1 are excerpts from the actual presentation; the right column shows the words or describes the images on the accompanying slides.[3] Pay attention to how the slides act as a complement to the speaker.

TABLE 6.1 JOBS'S iPHONE KEYNOTE PRESENTATION

STEVE'S WORDS	STEVE'S SLIDES
"The most advanced phones are called 'smartphones,' so they say."	Smartphone
"They typically combine a phone plus e-mail plus a baby Internet."	Smartphone Phone + Email + Internet
"The problem is they are not so smart and they are not so easy to use. They're really complicated. What we want to do is make a leapfrog product that is way smarter than any mobile device has ever been."	Smartphone Not so smart. Not so easy to use.
"So, we're going to reinvent the phone. We're going to start with a revolutionary user interface."	Revolutionary UI
"It is the result of years of research and development."	Revolutionary UI Years of research & development
"Why do we need a revolutionary user interface? Here are four smartphones: the Motorola Q, BlackBerry, Palm Treo, Nokia E62—the usual suspects."	Image of four existing smartphones: Motorola Q, BlackBerry, Palm Treo, and Nokia E62
"What's wrong with their user interface? The problem with them is in the bottom forty. It's this stuff right there [points to keyboards on the phones]. They all have these keyboards that are there whether you need them or not. And they all have these control	The top half of each image fades away, leaving just the bottom half— the keyboard

continued

TABLE 6.1 JOBS'S iPHONE KEYNOTE PRESENTATION (continued)

STEVE'S WORDS	STEVE'S SLIDES
buttons that are fixed in plastic and are the same for every application. Well, every application wants a slightly different user interface, a slightly optimized set of buttons just for it. And what happens if you think of a great idea six months from now? You can't add a button to these things. They're already shipped. So, what do you do?"	
"What we're going to do is get rid of all these buttons and just make a giant screen."	Image of iPhone
"How are we going to communicate with this? We don't want to carry around a mouse. So, what are we going to do? A stylus, right? We're going to use a stylus."	Image of iPhone on its side; a stylus fades in
"No [laughs]. Who wants a stylus? You have to get them out, put them away—you lose them. Yuck. Nobody wants a stylus."	Words appear next to image: Who wants a stylus?
"So, let's not use a stylus. We're going to use the best pointing device in the world—a pointing device that we're all born with. We're born with ten of them. We'll use our fingers."	Stylus fades out of frame as image of index finger appears next to iPhone
"We have invented a new technology called 'multi-touch,' which is phenomenal."	Finger fades out, and words appear: Multi-Touch
"It works like magic. You don't need a stylus. It's far more accurate than any touch display that's ever been shipped. It ignores unintended touches. It's supersmart. You can do multi-finger gestures on it, and boy have we patented it!" [laughter]	Words reveal upper right: Works like magic No stylus Far more accurate Ignores unintended touches Multi-finger gestures Patented

Make note of how Jobs asked rhetorical questions to advance the story. "Why do we need a revolutionary user interface?" he asked before introducing the problem. He even raised problems to his own solution. When he introduced the concept of replacing the keyboard with a touch screen, he rhetorically asked, "How are we going to communicate with this?" His ready answer was, "We're going to use the best pointing device in the world . . . our fingers."

Nobody really cares about your product or Apple's products or Microsoft's or any other company's, for that matter. What people care about is solving problems and making their lives a little better. As in the smartphone example in Table 6.1, Jobs described the pain they're feeling, gave them a reason for their pain (usually caused by competitors), and, as you will learn in Scene 7, offered a cure.

Making His Case to CNBC

"Why in the world would Apple want to jump into the handset market with so much competition and so many players?" asked CNBC's Jim Goldman in one of the few interviews Jobs granted immediately after the iPhone announcement. Jobs answered the question by posing a problem in need of a solution: "We used all the handsets out there, and boy is it frustrating. It's a category that needs to be reinvented. Handsets need to be more powerful and much easier to use. We thought we could contribute something. We don't mind if there are other companies making products. The fact is there were one billion handsets sold in 2006. If we just got 1 percent market share, that's ten million units. We've reinvented the phone and completely changed the expectations for what you can carry in your pocket."

"What message is this sending to your competitors?" asked Goldman.

"We're a product company. We love great products. In order to explain what our product is, we have to contrast it to what products are out there right now and what people use," said Jobs.[4] This last sentence revealed Jobs's approach to crafting a persuasive story. Explanations of new products or services require context, a relevance to a problem in your customer's life that is causing that person "pain." Once the pain is established, your listener will be much more receptive to a product or service that will alleviate that pain.

The Apple Religion

In his book *Buyology*, marketing guru Martin Lindstrom equates Apple's message with the same powerful ideas that propel widespread religions. Both appeal to a common vision and a specific enemy.

"Most religions have a clear vision," writes Lindstrom. "By that I mean they are unambiguous in their missions, whether it's to achieve a certain state of grace or achieve a spiritual goal. And, of course, most companies have unambiguous missions as well. Steve Jobs's vision dates back to the mid-1980s when he said, 'Man is the creator of change in this world. As such he should be above systems and structures, and not subordinate to them.' Twenty years and a few million iPods later, the company still pursues this vision."[5]

According to Lindstrom, who spent years studying the common traits of lasting brands, religions and brands such as Apple have another quality in common: the idea of conquering a shared enemy. "Having an identifiable enemy gives us the chance not only to articulate and showcase our faith, but also to unite ourselves with our fellow believers . . . this us-versus-them strategy attracts fans, incites controversy, creates loyalty, and gets us thinking—and arguing—and, of course, buying."[6]

Will It Eat Me?

Establishing the antagonist early is critical to persuasion, because our brains need a bucket—a category—in which to place a new idea. Think about it this way: your brain craves meaning before details. According to scientist John Medina, our brains were formed to see the big picture. Medina says that when primitive man saw a saber-toothed tiger, he asked himself, "Will it eat me?" and not, "How many teeth does it have?"

The antagonist gives your audience the big picture. "Don't start with the details. Start with the key ideas and, in a hierarchical fashion, form the details around these larger notions," writes Medina in his book *Brain Rules*.[7] In presentations, start with the big picture—the problem—before filling in the details (your solution).

Apple unveiled the Safari Web browser during Macworld 2003, designating it the fastest browser on the Mac. Safari would join several other browsers vying for attention in the face of Microsoft's juggernaut—Internet Explorer. At his persuasive best, Jobs set up the problem—introducing the antagonist— simply by asking a rhetorical question: "Why do we need our own browser?"[8] Before demonstrating the new features—filling in the details—he needed to establish a reason for the product's existence.

Jobs told the audience that there were two areas in which competitors such as Internet Explorer, Netscape, and others fell short: speed and innovation. In terms of speed, Jobs said Safari would load pages three times faster than Internet Explorer on the Mac. In the area of innovation, Jobs discussed the limitations of current browsers, including the fact that Google search was not provided in the main toolbar and that organizing bookmarks left a lot to be desired. "What we found in our research is that people don't use bookmarks. They don't use favorites very much because this stuff is complicated and nobody has figured out how to use it," Jobs said. Safari would fix the problems by incorporating Google search into the main toolbar and adding features that would allow users to more easily navigate back to previous sites or favorite Web pages.

One simple sentence is all you need to introduce the antagonist: "Why do you need this?" This one question allowed Jobs to review the current state of the industry (whether it was browsers, operating systems, digital music, or any other facet) and to set the stage for the next step in his presentation, offering the solution.

The $3,000-a-Minute Pitch

During one week in September, dozens of entrepreneurs pitch their start-ups to influential groups of media, experts, and investors at two separate venues—TechCrunch 50 in San Francisco and DEMO in San Diego. For start-up founders, these high-stakes presentations mean the difference between success and obsolescence. TechCrunch organizers believe that eight minutes is the ideal amount of time in which to communicate an idea. If you cannot express your idea in eight minutes, the thinking goes, you need to refine your idea. DEMO gives its presenters even less time—six minutes. DEMO also charges an $18,500 fee to present, or $3,000 per minute. If you had to pay $3,000 a minute to pitch your idea, how would you approach it?

The consensus among venture capitalists who attend the presentations is that most entrepreneurs fail to create an intriguing story line because they jump right into their product without explaining the problem. One investor told me, "You need to create a new space in my brain to hold the information you're about to deliver. It turns me off when entrepreneurs offer a solution without setting up the problem. They have a pot of coffee—their idea—without a cup to pour it in." Your listeners' brains have only so much room to absorb new information. It's as if most presenters try to squeeze 2 MB of data into a pipe that carries 128 KB. It's simply too much.

A company called TravelMuse had one of the most outstanding pitches in DEMO 2008. Founder Kevin Fleiss opened his pitch this way: "The largest and most mature online retail segment is travel, totaling more than $90 billion in the United States alone [establishes category]. We all know how to book a trip online. But booking is the last 5 percent of the process [begins to introduce problem]. The 95 percent that comes before booking—deciding where to go, building a plan—is where all the heavy lifting happens. At TravelMuse we make planning easy by seamlessly integrating content with trip-planning tools to provide a complete experience [offers solution]."[9] By introducing the category and the problem before introducing the solution, Fleiss created the cup to pour the coffee into.

Investors are buying a stake in ideas. As such, they want to know what pervasive problem the company's product addresses. A solution in search of a problem carries far less appeal. Once the problem and solution are established, investors feel comfortable moving on to questions regarding the size of the market, the competition, and the business model.

The Ultimate Elevator Pitch

The problem need not take long to establish. Jobs generally took just a few minutes to introduce the antagonist. You can do so in as little as thirty seconds. Simply create a one-sentence answer for the following four questions: (1) What do you do? (2) What problem do you solve? (3) How are you different? (4) Why should I care?

When I worked with executives at LanguageLine, in Monterey, California, we crafted an elevator pitch based on answers to the four questions. If we did our job successfully, the following pitch should tell you a lot about the company: "LanguageLine is the world's largest provider of phone interpretation services for companies who want to connect with their non-English-speaking customers [what it does]. Every twenty-three seconds, someone who doesn't speak English enters this country [the problem]. When he or she calls a hospital, a bank, an insurance company, or 911, it's likely that a LanguageLine interpreter is on the other end [how it's different]. We help you talk to your customers, patients, or sales prospects in 150 languages [why you should care]."

The Antagonist: A Convenient Storytelling Tool

Steve Jobs shared three things in common with former U.S. vice president turned global warming expert Al Gore: a commitment to the environment, a love for Apple (Al Gore sits on Apple's board), and an engaging presentation style.

Al Gore's award-winning documentary, *An Inconvenient Truth*, is a presentation designed with Apple's storytelling devices in mind. Gore gives his audience a reason to listen by establishing a problem everyone can agree on (critics may differ on the solution, but the problem is generally accepted).

Gore begins his presentation—his story—by setting the stage for his argument. In a series of colorful images of Earth taken from various space missions, he not only gets audiences to appreciate the beauty of our planet but also introduces the problem. Gore opens with a famous photograph called "Earthrise," the first look at Earth from the moon's surface. Then Gore reveals a series of photographs in later years showing signs of global warming such as melting ice caps, receding shorelines, and hurricanes. "The ice has a story to tell us," he says. Gore then describes the villain in more explicit terms: the burning of fossil fuels such as coal, gas, and oil has dramatically increased the amount of carbon dioxide in the earth's atmosphere, causing global temperatures to rise.

In one of the most memorable scenes of the documentary, Gore explains the problem by showing two colored lines (red and blue) representing levels of carbon dioxide and average temperatures going back six hundred thousand years. According to Gore, "When there is more carbon dioxide, the temperature gets warmer." He then reveals a slide that shows the graph climbing to the highest level of carbon dioxide in our planet's history—which represents where the level is today. "Now if you'll bear with me, I want to really emphasize this next point," Gore says as he climbs onto a mechanical lift. He presses a button, and the lift carries him what appears to be at least five feet. He is now parallel with the point on the graph representing current CO_2 emissions. This elicits a small laugh from his audience. It's funny but insightful at the same time. "In less than fifty years," he goes on to say, "it's going to continue to go up. When some of these children who are here are my age, here's where it's going to be." At this point, Gore presses the button again, and the lift carries him higher for about ten seconds. As he's tracking the graph upward, he turns to the audience and says, "You've heard of 'off the charts'? Well, here's where we're going to be in less than fifty years."[10] It's funny, memorable, and powerful at the same time. Gore takes facts, figures, and statistics and brings them to life.

Gore uses many of the same presentation and rhetorical techniques that we saw in a Steve Jobs presentation. Among them are the early introduction of the enemy, or the antagonist, rallying the audience around a common purpose. In a Jobs presentation, once the villain was clearly established, it was time to open the curtain to reveal the character who would save the day . . . the conquering hero.

DIRECTOR'S NOTES

» Introduce the antagonist early in your presentation. Always establish the problem before revealing your solution. You can do so by painting a vivid picture of your customers' pain point. Set up the problem by asking, "Why do we need this?"

» Spend some time describing the problem in detail. Make it tangible. Build the pain.

» Create an elevator pitch for your product using the four-step method described in this chapter. Pay particular attention to question number 2, "What problem do you solve?" Remember, nobody cares about your product. People care about solving their problems.

Reveal the Conquering Hero

The only problem with Microsoft is they just have no taste. And I don't mean that in a small way. I mean that in a big way.

—STEVE JOBS

Steve Jobs was a master at creating villains—the more treacherous, the better. Once Jobs introduced the antagonist of the moment (the limitation to current products), he introduced the hero, revealing the solution that would make your life easier and more enjoyable. In other words, an Apple product arrives in time to save the day. IBM played the antagonist in the 1984 television ad, as discussed in Scene 6. Jobs revealed the ad for the first time to a group of internal salespeople at an event in the fall of 1983.

Before showing the ad, Jobs spent several minutes painting "Big Blue" into a character bent on world domination. (It helped that IBM was known as Big Blue at the time. The similar ring to Big Brother was not lost on Jobs.) Jobs made Big Blue look more menacing than Hannibal Lecter:

It is 1958. IBM passes up the chance to a buy a new, fledgling company that has invented a new technology called xerography. Two years later, Xerox is born, and IBM has been kicking itself ever since. It is ten years later. The late sixties. Digital Equipment, DEC, and others invent the minicomputer. IBM dismisses the minicomputer as too small to do serious computing and therefore unimportant to their business. DEC grows to become a multihundred-million-dollar corporation, while IBM finally enters the minicomputer market. It is now ten years later. The late seventies. In 1977, Apple, a young, fledgling company on the West Coast, invents the Apple II, the first personal computer as we know it today [introduces the hero]. IBM dismisses the personal computer as too small to do serious computing and unimportant to their business [the villain overlooking the hero's qualities]. The early eighties. In 1981, Apple II has become the world's most popular computer, and Apple has grown into a $300 million company, becoming the fastest-growing corporation in American business history. With over fifty competitors vying for a share, IBM enters the personal computer market in November 1981, with the IBM PC. 1983. Apple and IBM emerge as the industry's strongest competitors, each selling over $1 billion in personal computers in 1983 [David has now matched Goliath]. The shakeout is in full swing. The first major firm goes bankrupt, with others teetering on the brink. It is now 1984. It appears IBM wants it all [the hero is about to spring into action]. Apple is perceived to be the only hope to offer IBM a run for its money. Dealers initially welcoming IBM with open arms now fear an IBM-dominated and -controlled future. They are increasingly and desperately turning back to Apple as the only force that will ensure their future freedom.[1]

The audience broke out into wild cheers as Jobs created a classic showdown. Jobs played his best James Bond. Just as the villain is about to destroy the world, Bond—or Jobs—enters the scene and calmly saves the day. Ian Fleming would be proud.

The Hero's Mission

The hero's mission in a Steve Jobs presentation was not necessarily to slay the bad guy, but to make our lives better. The introduction of the iPod on October 23, 2001, demonstrates this subtle but important difference.

It helps to understand the state of the digital music industry at the time. People were carrying portable CD players that looked monstrous compared with today's tiny iPods. The few existing digital music players were big and clunky or simply not that useful due to a small storage capacity that allowed only a few dozen songs. Some products, such as the Nomad Jukebox, were based on a 2.5-inch hard drive and, while portable, were heavy and were painfully slow to transfer songs from a PC. Battery life was so short that the devices were pretty much useless. Recognizing a problem in need of a solution, Jobs entered as the conquering hero.

"Why music?" Jobs asked rhetorically.

"We love music. And it's always good to do something you love. More importantly, music is a part of everyone's life. Music has been around forever. It will always be around. This is not a speculative market. And because it's a part of everyone's life, it's a very large target market all around the world. But interestingly enough, in this whole new digital-music revolution, there is no market leader. No one has found a recipe for digital music. We found the recipe."

Once Jobs whetted the audience's appetite by announcing that Apple had found the recipe, he had set the stage. His next step would be to introduce the antagonist. He did so by taking his audience on a tour of the current landscape of portable music players. Jobs explained that if you wanted to listen to music on the go, you could buy a CD player that held ten to fifteen songs, a flash player, an MP3 player, or a hard-drive device such as the Jukebox. "Let's look at each one," Jobs said.

A CD player costs about $75 and holds about ten to fifteen songs on a CD. That's about $5 a song. You can buy a flash player for $150. It holds about ten to fifteen songs, or about $10 a song. You can go buy an MP3 CD player that costs $150, and you can burn up to 150 songs, so you get down to a dollar a song. Or you can buy a hard-drive Jukebox player for $300. It holds about one thousand songs and costs thirty cents a song. We studied all these, and that's where we want to be [points to "hard drive" category on slide]. We are introducing a product today that takes us exactly there, and that product is called iPod.

With that, Jobs introduced the hero, the iPod. The iPod, he said, is an MP3 music player that plays CD-quality music. "But the biggest thing about iPod is that it holds a thousand songs. This is a quantum leap because for most people, it's their entire music library. This is huge. How many times have you gone on the road and realized you didn't bring the CD you wanted to listen to? But the coolest thing about iPod is your entire music library fits in your pocket. This was never possible before."[2] By reinforcing the fact that one's entire music library could fit in a pocket, Jobs reinforced the hero's (iPod) most innovative quality, reminding the audience that this was never possible until Apple appeared to save the day.

After the iPod's introduction, journalistist Mike Langberg wrote an article in which he pointed out that Creative (the maker of the original Nomad Jukebox) saw the opportunity in portable music players before Apple and unveiled a 6 GB hard-drive player in September 2000; Apple followed with its first iPod a year later. "But," he noted, "Creative lacks Apple's not-so-secret weapon: founder, chairman, and chief evangelist, Steve Jobs."[3]

"I'm a Mac." "I'm a PC."

The "Get a Mac" advertising campaign kicked off in 2006 and quickly became one of the most celebrated and recognizable television campaigns in recent corporate history. Comedian John Hodgman played "the PC," while actor Justin Long played the "Mac guy." Both stood against a stark white background, and the ads typically revolved around a story line in which the PC character was stuffy, slow, and frustrated, whereas the Mac had a friendly, easygoing personality. The ads played out the villain (PC) and hero (Mac) plot in thirty-second vignettes.

In one early ad "Angel/Devil," the Mac character gives PC an iPhoto book. An "angel" and a "devil" appear (the PC character dressed in a white suit and a red suit). The angel encourages PC to compliment Mac, while the devil prods PC to rip the book in half. The metaphor is clear. I'm a Mac/I'm a PC could be titled "I'm the good guy/I'm the bad guy."[4]

Once the hero is established, the benefit must be made clear. The one question that matters to people—Why should I care?—must be answered immediately. In an ad titled "Out of the Box," both characters pop out of boxes. The conversation goes like this:

> **MAC:** Ready to get started?
>
> **PC:** Not quite. I've got a lot to do. What's your big plan?
>
> **MAC:** Maybe make a home movie, create a website, try out my built-in camera. I can do it all right out of the box. What about you?
>
> **PC:** First, I've got to download those new drivers, I have to erase the trial software that came on my hard drive, and I've got a lot of manuals to read.
>
> **MAC:** Sounds like you've got a lot of stuff to do before you do any stuff. I'm going to get started, because I'm kind of excited. Let me know when you're ready. [Jumps out of box]
>
> **PC:** Actually, the rest of me is in some other boxes. I'll meet up with you later.

Some observers have criticized Apple's campaign, saying it smacked of smug superiority. Whether you liked the ads or hated them, there is no question they were effective, if only to keep people talking about Apple. In fact, the ads were so successful that Microsoft countered with an ad campaign of its own showing famous and not-so-famous people in all walks of life proudly proclaiming, "I'm a PC." But Apple had landed the first punch, painting the PC as nerdy and Apple as the cool kid you really want to be like. The Microsoft ads are fun to watch but lack the emotional punch of Apple's ads, for one reason—there's no villain.

Problem and Solution in Thirty Seconds

With more than 1.5 million applications available for the iPhone, the App Store has been a resounding success for Apple. The company features some individual apps in television and print ads for the iPhone and iPod Touch. The television ads are effective because in thirty seconds they paint a picture of a problem and offer a solution.

For example, in one ad for an app called Shazam, a narrator says, "You know when you don't know what song is playing and it's driving you crazy? [introduces problem] With the Shazam app, you just hold up your iPhone to the song, and within seconds you will know who sings it and how to get it."[5] The taglines are always the same: "That's the iPhone. Solving life's dilemmas one app at a time."

In thirty seconds, the commercials succeed in raising a problem and solving those problems one app at a time. The ads prove that establishing problems and offering solutions need not be time consuming. Don't spend too much time getting to the punch line.

Jobs Didn't Sell Computers; He Sold an Experience

After identifying the villain and introducing the hero, the next step in the Apple narrative is to show how the hero clearly offers the victim—the consumer—an escape from the villain's grip. The solution must be simple and free of jargon. In 2010, if you visited the Apple site, for instance, you would have found a list of the top reasons on "why you'll love a Mac."[6] The list included specific benefits and largely avoided complicated technical language. As a case in point, instead of saying that a MacBook Pro came with an Intel Core 2 Duo 2.4 GHz, 2 GB, 1,066 MHz, DDR3 SDRAM, and a 250 GB Serial ATA 5,400 rpm, the site listed direct benefits to the customer: "It's gorgeous inside and out; it does what a PC does, only better; it has the world's most advanced operating system, and then some; it's a pleasure to buy and own." You see, your target customers are not buying a

2.4 GHz multicore processor. They are buying the *experience* the processor provides.

Unlike his competitors, Jobs largely avoided mind-numbing data, stats, and jargon in his presentations. During Macworld 2006, Jobs added his famous "One more thing" signature phrase near the end of the presentation. The one more thing turned out to be the new MacBook Pro with an Intel Core 2 microprocessor, marking the first Intel chips in Mac notebooks. Jobs took a few minutes to clearly outline the problem and introduce the hero's tangible benefits, in plain and simple language.

"There's been this pesky little problem in the PowerBooks," Jobs said.

"It's not a secret that we've been trying to shoehorn a G5 [IBM microprocessor] into the PowerBook and have been unable to do so because of its power consumption. It's unrealistic in such a small package. We've done everything possible engineeringwise. We've consulted every possible higher authority [shows a slide with a photograph of the pope, drawing a huge laugh]."

Replacing the existing microprocessor with an Intel Core Duo, Jobs explained, yielded much better performance in a smaller package.

> Today we are introducing a new notebook computer we are calling the MacBook Pro. It has an Intel Core Duo chip in it, the same as we're putting in the new iMac, which means there will be dual processors in every MacBook Pro. What does this yield? It's four to five times faster than the PowerBookG4. These things are screamers . . . The new MacBook Pro is the fastest Mac notebook ever. It's also the thinnest. It's got some amazing new features. It has a 15.4-inch wide-screen display that is as bright as our cinema displays. It's a gorgeous display. It's got an iSight camera built in. Now you can have videoconferencing right out of the box on the go. It's great. Videoconferencing to go. This is heaven.[7]

You may or may not agree that a portable webcam is "heaven," but Jobs knew his audience and voiced what was, to those present, a serious problem in need of a solution.

This skill, the ability to create a villain and sell the benefit behind the hero's solution, was a Steve Jobs messaging technique that appeared in nearly every presentation and interview he gave. When Jobs agreed to be interviewed for Smithsonian's oral and video history series, he said that perseverance separates the successful entrepreneurs from the nonsuccessful ones. Perseverance, he said, comes from passion. "Unless you have a lot of passion about this, you're not going to survive. You're going to give it up. So, you've got to have an idea or a problem or a wrong that you want to right that you're passionate about. Otherwise, you're not going to have the perseverance to stick it through. I think that's half the battle right there."[8]

Jobs was the Indiana Jones of business. Just as great movie characters vanquish the villain, Jobs identified a common enemy, conquered that enemy, and won over the hearts and minds of his audience as he walked off into the sunset, leaving the world a better place.

DIRECTOR'S NOTES

» Describe the state of the industry (or product category) as it currently stands, followed by your vision of where it could be.

» Once you have established the antagonist—your customers' pain point—describe in plain English how your company, product, or service offers a cure for that pain.

» Remember, Steve Jobs believed that unless you're passionate about a problem that you want to make right, you won't have the perseverance to stick it out.

Obey the Ten-Minute Rule

Your audience checks out after ten minutes. Not in eleven minutes, but ten. We know this valuable fact thanks to research into cognitive functioning. Simply put, the brain gets bored. According to molecular biologist John Medina, "The brain seems to be making choices according to some stubborn timing pattern, undoubtedly influenced by both culture and gene."[1] Medina says peer-reviewed studies confirm the ten-minute rule, as do his own observations. In every college course Medina teaches, he asks the same question: "Given a class of medium interest, not too boring and not too exciting, when do you start glancing at the clock, wondering when the class will be over?" The answer is always exactly the same—ten minutes.

Steve Jobs did not give the brain time to get bored. In a thirty-minute period, his presentations included demonstrations, a second or even third speaker, and video clips. Jobs was well aware that even his gifts of persuasion were no match for a tired brain constantly seeking new stimuli.

Exactly ten minutes into his presentation at Macworld 2007—and not a second more—Jobs revealed a new Apple television commercial for iTunes and iPods (the one with a dark silhouette of people dancing in front of brightly colored backgrounds—the silhouettes are holding iPods, and the stark white earphones noticeably stick out). "Isn't that great?" Jobs said as the commercial ended.[2] Jobs essentially provided an "intermission" between the first act of his presentation (music) and the second (the launch of Apple TV, a product designed to play iTunes content on a widescreen TV).

Obey the ten-minute rule and give your listeners' brains a break. Here we go . . . on to Act 2: delivering the experience.

ACT 2

Deliver the Experience

Steve Jobs did not deliver a presentation. He offered an experience. Imagine visiting New York City to watch an award-winning play on Broadway. You would expect to see multiple characters, elaborate stage props, stunning visual backgrounds, and one glorious moment when you knew that the money you spent on the ticket was well worth it. In Act 2, you will discover that a Steve Jobs presentation contained each of these elements, which helped Jobs create a strong emotional connection between himself and his audience.

Just as in Act 1, each scene will be followed by a summary of specific and tangible lessons you can easily apply today. Following is a short description of each scene in this act:

» **SCENE 8: "Channel Their Inner Zen."** Simplification is a key feature in all of Apple's designs. Jobs applied the same approach to the way he created his slides. Every slide was simple, visual, and engaging.

» **SCENE 9: "Dress Up Your Numbers."** Data is meaningless without context. Jobs made statistics come alive and, most important, discussed numbers in a context that was relevant to his audience.

» **SCENE 10: "Use 'Amazingly Zippy' Words."** The "mere mortals" who experienced an "unbelievable" Steve Jobs presentation found it "cool," "amazing," and "awesome." These are just some of the zippy words Jobs used frequently. Find out why Jobs used the words he did and why they worked.

» **SCENE 11: "Share the Stage."** Apple is a rare company whose fortunes are closely tied to its cofounder. Despite the fact that Apple has a deep bench of brilliant leaders, many observers say that when Jobs was alive, Apple was a one-man show. Perhaps. But Jobs treated presentations as a symphony.

» **SCENE 12: "Stage Your Presentation with Props."** Demonstrations played a very important supporting role in every Jobs presentation. Learn how to deliver demos with pizzazz.

» **SCENE 13: "Reveal a 'Holy Shit' Moment."** From his earliest presentations, Jobs had a flair for the dramatic. Just when you thought you had seen all there was to see or heard all there was to hear, Jobs would spring a surprise. The moment was planned and scripted for maximum impact.

Channel Their Inner Zen

Simplicity is the ultimate sophistication.

—STEVE JOBS, QUOTING LEONARDO DA VINCI

Simplicity is one of the most important concepts in all Apple designs—from computers, to music players, to phones, and even to the retail store experience. "As technology becomes more complex, Apple's core strength of knowing how to make very sophisticated technology comprehensible to mere mortals is in ever greater demand,"[1] Jobs told a *New York Times* columnist writing a piece about the iPod in 2003.

Apple's design guru, Jony Ive, was interviewed for the same *New York Times* article and noted that Jobs wanted to keep the original iPod free of clutter and complexity. What the team removed from the device was just as important as what they kept in. "What's interesting is that out of that simplicity, and almost that unashamed sense of simplicity, and expressing it, came a very different product. But difference wasn't the goal. It's actually very easy to create a different thing. What was exciting is starting to realize that its difference was really a consequence of this quest to make it a very simple thing,"[2] Ive said. According to Ive, complexity would have meant the iPod's demise.

Jobs made products easy to use by eliminating features and clutter. This process of simplification translated to the way Jobs designed his slides as well. "It's laziness on the presenter's part to put everything on one slide," writes Nancy Duarte.[3] Where most presenters add as many words as possible to a slide, Jobs removed and removed and removed.

A Steve Jobs presentation was strikingly simple, visual, and devoid of bullet points. That's right—no bullet points. Ever. Of course, this raises the question, would a PowerPoint presentation without bullets still be a PowerPoint presentation? The answer is yes, and a much more interesting one. New research into cognitive functioning—how the brain works—proves that bullet points are the *least* effective way to deliver important information. Neuroscientists are finding that what passes as a typical presentation is usually the worst way to engage your audience.

"The brain is fundamentally a lazy piece of meat," writes Dr. Gregory Berns in *Iconoclast*.[4] In other words, the brain doesn't like to waste energy; it has evolved to be as efficient as possible. Presentation software such as PowerPoint makes it far too easy to overload the brain, causing it to work *way* too hard. Open PowerPoint, and the standard slide template has room for a title and subtitles, or bullets. If you are like most presenters, you write a title to the slide and add a bullet, a subbullet, and often a sub-subbullet. The result looks like the sample slide in Figure 8.1.

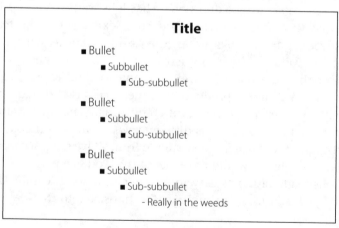

Figure 8.1 A typical, boring PowerPoint template.

This slide format gives me the willies. It should scare the heck out of you, too. Designer Garr Reynolds calls these creations "slideuments," an attempt to merge documents with slides. "People think they are being efficient and simplifying things," according to Reynolds. "A kind of kill-two-birds-with-one-stone approach. Unfortunately, the only thing 'killed' is effective communication."[5] Reynolds argues that PowerPoint, used effectively, can complement and enhance a presentation. He is not in favor of ditching PowerPoint. He is, however, in favor of ditching the use of "ubiquitous" bulleted-list templates found in both PowerPoint and Keynote. "And it's long past time that we realized that putting the same information on a slide in text form that is coming out of our mouths usually does not help—in fact, it hurts our message."[6]

Creating Steve Jobs–like slides will make you stand out in a big way, if only because so few people create slides the way he did. Your audience will be shocked and pleased, quite simply because nobody else did it. Before we look at *how* he did it, though, let's explore *why* he did it. Steve practiced Zen Buddhism. According to biographers Jeffrey Young and William Simon, Jobs began studying Zen in 1976.[7] A Zen Buddhist monk even officiated at his wedding to Lauren Powell in 1991.

A central principle of Zen is a concept called *kanso*, or simplicity. According to Reynolds, "The Japanese Zen arts teach us that it is possible to express great beauty and convey powerful messages through simplification."[8] Simplicity and the

No More Pencils

> We've been trained since youth to replace paying attention with taking notes. That's a shame. Your actions should demand attention. (Hint: bullets demand note taking. The minute you put bullets on the screen you are announcing, "Write this down, but don't really pay attention to it now.") People don't take notes when they go to the opera.[9]
>
> —SETH GODIN, SETH'S BLOG

elimination of clutter is a design component that Jobs incorporated into his products and slides. In fact, most everything about his approach to life was all-out Zen.

In 1982, photographer Diana Walker took a portrait of Jobs in the living room of his house. The room was huge, with a fireplace and ceiling-to-floor windows. Jobs sat on a small rug on a wooden floor. A lamp stood next to Jobs. Behind him were a record player and several albums, some of which were strewn on the floor. Now, Jobs could surely have afforded some furniture. He was, after all, worth more than $100 million when the photograph was taken. Jobs brought the same minimalist aesthetic to Apple's products. "One of the most important parts of Apple's design process is simplification," writes Leander Kahney in *Inside Steve's Brain*.[10]

"Jobs," says Kahney, "is never interested in technology for technology's sake. He never loads up on bells and whistles, cramming features into a product because they're easy to add. Just the opposite. Jobs pares back the complexity of his products until they are as simple and as easy to use as possible."[11]

When Apple first started in the 1970s, the company's ads had to stimulate demand for computers among ordinary consumers who, frankly, didn't quite see the need for these new devices. According to Kahney, "The ads were written in simple, easy-to-understand language with none of the technical jargon that dominates competitors' ads, who, after all, were trying to appeal to a completely different market—hobbyists."[12] Jobs kept his messages simple ever after.

The influential German painter Hans Hofmann once said, "The ability to simplify means to eliminate the unnecessary so that the necessary may speak." By removing clutter—extraneous information—from his products and presentations, Jobs achieved the ultimate goal: ease of use and clarity.

Macworld 2008: The Art of Simplicity

To gain a fuller appreciation of Jobs's simple slide creations, I have constructed a table of excerpts from his Macworld 2008 keynote presentation. The column on the left in Table 8.1

TABLE 8.1 EXCERPTS FROM JOBS'S MACWORLD 2008 KEYNOTE

STEVE'S WORDS	STEVE'S SLIDES
"I just want to take a moment and look back to 2007. Two thousand seven was an extraordinary year for Apple. Some incredible new products: the amazing new iMac, the awesome new iPods, and of course the revolutionary iPhone. On top of that, Leopard and all of the other great software we shipped in 2007."	2007
"It was an extraordinary year for Apple, and I want to just take a moment to say thank you. We have had tremendous support by all of our customers, and we really, really appreciate it. So, thank you for an extraordinary 2007."	Thank you.
"I've got four things I'd like to talk to you about today, so let's get started. The first one is Leopard."	1
"I'm thrilled to report that we have delivered over five million copies of Leopard in the first ninety days. Unbelievable. It's the most successful release of Mac OS X ever."	5,000,000 copies delivered in first 3 months

contains his actual words, and the column on the right contains the text on the accompanying slides.[13]

In four slides, Jobs's presentation contained fewer words by far than what most other presenters cram onto one slide alone. Cognitive researchers like John Medina at the University of Washington have discovered that the average PowerPoint slide contains forty words. Jobs's first four slides had a grand total of seven words, three numbers, one date, and no bullet points.

Let's Rock

On September 9, 2008, Jobs revealed new features for the iTunes music store and released new iPod models for the holiday season. Prior to the event—dubbed "Let's Rock"—observers speculated that Jobs might be in ill health, given his gaunt appearance. (In January 2009, Apple revealed that Jobs had been losing weight due to a hormone imbalance and would take a leave of absence for treatment.) Jobs addressed the rumor as soon as he stepped onstage. He did so without saying a word about it. He let a slide do the talking (see Table 8.2).[14] It was simple and unexpected. It generated cheers and deflected the tension. The rest of the introduction was equally as compelling for its simplicity.

Make note of the words and figures on the slides in the table. The words on the slide match the exact words that Jobs used to deliver his message. When Jobs said, "We're going to talk about music," the only word the audiences saw was "Music." The words acted as a complement.

If you deliver a point and your slide has too many words—and words that do not match what you say—your audience will have a hard time focusing on both you and the slide. In short, wordy slides detract from the experience. Simple slides keep the focus where it belongs—on you, the speaker.

Empirical Evidence

Empirical studies based on hard data, not opinions, prove that keeping your slides simple and free of extraneous information is the best way to engage your audience. Dr. Richard Mayer teaches educational psychology at the University of California, Santa Barbara, and has been studying multimedia learning since 1991. His theories are based on solid, empirical studies published in peer-reviewed journals. In a study titled "A Cognitive Theory of Multimedia Learning," Mayer outlined fundamental principles of multimedia design based on what scientists know about cognitive functioning. Steve Jobs's slides adhered to each of Mayer's principles:

MULTIMEDIA REPRESENTATION PRINCIPLE
"It is better to present an explanation in words and pictures than solely in words," writes Mayer.[15] According to Mayer, learners can

TABLE 8.2 EXCERPTS FROM JOBS'S 2008 "LET'S ROCK" PRESENTATION

STEVE'S WORDS	STEVE'S SLIDES
"Good morning. Thank you for coming this morning. We have some really exciting stuff to share with you. Before we do, I just wanted to mention this [gestures toward screen]."	The reports of my death are greatly exaggerated.
"Enough said. So, let's get on with the real topic of this morning, which is music. We're going to talk about music today, and we've got a lot of fun, new offerings."	Music
"So, let's start with iTunes."	iTunes
"iTunes, of course, is the ubiquitous music and video player married with the largest online content store in the world."	Image of iTunes home page
"iTunes now offers over eight and a half million songs. It's amazing. We started with two hundred thousand. We now have over eight and a half million songs."	8,500,000 songs
"Over one hundred and twenty-five thousand podcasts."	125,000 podcasts
"Over thirty thousand episodes of TV shows."	30,000 episodes of 1,000 TV shows
"Twenty-six hundred Hollywood movies."	2,600 Hollywood movies
"And, as of very recently, we now offer over three thousand applications for iPhone and iPod Touch."	3,000 applications for iPhone & iPod Touch
"And over the years, we've built up a great customer base. We're very pleased to announce that we've got over sixty-five million accounts in iTunes now. It's fantastic: sixty-five million customers."	65,000,000 accounts with credit cards

Two-Minute Warning

The task of leaders is to simplify. You should be able to explain where you have to go in two minutes.[16]

—JEROEN VAN DER VEER, FORMER CEO, ROYAL DUTCH SHELL

more easily understand material when it is presented in both words *and* pictures. In Mayer's experiments, groups that were exposed to multisensory environments—texts and pictures, animation, and video—always had much more accurate recall of the information, in some cases up to twenty years later!

CONTIGUITY PRINCIPLE

"When giving a multimedia explanation, present corresponding words and pictures contiguously rather than separately," Mayer advises.[17] In Mayer's experiments, he exposed students to certain types of information and then tested them on what they had learned. Those students who had read a text containing captioned illustrations near the corresponding words performed 65 percent better than those students who had read only plain text. Mayer says this principle is not surprising if you know how the brain works. When the brain is allowed to build two mental representations of an explanation—a verbal model and a visual model—the mental connections are that much stronger.

SPLIT-ATTENTION PRINCIPLE

Mayer also advises, "When giving a multimedia explanation, present words as auditory narration rather than visual on-screen text."[18] When presenting information, words delivered orally have greater impact than words read by your audience on a slide. Having too many words to process overloads the brain.

COHERENCE PRINCIPLE

"When giving a multimedia explanation," writes Mayer, "use few rather than many extraneous words and pictures."[1] Shorter presentations with more relevant information are more consistent with cognitive-learning theories. In sum, adding redundant or irrelevant information will impede, rather than aid, learning.

Mayer says an ideal slide would contain an image along with a simple line drawing directing the eye to the area that you want the viewer to see. This is called "signaling," and it is based on the scientific premise that your audience should not have to waste cognitive resources trying to find their place on the screen. Now, keep this in mind as we return to the "Let's Rock" event. About six minutes into the presentation, Jobs described a new feature available on iTunes—Genius (see Table 8.3).[20]

What could be easier to follow than simple line arrows pointing to the relevant area of a slide? Line drawings, few words, and a rich library of colorful images and photographs make up the majority of Jobs's slides. Simplicity—the elimination of clutter—is the theme that ties them all together.

The "McPresentation"

Critics once derided *USA Today* as "McPaper" for its short, easy-to-read stories. They're not laughing now. *USA Today* boasts the largest circulation of any newspaper in the United States. Readers love the colorful and bold graphics, charts, and photographs. After *USA Today* launched in 1982, many daily newspapers had no choice but to follow with shorter stories, splashes of color, and more photographs.

USA Today became famous for its "snapshots," stand-alone charts carried on the lower left of the main sections (i.e., News, Sports, Money, Life). They are easy-to-read statistical graphics that present information on various issues and trends in a visually appealing way. These graphics are among the best learning tools to create more visual slides. Study them. You'll see Richard Mayer's theory in action. Statistics share the slide with images, making the information more memorable. For an index of *USA Today* "snapshots," visit usatoday.com/snapshot/news/snapndex.htm.

TABLE 8.3 MORE EXCERPTS FROM JOBS'S 2008
"LET'S ROCK" PRESENTATION

STEVE'S WORDS	STEVE'S SLIDES
"We're introducing a new feature called Genius. Genius is pretty cool."	Genius
"What Genius does is automatically allow you to make playlists from songs in your music library that go great together, with just one click. It helps you rediscover music from your own music library and make great playlists that you probably wouldn't think of making any other way, and it really works well with just one click."	Automatically make playlists from songs in your library that go great together—with just one click
"So, that's what Genius is. Here's what it looks like. Let's say you're listening to a song—in my case, a Bob Dylan song."	Image of an iTunes library screen shot with a song highlighted
"There's a Genius button down here in the corner. You push that, and voilà—you've made a Genius playlist. In addition, you can bring up the Genius sidebar that makes recommendations from the iTunes store of music you might want to buy."	Animated circle appears and surrounds small Genius logo at bottom right of screen
"So, how does all this work? Well, we've got the iTunes store in the cloud, and we've added Genius algorithms to it."	Simple cloud line drawing with Genius logo inside
"So, you've got your music library. If you turn on Genius, it's going to send up information about your music library to iTunes so we can learn about your musical tastes. This information is sent completely anonymously."	Image of iTunes music library; arrow appears moving up from iTunes to cloud
"But it's not just information from you, because we are going to combine your information with the knowledge of millions of iTunes users as well."	Many images of iTunes music libraries appear alongside original
"And so, you're going to send your information up, and so are they."	Arrow up from original image to cloud, followed by more than a dozen arrows from other images

STEVE'S WORDS	STEVE'S SLIDES
"And as that happens, Genius just gets smarter, and smarter, and smarter."	Genius logo in cloud replaced with word "Smarter"
"Everybody benefits. When we send back down Genius results to you, they are tailored to your music library."	Arrow appears moving downward from cloud to iTunes library image
"So, automatically make playlists from songs in your library that go great together, with just one click. That's what Genius is about." [moves to demo]	

White Space

According to Garr Reynolds, there was a clear Zen aesthetic to Jobs's slides. "In Jobs's slides, you can see evidence of restraint, simplicity, and powerful yet subtle use of empty space."[21] Top designers such as Reynolds say the biggest mistake business professionals make is filling up every centimeter of the slide.

Nancy Duarte describes white space as giving your slides visual breathing room. "Visible elements of a slide often receive the most focus. But you need to pay equal attention to how much space you leave open . . . It's OK to have clear space—clutter is a failure of design."[22] Duarte says it's "laziness" on the part of the presenter to put everything on one slide.

Dense information and clutter requires too much effort for your audience. Simplicity is powerful. Empty space implies elegance, quality, and clarity. To see examples of how designers use space, visit some slide design contest winners at Slideshare. net (blog.slideshare.net/2007/05/07/contest-results-2).

Picture Superiority Effect

By now I hope you have decided to gather up your current slides, especially those with bullet points, and burn them. At least burn them digitally by deleting them and emptying your recycle bin so you can never retrieve those slides again. The argument for the visual representation of ideas is such a powerful concept that psychologists have a term for it: the picture superiority effect (PSE).[23] Researchers have discovered that visual and verbal information are processed differently along multiple "channels" in your brain. What this means for you and your next presentation is simple: your ideas are much more likely to be remembered if they are presented as pictures instead of words.

Scientists who have advanced the PSE theory believe it represents a powerful way of learning information. According to John Medina, a molecular biologist at the University of Washington School of Medicine, "Text and oral presentations are not just less efficient than pictures for retaining certain types of information; they are *way* less efficient. If information is presented orally, people remember about 10 percent, tested seventy-two hours after exposure. That figure goes up to 65 percent if you add a picture."[24]

Pictures work better than text because the brain sees words as several tiny pictures. According to Medina, "My text chokes you, not because my text is not enough like pictures but because my text is too much like pictures. To our cortex, unnervingly, there is no such thing as words."[25]

Steve's Love of Photos

On June 9, 2008, Steve Jobs announced the introduction of the iPhone 3G at the WWDC. He used eleven slides to do so, employing the concept of PSE to its fullest. Only one slide contained words ("iPhone 3G"). The others were all photographs. Take a look at Table 8.4.[26]

Given the same information, a mediocre presenter would have crammed all of it onto one slide. It would have looked something like the slide in Figure 8.2. Which do you find more memorable: Jobs's eleven slides or the one slide with a bulleted list of features?

When Steve Jobs introduced the MacBook Air as "the world's thinnest notebook," one slide showed a photograph of the

TABLE 8.4 JOBS'S WWDC 2008 KEYNOTE

STEVE'S WORDS	STEVE'S SLIDES
"As we arrive at iPhone's first birthday, we're going to take it to the next level."	Photo of birthday cake, with white frosting, strawberries, and one candle in the middle
"Today we're introducing the iPhone 3G. We've learned so much with the first iPhone. We've taken everything we've learned and more, and we've created the iPhone 3G. And it's beautiful."	iPhone 3G
"This is what it looks like [turns and gestures toward screen; audience laughs]. It's even thinner at the edges. It's really beautiful."	Side view of iPhone, so slim that it's hard to see on the slide and takes up very little space—an example of using empty space to communicate an idea
"It's got a full plastic back. It's really nice."	Full-screen view of the back
"Solid metal buttons."	Another side view of the device, where buttons are visible
"The same gorgeous 3.5-inch display."	Photo of front, showing display
"Camera."	Close-up photo of camera
"Flush headphone jack so you can use any headphones you like."	Close-up of headphone jack
"Improved audio. Dramatically improved audio."	Another photo from top of the device
"It's really, really great. And it feels even better in your hand, if you can believe it."	Returns to first side-view photo
"It's really quite wonderful. The iPhone 3G."	iPhone 3G

iPhone 3G
• Thinner at the edges
• Full plastic back
• Solid metal buttons
• 3.5-inch display
• Built-in camera
• Flush headphone jack
• Improved audio

Figure 8.2 Dull slides have no images and too many words.

new computer on top of an envelope, which was even larger than the computer itself. That's it. No words, no text boxes, no graphs, just the photo. How much more powerful can you get? The picture says it all. For illustrative purposes, I created the slide in Figure 8.3 as an example of a typical slide that a mediocre presenter would have created to describe a technical product. (Believe it or not, this mock slide is gorgeous compared with many slides I have actually seen in technical presentations delivered by subpar presenters.) It's a mishmash of fonts, styling, and text. Not memorable and truly awful.

In contrast, Figure 8.4 shows one of Jobs's slides from the Macbook Air presentation. The majority of his slides for this presentation looked very similar, featuring mostly photographs. He referred customers to the Apple website for more technical information; visuals dominated the keynote. Clearly, presenting a technical product in such a way as Jobs did for the Macbook Air is far more effective.

It takes confidence to deliver your ideas with photographs instead of words. Since you can't rely on the slides' text as a crutch, you must have your message down cold. But that was the difference between Jobs and millions of average communicators in business today. Jobs delivered his ideas simply, clearly, and confidently.

Simplify Everything

Simplicity applied to Jobs's slides as well as the words he carefully chose to describe products. Just as Jobs's slides were free

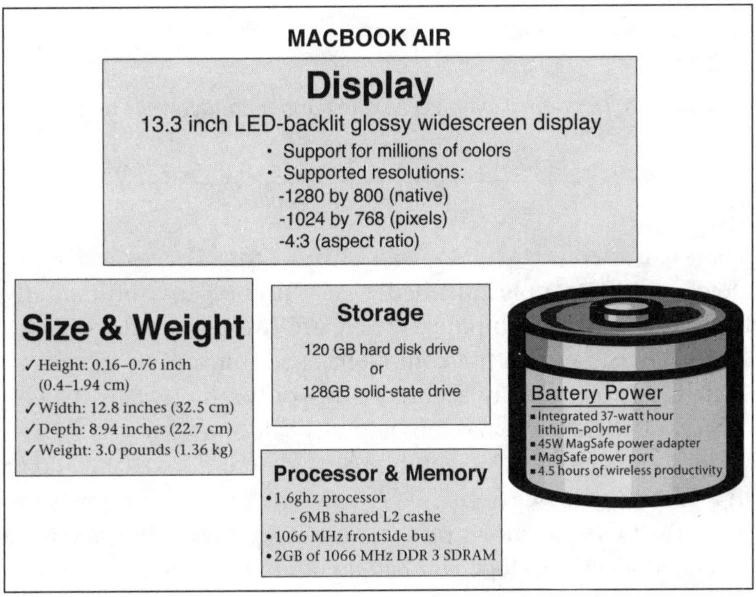

MACBOOK AIR

Display

13.3 inch LED-backlit glossy widescreen display
- Support for millions of colors
- Supported resolutions:
-1280 by 800 (native)
-1024 by 768 (pixels)
-4:3 (aspect ratio)

Size & Weight
✓ Height: 0.16–0.76 inch
(0.4–1.94 cm)
✓ Width: 12.8 inches (32.5 cm)
✓ Depth: 8.94 inches (22.7 cm)
✓ Weight: 3.0 pounds (1.36 kg)

Storage
120 GB hard disk drive
or
128GB solid-state drive

Battery Power
- Integrated 37-watt hour
lithium-polymer
- 45W MagSafe power adapter
- MagSafe power port
- 4.5 hours of wireless productivity

Processor & Memory
- 1.6ghz processor
 - 6MB shared L2 cashe
- 1066 MHz frontside bus
- 2GB of 1066 MHz DDR 3 SDRAM

Figure 8.3 An ugly slide with too much information, too many different fonts, and inconsistent styling.

Figure 8.4 Jobs's slides are strikingly simple and visually engaging.

TONY AVELAR/AFP/Getty Images

Einstein's Theory of Simplicity

> *If you can't explain it simply, you don't understand it well enough.*
>
> —ALBERT EINSTEIN

from extraneous text, so were his words. For example, in October 2008, Apple unveiled a new line of environmentally friendly MacBook computers. There are two principal ways Jobs could have described the computers. The column on the left in Table 8.5 is technically accurate but wordy; the text in the column on the right is what Jobs actually said.[27]

Jobs replaced lengthy sentences with descriptions that could fit in a Twitter post (see Scene 4). Simple sentences are simply easier to recall. Table 8.6 shows other examples of how Jobs *could* have described a new product, compared with what he actually said.

Plain English Campaign

If you need help writing crisp, clear sentences, the Plain English Campaign can help. Since 1979, this UK-based organization has been leading the fight to get governments and corporations to simplify their communications. The site is updated weekly with examples of the most complex, unintelligible business language submitted by readers around the world. The organizers define plain English as writing that the intended audience can read,

TABLE 8.5 DESCRIBING THE ENVIRONMENTALLY
 FRIENDLY MACBOOK

WHAT STEVE COULD HAVE SAID	WHAT STEVE ACTUALLY SAID
The new MacBook family meets the most stringent Energy Star standards and contains no brominated flame retardants. It uses only PVC-free internal cables and components and features energy-efficient LED-backlit displays that are mercury free.	"They are the industry's greenest notebooks."

TABLE 8.6 POSSIBLE VERSUS ACTUAL DESCRIPTIONS IN JOBS'S PRESENTATIONS

WHAT STEVE COULD HAVE SAID	WHAT STEVE ACTUALLY SAID
MacBook Air measures 0.16 inch at its thinnest point, with a maximum height of 0.76 inch.	"It's the world's thinnest notebook."
Time Capsule is an appliance combining an 802.11n base station with a server-grade hard disk that automatically backs up everything on one or more Macs running Leopard, the latest release of the Mac OS X operating system.	"With Time Capsule, plug it in, click a few buttons, and voilà—all the Macs in your house are backed up automatically."
Mac OS X features memory protection, pre-emptive multitasking, and symmetric multi-processing. It includes Apple's new Quartz 2D graphics engine based on the Internet-standard portable document format.	"Mac OS X is the most technically advanced personal computer operating system ever."

understand, and act upon the first time they read (or hear) it. The website has free guides on how to write in plain English as well as marvelous before-and-after examples, such as the ones in Table 8.7.[28]

Nearly everything you say in any memo, e-mail, or presentation can be edited for conciseness and simplicity. Remember that simplicity applies not just to the words on the slides but also to the words that come out of your mouth.

Author and advertising expert Paul Arden said that people go to a presentation to see you, not to read your words. He offered this tip: "Instead of giving people the benefit of your wit and wisdom (words), try painting them a picture. The more strikingly visual your presentation is, the more people will remember it."[29]

Leonardo da Vinci stated, "Simplicity is the ultimate sophistication." One of the most celebrated painters in history, he understood the real power of simplicity, as did Steve Jobs. When you discover this concept for yourself, your ideas will become far more persuasive than you could ever imagine.

TABLE 8.7 BEFORE-AND-AFTER EXAMPLES FROM THE PLAIN ENGLISH CAMPAIGN

BEFORE	AFTER
If there are any points on which you require explanation or further particulars we shall be glad to furnish such additional details as may be required by telephone.	If you have any questions, please call.
High-quality learning environments are a necessary precondition for facilitation and enhancement of the ongoing learning process.	Children need good schools to learn properly.
It is important that you shall read the notes, advice and information detailed opposite then complete the form overleaf (all sections) prior to its immediate return to the Council by way of the envelope provided.	Please read the notes before you fill in the form. Then send it back to us as soon as possible in the envelope provided.

DIRECTOR'S NOTES

» Avoid bullet points. Always. Well, almost always. Bullet points are perfectly acceptable on pages intended to be read by your audience, like books, documents, and e-mails. In fact, they break up the text quite nicely. Bullet points on presentation slides should be avoided. Pictures are superior.

» Focus on one theme per slide, and complement that theme with a photograph or image.

» Learn to create visually aesthetic slides. Above all, keep in mind that you do not have to be an artist to build slides rich in imagery. Visit carminegallo.com for a list of resources.

Dress Up
Your Numbers

**We have sold four million iPhones to date. If you
divide four million by two hundred days, that's
twenty thousand iPhones every day on average.**

—STEVE JOBS

On October 23, 2001, Apple launched a digital music
player that would revolutionize the entire music
industry—the iPod. At $399, however, it was an
expensive gadget. The iPod stored songs on a five-
gigabyte drive, but the number itself—5 GB—meant very little to
the average music lover. In his keynote presentation, Jobs made
that number more meaningful by saying that 5 GB provided
enough storage for one thousand songs. While that sounds more
impressive, it still did not provide a compelling value, since competitors were offering devices containing more storage at a lower
price. But wait, Jobs assured his audience, there's more. Jobs said
the new iPod weighed 6.5 ounces and was so small that it could
"fit in your pocket." When Jobs pulled one out of his own pocket,
it immediately clicked with the audience. The iPod's slogan said
it all: "1,000 songs in your pocket."[1]

Rarely do numbers resonate with people until those numbers
are placed in a context that people can understand, and the
best way to help them understand is to make those numbers
relevant to something with which they are already familiar. Five
gigabytes may mean nothing to you, but one thousand songs

in your pocket opens up an entirely new way for you to enjoy music.

Jobs dressed up numbers to make them more interesting. *Rolling Stone* reporter Jeff Goodell once asked Jobs what he thought about Apple's market share's being "stuck" at 5 percent in the United States. (The interview took place in 2003. As of this writing, Apple's market share of the computer industry is 10 percent.) The average reader might consider a 5 percent market share to be tiny. Jobs put the number in perspective when he described it this way: "Our market share is greater than BMW or Mercedes in the car industry. And yet, no one thinks BMW or Mercedes are going away and no one thinks they're at a tremendous disadvantage because of their market share. As a matter of fact, they're both highly desirable products and brands."[2] A 5 percent market share sounded low but became much more interesting when Jobs put it into context using the automobile analogy. Comparing Apple's market share to that of two admired brands told the story behind the numbers.

Twice as Fast at Half the Price

Data transfers on the original iPhone were often painfully slow on AT&T's standard cellular network (EDGE). Apple solved the problem with the launch of iPhone 3G on June 9, 2008. In the presentation, Jobs said the new iPhone was 2.8 times faster than EDGE, but he didn't stop there. Jobs put the figure into a context that normal Web surfers would understand and appreciate. He showed two images back to back—a National Geographic website loading on the EDGE network and also on the new 3G high-speed network. The EDGE site took fifty-nine seconds to fully load. The 3G site took only twenty-one seconds.[3] Further, Apple offered customers a bonus by lowering the price.

According to Jobs, consumers would be getting a phone that was twice as fast at half the price. Average presenters spew numbers with no context, assuming their audience will share their excitement. Jobs knew that numbers might have meaning to the most ardent fans but are largely meaningless to the majority of potential customers. Jobs made his numbers specific, relevant, and contextual.

Specific. Relevant. Contextual.

Let's take a look at two other examples in which Jobs made numbers specific, relevant, and contextual. On February 23, 2005, Apple added a new iPod to its lineup. The iPod featured 30 GB of storage. Now, most consumers could not tell you what 30 GB means to them. They know it's "better" than 8 GB, but that's about it. Jobs would have never announced a number that big without context, so he broke it down in language his audience could understand. He said 30 GB of storage is enough memory for 7,500 songs, 25,000 photos, or up to 75 hours of video. The description was specific (7,500 songs, versus "thousands" of songs), relevant to the lives of his audience (people who want mobile access to songs, photos, and video), and contextual because he chose to highlight numbers that his core audience of consumers would care about most.

In a second example, Jobs chose Macworld 2008 to hold a two-hundredth-day birthday celebration for the iPhone. Jobs said, "I'm extraordinarily pleased that we have sold four million iPhones to date." He could have stopped there (and most presenters would have done just that), but Jobs being Jobs, he continued: "If you divide four million by two hundred days, that's twenty thousand iPhones every day on average." Jobs could have stopped there as well, but he kept going, adding that the iPhone had captured nearly 20 percent of the market in that short period. OK, you might be saying, surely Jobs would have stopped there. He didn't.

"What does this mean in terms of the overall market?" he asked.[4] He then showed a slide of the U.S. smartphone market share with competitors RIM, Palm, Nokia, and Motorola. RIM's BlackBerry had the highest market share at 39 percent. The iPhone came in second at 19.5 percent. Jobs then compared iPhone's market share to that of all of the other remaining competitors. Jobs concluded that the iPhone matched the combined market share of the remaining three competitors—in the first ninety days of shipments. The numbers, of course, were very specific, relevant to the category, and, above all, contextual (Jobs was addressing investors). By comparing the iPhone against well-established competitors, Jobs made this achievement—selling four million units in the first quarter—far more remarkable.

Dress Up Numbers with Analogies

When I worked with SanDisk executives to prepare them for a major announcement at the 2008 Consumer Electronics Show in Las Vegas, we took a page from the Steve Jobs playbook. The maker of flash memory cards was introducing a card small enough to fit into a cell phone's micro SD slot. That's very tiny. Even bigger news was that it held 12 GB of storage in that small form factor. Now, only gadget geeks would find 12 GB exciting. So, we had to dress up the numbers à la Steve Jobs. Our final announcement went something like this:

"Today we're announcing the first 12 GB memory card for cell phones. It has fifty billion transistors. Think of each transistor as an ant: if you were to put fifty billion end to end, they would circle the globe twice. What does this mean to you? Enough memory to store six hours of movies. Enough memory to listen to music while traveling to the moon . . . and back!"

The number 12 GB is largely uninteresting unless you truly understand the implications of the achievement and what it means to you. When SanDisk compared fifty billion transistors to the number of ants that could circle the globe, the company was using an analogy to jazz up the numbers. Analogies point out similar features between two separate things. Sometimes, analogies are the best way to put numbers into a context that people can understand.

The more complex the idea, the more important it is to use rhetorical devices such as analogies to facilitate understanding. For example, on November 17, 2008, Intel released a powerful new microprocessor named the Core i7. The new chip represented a significant leap in technology, packing 730 million transistors on a single piece of silicon. Engineers described the technology as "breathtaking." But that's because they're engineers. How could the average consumer and investors appreciate the profound achievement? Vice President and General Manager, John Barton, found the answer.

In an interview with the *New York Times*, Barton said an Intel processor created twenty-seven years earlier had 29,000 transistors; the i7 boasted 730 million transistors on a chip the same size. He equated the two by comparing the city of Ithaca, New York (population 30,500), with the continent of Europe. "Ithaca is quite complex in its own right, if you think about all that goes on. If we scale up the population to 730 million, we come to Europe at about the right size. Now take Europe and shrink it until it all fits in the same land mass as Ithaca."[5]

Number Smiths

Every industry has numbers, and nearly every presenter in every industry fails to make numbers interesting and meaningful. For the rest of this scene, let's examine several examples of individuals and companies who have accomplished what Jobs did in every presentation—made numbers meaningful.

DEFINING ONE THOUSAND TRILLION

On June 9, 2008, IBM issued a press release touting a superfast supercomputer. As its name suggests, Roadrunner was one really quick system. It operated at one petaflop per second. What's a petaflop? Glad you asked. It's one thousand trillion calculations per second. IBM realized that the number would be meaningless to the vast majority of readers, so it added the following description:

> How fast is a petaflop? Lots of laptops. That's roughly equivalent to the combined computing power of 100,000 of today's fastest laptop computers. You would need a stack of laptops 1.5 miles high to equal Roadrunner's performance.

It would take the entire population of the earth—about six billion—each of us working a handheld calculator at the rate of one second per calculation, more than 46 years to do what Roadrunner can do in one day.

If it were possible for cars to improve their gas mileage over the past decade at the same rate that supercomputers have improved their cost and efficiency, we'd be getting 200,000 miles to the gallon today.[6]

The comparisons were compelling and caught the attention of the media. In 2008, if you conducted a Google search for "IBM + Roadrunner + 1.5 miles," the search returned nearly twenty thousand links to articles that used IBM's comparison word for word from the press release. The analogy worked.

$700 BILLION BAILOUT

The bigger the number, the more important it is to place the number into a context that makes sense to your audience. For example, in October 2008, the U.S. government bailed out banks and financial institutions to the tune of $700 billion. That's the numeral 7 followed by eleven zeros, a number so large that few of us can get our minds around it. *San Jose Mercury News* reporter Scott Harris put the number into a context his Silicon Valley readers could understand: $700 billion is twenty-five times the combined wealth of the Google guys. It is the equivalent of 350 billion venti lattes at Starbucks or 3.5 billion iPhones. The government could write checks for $2,300 to every man, woman, and child in America or provide free education for twenty-three million college students. Few people can grasp the concept of 700 billion, but they know lattes and college tuitions. Those numbers are specific and relevant.[7]

CHIPPING DOWN $13 TRILLION

Environmental groups go to great lengths to make numbers more meaningful. They must if they hope to persuade individuals to break deeply ingrained habits and routines that might contribute to damaging climate change. The numbers are simply too big (and seemingly irrelevant) without connecting the dots. For example, try telling someone that in 2006 alone, the United States produced thirteen trillion pounds of carbon dioxide (CO_2). It sounds like a humongous number, but what does it mean? There is no context. Thirteen trillion could be small or large in comparison with other countries. And frankly, what would it mean to the average person? The number itself won't persuade people to change their habits.

Al Gore's website broke the number down further, claiming the average American was responsible for 44,000 pounds of CO_2 emissions per year, while the world average was 9,600 pounds per individual. That's specific and contextual. The site then made the number even more relevant by telling its readers what might happen if that number didn't come down: heat waves would be more frequent and intense, droughts and wildfires would occur more often, and more than a million species could be driven to extinction in the next fifty years.

Scientists at NOAA (National Oceanic and Atmospheric Administration) are also catching on. Senior scientist Susan Solomon once told the *New York Times* that if the burning of fossil fuels continues at its present rate, carbon dioxide emissions could reach 450 parts per million. What does that figure mean? According to Solomon, at 450 parts per million, rising seas will threaten coastal areas around the world, and western Australia could expect 10 percent less rainfall. "Ten percent may not seem like a high number," said Solomon, "but it is the kind of number that has been seen in major droughts in the past, like the Dust Bowl."[8]

Whether or not you believe in global warming, climate change experts such as Al Gore and Susan Solomon are masters at making large numbers meaningful, and by doing so, they hope to persuade governments and individuals to take the action they deem necessary to solve the problem.

CHANGE YOUR DIET OR PAY THE ULTIMATE PRICE

What if you knew nothing about blood pressure and a doctor told you your blood pressure was 220 over 140? Would you be motivated to change your diet and exercise habits? Perhaps not until those numbers are put into context that makes sense to you. One doctor I know once told a patient, "Your blood pressure is 220 over 140. We consider 120 over 80 to be normal. Your blood pressure is severely high. That means you have a much higher risk of having a heart attack, kidney disease, and stroke. In fact, with numbers this high, you could drop dead at any minute by blowing your gourd. The arteries in your brain will literally burst." By being specific, relevant, and contextual, the doctor made his point and motivated his patient to make changes right away!

Regardless of what industry you're in, the numbers you throw around will have little impact on your audience unless, and until, you make them meaningful. Numbers out of context are simply unimpressive. Whether you're presenting the data behind a new technology or a particular medical condition, comparing the number to something your listeners can relate to will make your message far more interesting, impactful, and ultimately persuasive.

DIRECTOR'S NOTES

» Use data to support the key theme of your presentation. As you do, consider carefully the figures you want to present. Don't overwhelm your audience with too many numbers.

» Make your data specific, relevant, and contextual. In other words, put the numbers into a context that is relevant to the lives of your listeners.

» Use rhetorical devices such as analogies to dress up your numbers.

Use "Amazingly Zippy" Words

Plug it in. Wirrrrrr. Done.

—STEVE JOBS, DESCRIBING THE SONG TRANSFER FEATURE
OF THE FIRST IPOD, *FORTUNE*, NOVEMBER 2001

Steve Jobs introduced an upgrade to the iPhone at Apple's Worldwide Developers Conference on June 9, 2008. The iPhone 3G was twice as fast as the original model, supporting the speedier third-generation AT&T data network. A 3G network has a potential transfer speed of 3 Mbps, versus 144 Kbps on a slower, 2G (second-generation) network. Simply put, 3G is better for accessing the Internet and downloading large multimedia files on a mobile phone. Jobs made it even simpler. "It's amazingly zippy," he said.[1]

Jobs spoke in simple, clear, and direct language, free of the jargon and complexity so common in business communications. Jobs was one of the few business leaders who could confidently call a product "amazingly zippy." In an interview for *Fortune* magazine, he was asked to describe the interface of Apple's new OS X operating system. "We made the buttons on the screen look so good, you'll want to lick them," he said.[2] Even if you thought Jobs was grandstanding from time to time, his choice of words put a smile on your face. He chose words that were fun, tangible, and uncommon in most professional business presentations.

Jobs, Gates, and the Plain English Test

Tech reporter Todd Bishop wrote a clever piece at the urging of his readers. He ran the transcripts from four presentations in 2007 and 2008 (Steve Jobs's Macworld keynotes and Bill Gates's Consumer Electronics Show presentations) through a software tool that analyzes language. In general, the lower the numerical score, the more understandable the language.

Bishop used an online software tool provided by UsingEnglish .com.[3] The tool analyzes language based on four criteria:

1. Average number of words per sentence.
2. Lexical density—how easy or difficult a text is to read. Text with "lower density" is more easily understood. In this case, a lower percentage is better.
3. Hard words—average number of words in a sentence that contain more than three syllables. In this case, a higher percentage is worse because it implies there are more "hard words" in the text that are generally less understood by the average reader.
4. Fog index—the number of years of education a reader theoretically would require to understand the text. For example, the *New York Times* has a fog rating of 11 or 12, while some academic documents have a fog rating of 18. The fog index simply means that short sentences written in plain English receive a better score than sentences written in complicated language.

It should be no surprise that Jobs did noticeably better than Gates when their language was put to the test. Table 10.1 compares the results for both 2007 and 2008.[4]

In each case, Jobs performed significantly better than Gates when it came to using terms and language people could easily understand. Jobs's words were simpler, his phrases were less abstract, and he used fewer words per sentence.

TABLE 10.1 LANGUAGE COMPLEXITY: STEVE JOBS VERSUS BILL GATES

PRESENTER/EVENT	STEVE JOBS, MACWORLD	BILL GATES, INTERNATIONAL CONSUMER ELECTRONICS SHOW
Jobs's 2007 Macworld Keynote and Gates's 2007 CES Keynote		
Average words/ sentence	10.5	21.6
Lexical density	16.5%	21.0%
Hard words	2.9%	5.11%
Fog index	5.5	10.7
Jobs's 2008 Macworld Keynote and Gates's 2008 CES Keynote		
Average words/ sentence	13.79	18.23
Lexical density	15.76%	24.52%
Hard words	3.18%	5.2%
Fog index	6.79	9.37

Table 10.2 compares some exact phrases from the 2007 presentations. Excerpts from Bill Gates's remarks are in the right column.[5] The left column contains excerpts from Steve Jobs.[6]

Where Gates was obtuse, Jobs was clear. Where Gates was abstract, Jobs was tangible. Where Gates was complex, Jobs was simple.

Now, I can hear you saying, "Bill Gates might not speak as simply as Jobs did, but he's the richest guy in the world, so he must have done something right." You're correct. He did. Gates invented Windows, the operating system installed in 90 percent of the world's computers. You, however, did not. Your audience will not let you get away with language they'll accept

TABLE 10.2 VERBIAGE IN GATES'S 2007 CES KEYNOTE VERSUS JOBS'S 2007 MACWORLD KEYNOTE

STEVE JOBS, 2007 MACWORLD	BILL GATES, 2007 INTERNATIONAL CONSUMER ELECTRONICS SHOW
"You know, it was just a year ago that I was up here and announced that we were going to switch to Intel processors. It was a huge heart transplant to Intel microprocessors. And I said that we would do it over the coming twelve months. We did it in seven months, and it's been the smoothest and most successful transition that we've ever seen in the history of our industry."	"The processors are now opening the memory capability up to 64-bit, and that's a transition we're making without a lot of incompatibility, without paying a lot of extra money. Software, the old 32-bit software, can run, but if you need to get more space, it's just there."
"Now I'd like to tell you a few things about iTunes that are pretty exciting . . . We are selling over five million songs a day now. Isn't that unbelievable? That's fifty-eight songs every second of every minute of every hour of every day."	"The process we've been through over this year—there was a beta 2—got out to over two million people. The release candidate, which was our last chance for feedback, got out to over five million. We had a lot of in-depth things where we went in and sat and interviewed people using Windows Vista in family situations. We did that in seven different countries. We did incredible performance simulation, getting over sixty years equivalent of performance testing with all the common mix of applications that were out there."
"We've got awesome TV shows on iTunes. As a matter of fact, we have over 350 TV shows that you can buy episodes from on iTunes. And I'm very pleased to report that we have now sold fifty million TV shows on iTunes. Isn't that incredible?"	"Microsoft Office has got a new user interface; it's got new ways of connecting up to Office Live services and SharePoint, but the discoverability of the richness is advanced dramatically by that user interface."

from Gates. If your presentations are confusing, convoluted, and full of jargon, you will miss an opportunity to engage and excite your listeners. Strive for understanding. Avoid lexical density.

You might have noticed that many of Jobs's favorite words were the type of words most people use in everyday watercooler conversation: "amazing," "incredible," "gorgeous." Most presenters change their language for a pitch or presentation. Jobs spoke the same way onstage as he did offstage. He had confidence in his brand and had fun with the words he chose. Some critics might say his language bordered on hyperbole, but Jobs echoed the sentiments shared by millions of his customers.

Of course, you should use words that authentically represent your service, brand, or product. A financial adviser recommending a mutual fund to a client would appear insincere (and probably dishonest) if he or she said, "This new mutual fund will revolutionize the financial industry as we know it. It's amazing, and you need to invest your money in it right now." Instead, the financial adviser could say, "Mutual funds are amazing products that will help your money grow while lowering your risk. There are thousands of funds available, but I'm especially excited about a new one. Let me tell you more about it . . ." In the latter statement, our financial adviser has chosen words that are simple and emotional while still maintaining his or her professionalism and integrity.

Don't be afraid of using simple words and descriptive adjectives. If you genuinely find a product "amazing," go ahead and say so. After all, if you're not excited about it, how do you expect the rest of us to be?

Avoid Jargon Creep

Jargon rarely crept into Jobs's language. His words were conversational and simple. Jargon—language that is specific to a particular industry—creates a roadblock to the free and easy exchange of ideas. I have attended countless meetings in which two people who work for different divisions of the same company cannot understand the jargon used by the other. Jargon and buzzwords are meaningless and empty and will most certainly make you *less* understandable and therefore less persuasive.

Mission statements are the worst culprits of jargon creep. Mission statements typically are long, convoluted, jargon-laden paragraphs created in multiple committee meetings and destined to be forgotten. They are replete with jargon and murky words you would have rarely heard from Jobs, such as "synergy," "principle-centered," and "best of breed." These expressions are nonsense, yet on any given day, employees in companies around the world are sitting in committee meetings to see just how many such words can be crammed into a single sentence.

Apple's mission statement, on the other hand, is simple, clear, and impactful. It's full of emotive words and tangible examples. It reads (emphasis added):

> Apple *ignited* the personal computer revolution in the 1970s with the Apple II and *reinvented* the personal computer with the Macintosh. Today, Apple continues to *lead* the industry in *innovation* with its award-winning computers, OS X operating system, and iLife and professional applications. Apple is also *spearheading* the digital media revolution with its iPod portable music and video players and iTunes online store, and has entered the mobile phone market with its *revolutionary* iPhone.[7]

The words Jobs chose to announce a new product had three characteristics: they were simple, concrete, and emotionally charged.

>> **Simple.** Free of jargon and with few syllables.
>> **Concrete.** Very specific phrases. Short, tangible descriptions instead of long, abstract discussions.
>> **Emotional.** Descriptive adjectives.

Examples of each of these three characteristics appeared in Jobs's introduction of the MacBook Air: "This is the MacBook Air. You can get a feel for how thin it is [concrete]. It has a full-size keyboard and display [simple]. Isn't it amazing [emotional]? This is

A Guru Who Keeps It Simple

It was hard to miss financial guru Suze Orman in 2008 and 2009 when the global financial markets were collapsing. In addition to appearing on her own CNBC show, the bestselling author was a frequent guest on shows such as "Oprah" and "Larry King Live." Banks and financial companies were also using her in advertisements meant to alleviate their customers' fears. I interviewed Orman several times and found her to be surprisingly candid about the secret to her success as a communicator.

"How do you make complicated financial topics easy to understand?" I once asked.

"Too many people want to impress others with the information they have so others think the speaker is intelligent," Orman responded.[8]

"But Suze," I said, "If your message is too simple, don't you risk not being taken seriously?"

I don't care what people think about it. All I care about is that the information I'm imparting empowers the listener or reader of my material . . . If your intention is to impart a message that will create change for the person listening, then if you ask me, it is respectful to that person to make the message as simple as possible. For example, if I gave you directions to how to get to my house, you would want me to give you the simplest directions to get there. If I made it more complicated, you would not be better off. You might get aggravated and give up. If it were simple, chances are you will get in your car and try to get to my house rather than giving up and saying it's not worth it. Others criticize simplicity because they need to feel that it's more complicated. If everything were so simple, they think their jobs could be eliminated. It's our fear of extinction, our fear of elimination, our fear of not being important that leads us to communicate things in a more complex way than we need to."[9]

what it looks like. Isn't it incredible [emotional]? It's the world's thinnest notebook [simple]. It has a gorgeous 13.3-inch wide-screen display and a phenomenal full-sized keyboard [emotional and concrete]. I'm stunned our engineering team could pull this off [emotional]."[10]

Table 10.3 lists even more examples of specific, concrete, and emotional phrases from the Jobs repertoire of language. This is just a small sample. Every Jobs presentation contained similar language.

Jargon: A Sure Way to Upset Jack Welch

Jack Welch made the observation, "Insecure managers create complexity." During his twenty years as GE's top executive, the conglomerate grew from $13 billion in revenue to $500 billion. Welch was on a mission to "declutter" everything about the company, from its management processes to its communication. He despised long, convoluted memos, meetings, and presentations.

In his book *Jack: Straight from the Gut*, Welch describes meetings that left him "underwhelmed." If you wanted to upset the new CEO, all you had to do was talk over his head. Welch would say, "Let's pretend we're in high school . . . take me through the basics." He recounts his first meeting with one of his insurance leaders. Welch asked some simple questions about terms he was unfamiliar with. He writes, "So I interrupted him to ask: 'What's the difference between facultative and treaty insurance?' After fumbling through a long answer for several minutes, an answer I wasn't getting, he finally blurted out in exasperation, 'How do you expect me to teach you in five minutes what it has taken me twenty-five years to learn!' Needless to say, he didn't last long."[11]

Speaking in jargon carries penalties in a society that values speech free from esoteric, incomprehensible bullshit. Speaking over people's heads may cost you a job or prevent you from advancing as far as your capabilities might take you otherwise.

TABLE 10.3 SPECIFIC, CONCRETE, AND EMOTIONAL PHRASES IN JOBS'S PRESENTATIONS

EVENT	PHRASE
Apple Music Event, 2001	"The coolest thing about iPod is your entire music library fits in your pocket."[12]
Introduction of the world's first seventeen-inch widescreen notebook, Macworld 2003	"I asked you to buckle up. Now I want you to put on your shoulder harness."[13]
Referencing the current Titanium PowerBook, Macworld 2003	"The number one lust object."[14]
Describing the new seventeen-inch PowerBook, Macworld 2003	"It's stunning. It is the most incredible product we have ever made. Look at that screen. It's amazing. Look at how thin it is. Isn't that incredible? When it's closed, it's only one inch think. It's beautiful, too. This is clearly the most advanced notebook computer ever made on the planet. Our competitors haven't even caught up with what we introduced two years ago; I don't know what they're going to do about this."[15]
Jobs's description of the original Macintosh	"Insanely great."
Persuading PepsiCo president John Sculley to become Apple's CEO	"Do you want to spend the rest of your life selling sugared water or do you want a chance to change the world?"
Quote in *Triumph of the Nerds*	"We're here to put a dent in the universe."[16]
Discussing CEO Gil Amelio's reign at Apple	"The products suck! There's no sex in them anymore!"[17]
Jobs creating a new word for the launch of a new iPod, September 2008	"iPod Touch is the funnest iPod we've ever created."[18]
Unveiling the first seventeen-inch notebook computer, January 7, 2003	"A giant leap beyond PC notebooks. Miraculously engineered."[19]

Some people will look at the language in this table and say Jobs was a master of hype. Well, hype is hype only if there's no "there" there. It would have been hard to argue with Jobs that the Macintosh (the first easy-to-use computer with a graphical interface and mouse) wasn't "insanely great" or that products like the MacBook Air weren't "stunningly" thin.

Jobs wasn't a hype-master as much as he was the master of the catchphrase. The folks at Apple think long and hard about the words used to describe a product. Language is intended to stir up excitement and create a "must-have" experience for Apple's customers. There's nothing wrong with that. Keep in mind that the majority of business language is gobbledygook—dull, abstract, and meaningless. Steve Jobs was anything but dull. Inject some zip into your words.

It's Like This . . .

Another way to add zip to your language is to create analogies, comparing an idea or a product to a concept or product familiar to your audience. When Steve Jobs shook up a market category with the introduction of an entirely new product, he went out of his way to compare the product to something that was widely understood, commonly used, and well known. Here are some examples:

>> "Apple TV is like a DVD player for the twenty-first century" (Introduction of Apple TV, January 9, 2007)
>> "iPod Shuffle is smaller and lighter than a pack of gum" (Introduction of iPod Shuffle, January 2005)
>> "iPod is the size of a deck of cards" (Introduction of iPod, October 2001)

When you find an analogy that works, stick with it. The more you repeat it, the more likely your customers are to remember it. If you do a Google search for articles about the products just mentioned, you will find thousands of links with the exact

A Cure for Bad Pitches

Don't sell solutions; create stories instead. The *New York Times* columnist David Pogue loves a good pitch. He says the majority of his columns come from pitches. What he doesn't want to hear is jargon. Surprisingly, PR professionals are among the worst offenders (surpassed only by bureaucrats, senior managers, and IBM consultants). Pogue argues that buzzwords (terminology such as "integrated," "best of breed," "B2B," and "consumer-centric") are unnecessary. The ideal pitch is a short paragraph telling Pogue exactly what the product is and does. For example, one company wrote Pogue and said it had a new laptop that could be dropped from six feet, could be dunked in water, and could survive three-hundred-degree heat and still work. This clever description was enough to grab Pogue's attention.

The Bad Pitch blog is a must-read for PR, marketing, and sales professionals. The site carries actual pitches from PR professionals who should know better than to issue impenetrable jargon masking as a press release.

Here's an example: "Hope you're well. I'd like to introduce you to _____, a new, place-based out-of-home digital network that delivers relevant, localized media within the rhythm of consumers' daily rituals, like afternoon coffee or sandwiches at lunch." This particular pitch came from a company that puts video billboards in delis. Why couldn't they just say that? It's too simple, that's why. People are afraid of simplicity. This is not an isolated example. The site is updated daily with pitches from large and small PR agencies as well as small and large corporations. Apple pitches rarely make the site, because the company's press releases tell a story in the same conversational language that Jobs uses in his presentations.

As the site's mantra explains, "A good pitch disappears and turns into the story; a bad pitch becomes the story." Follow the blog posts at http://badpitch.blogspot.com.

comparisons that Jobs himself used. Following are the three analogies just reviewed (in the format of a search phrase) and the number of links to articles using those phrases:

» Apple TV + DVD player for twenty-first century: 160,000 links
» iPod Shuffle + pack of gum: 32,200 links
» iPod + deck of cards: 889,000 links

Your listeners and viewers are attempting to categorize a product—they need to place the concept in a mental bucket. Create the mental bucket for them. If you don't, you are making their brains work too hard. According to Emory University psychology professor Dr. Gregory Berns, the brain wants to consume the least amount of energy. That means it doesn't want to work too hard to figure out what people are trying to say. "The efficiency principle has major ramifications," he states. "It means the brain takes shortcuts whenever it can."[20] Analogies are shortcuts.

Nothing will destroy the power of your pitch more thoroughly than the use of buzzwords and complexity. You're not impressing anyone with your "best-of-breed, leading-edge, agile solutions." Instead, you are putting people to sleep, losing their business, and setting back your career. Clear, concise, and "zippy" language will help transform your prospects into customers and customers into evangelists. Delight your customers with the words you choose—stroke their brains' dopamine receptors with words that cause them to feel good whenever they think of you and your product. People cannot follow your vision or share your enthusiasm if they get lost in the fog.

Word Fun with Titles

Your customers are your most potent evangelists. I recall a conversation with one of my clients, Cranium founder Richard Tait, who said he sold one million games with no advertising, all word of mouth. "Never forget that your customers are your sales force," he told me.

His customers—he calls them "Craniacs"—want to have fun. Since fun was the name of the game, so to speak, Tait decided that every facet of the company should have some whimsy associated with it. He started with job titles. Cranium employees are allowed to make up their own titles. For example, Tait is not Cranium's CEO. He is the Grand Poo-Bah. No kidding. It's on his business card.

You might think it's silly, but I'll tell you that when I first walked into the company's Seattle headquarters, I was hit with a wave of fun, enthusiasm, and engagement the likes of which I had never seen before and I have never seen since.

DIRECTOR'S NOTES

» Unclutter your copy. Eliminate redundant language, buzzwords, and jargon. Edit, edit, and edit some more.

» Run your paragraphs through the UsingEnglish tool to see just how "dense" it is.

» Have fun with words. It's OK to express enthusiasm for your product through superlatives or descriptive adjectives. Jobs thought the buttons on the Macintosh screen looked so good that you would want to "lick" them. That's confidence.

Share the Stage

**Don't be encumbered by history. Go out
and create something wonderful.**

—ROBERT NOYCE, INTEL COFOUNDER

A t Macworld on January 10, 2006, Jobs announced that the new iMac would be the first Apple computer with an Intel processor inside. Earlier the previous year, Jobs had announced that the "brain transplant" would begin in June 2006. On January 10, he told the audience that he wanted to give everyone an update on the schedule. As he began, dry-ice-created smoke wafted upward in the middle of the stage. A man walked out wearing the famous bunny suit worn in Intel's ultrasterile microprocessor manufacturing plants. The man was carrying a wafer, one of the thin, round slices of silicon from which chips are made. He walked over to Jobs and shook hands. As the lights came up, it became obvious that the person in the bunny suit was none other than Intel CEO Paul Otellini.

"Steve, I wanted to report that Intel is ready," Otellini said as he handed Jobs the wafer. "Apple is ready, too," said Jobs. "We started a partnership less than a year ago to make this happen," Jobs told the audience. "Our teams have worked hard together to make this happen in record time. It's been incredible to see how our engineers have bonded and how well this has gone."[1] Otellini credited the Apple team in return. The two men talked about the achievement, they shook hands again, and Otellini left the stage. Jobs then turned to the audience and revealed the surprise: Apple would be rolling out the first Mac with Intel processors, not in June as originally announced, but *today*. See Figure 11.1.

Few companies are more closely associated with their founders than Apple is with Jobs. Regardless, Jobs himself was more than happy to share the spotlight with employees and partners onstage. A Jobs presentation was rarely a one-man play. He featured supporting characters who performed key roles in the narrative.

Microsoft founder Bill Gates was one of the most unexpected partners to share the stage with Jobs. In 1997, at the Macworld Expo in Boston, Jobs, who had recently returned to Apple as interim CEO, told the audience that in order to restore Apple to health, some relationships had to be revisited. He announced that Microsoft's Internet Explorer would be the default browser on the Macintosh and that Microsoft would make a strategic investment of $150 million in the company. On that note, he introduced a "special guest," live via satellite. When Bill Gates appeared, you could hear some cheering, along with a lot of boos. Gates spoke for a few minutes and graciously expressed his admiration for what Apple had accomplished.

Figure 11.1 Steve Jobs sharing the stage with Intel CEO Paul Otellini.
Photo by Justin Sullivan/Getty Images

Jobs returned to the stage and, knowing that many people would be unhappy, sounded like a stern father as he admonished the audience to embrace the relationship. "If we want to move forward and see Apple happy and prospering, we have to let go of this notion that for Apple to win, Microsoft has to lose," Jobs said. "If we screw up, it's not somebody else's fault; it's our fault . . . If we want Microsoft Office on the Mac, we'd better treat the company that puts it out with a little bit of gratitude."[2]

Great actors are often said to be "giving"; they help other actors in the scene give better performances. When Jobs introduced another person onstage—an employee, a partner, or a former nemesis such as Gates—he was the most giving of performers. Everyone needs to shine for the good of the show.

The Brain Craves Variety

The brain doesn't pay attention to boring things. Not that Jobs was boring. Far from it. However, our brains crave variety. No one, no matter how smooth and polished, can carry an audience for long before his or her listeners start to glance at their watches. Great speechwriters have known this for years. Speeches written for John F. Kennedy, Ronald Reagan, and Barack Obama were scripted to last no longer than twenty minutes. A Jobs keynote presentation lasted much longer, of course, closer to 1.5 hours, but Jobs kept it interesting by incorporating demonstrations, video clips, and—very important—guest speakers.

Know What You Don't Know

In October 2008, Apple introduced new MacBook laptops crafted from single blocks of aluminum. The design breakthrough allowed Apple to build mobile computers that were lighter and stronger than previous designs. "Let's talk about notebooks. We want to talk about some technologies and discoveries that we've made that help us build notebooks in some new ways," Jobs said.[3] However, instead of describing the new process himself,

Jobs introduced Jony Ive, Apple's then senior vice president of design (he has since become Apple's Chief Design Officer).

Ive walked onstage, Jobs took a seat, and Ive gave the audience a six-minute crash course on notebook design. He explained how the new process allowed Apple to start with a 2.5-pound slab of aluminum and carve it out until the final frame weighed just one-quarter of a pound. The result was a stronger, thinner, and lighter computer. Jobs retook the stage and concluded the segment by thanking Ive and reaffirming the headline of the segment: "A new way to build notebooks." Jobs may have had his hands all over Apple, but he knew what he didn't know. Jobs shared the spotlight with other actors, who added credibility and excitement to the plot.

Your Best Sales Tool

When Apple launched an online movie-rental service, Jobs announced the list of studios that would make films available for online rentals via iTunes. The list included all the heavy-weights—Touchstone, Sony, Universal, MGM, Walt Disney, and others. Still, Apple faced skepticism. The company was launching a movie-rental service in a field with established competitors such as Blockbuster and Netflix. Apple was betting that people would want the choice of watching their movies on their computers, iPods, iPhones, or wide-screen television sets via Apple TV. Jobs added credibility to the initiative by sharing the stage with one of Apple's key partners.

"We have support from every major studio," said Jobs. "The first studio to sign up was Twentieth Century Fox. We've developed a really great working relationship with Fox. It's my pleasure to introduce the chairman and CEO of Twentieth Century Fox, Jim Gianopulos."

An enthusiastic Gianopulos bounded onto the stage and talked about what people want: great movies; easy access; convenience; control over where, when, and how they watch movies; and the ability to take the movie with them wherever they go. "When Steve came to us with the idea, it was a no-brainer. It was the most exciting, coolest thing we've ever heard," Gianopulos said. "Video rentals are not a new thing. But there was music and then iPod. There was the phone and then iPhone. Apple does things in an intuitive, insightful, and innovative way. It will be a transformative version of the rental model, and we're incredibly excited about it. We couldn't be happier and prouder of our partnership."[4]

Gianopulos had provided Jobs with a company's best sales tool—a customer's endorsement. Best of all, the two men appeared side by side. A reference is good. A customer or partner physically sharing the stage is even better.

Number One Reason People Buy

Your customers are always mindful of budgets, but in tough economic times they are even more so, casting a critical eye on every last dollar. Prospects do not want to act as a beta group. Your product must deliver what it promises—saving your customers money, making them money, or providing the tools to make more efficient use of the money they have. Testimonials and endorsements are persuasive because, as discussed earlier, word of mouth is the number one influencer of purchasing decisions.

Successful companies know that a pool of reputable and satisfied customers is critical for sales success. In fact, some companies even have specific employees whose job it is to gather case studies and distribute them to their prospects. Most small business owners do not have the resources to designate a "case study" specialist, but they can easily adopt some of the techniques used by the world's most successful companies. One proven strategy is to steal a page from the Apple playbook and invite your customers to share the spotlight, either in person, on video, or, at the very least, through quotes.

Don't forget the media. Sharing the stage with publications that rave about your product will bolster your message. Jobs had a love-hate relationship with the media, but for presentation purposes, there was a lot of love in the room. In the first few minutes of his Macworld 2008 keynote address, Jobs announced that Leopard (the latest version of the OS X operating system) had sold five million copies in its first ninety days,

Twenty-First-Century Case Study

The case study remains an important marketing tool. Most of us are familiar with white papers or simple case studies featured on a company's website, but as video and audio become much less expensive to create and distribute online, some innovative companies are tapping into the power of YouTube to deliver customer evidence. Creating an inexpensive video of a customer testimonial and posting it on YouTube carries as much weight as a slick marketing production. Posting video and audio testimonials on your site and incorporating them into your presentations will add another valuable layer of authenticity and credibility to your story.

If you are a business owner or an entrepreneur, it is important to develop a list of customers you can use as references. In fact, a customer who offers a testimonial is worth more than one who doesn't. Look for customers who will help you win new customers. Then, give them a *reason* to offer a reference. This could be as simple as offering a deeper relationship with your company, such as providing more access to you or your staff when your customer has questions. Other benefits might include access to product teams, input into new designs or products, and visibility.

Give your partners a reason to participate, and once they do, incorporate them into your presentations. Most customers will not be available for your presentation, but try the next best thing: insert a video testimonial into your presentation. It might not have the same impact as Paul Otellini appearing onstage with Jobs, but it might give you a step up on your competitors.

marking the most successful release of OS X. He also made sure that everyone knew that Leopard had been a hit with the media. "The press has been very kind. It's been a critical success as well as a commercial success," said Jobs.[5] As Jobs read reviews from major technology influencers, a slide appeared with their quotes. Here are the endorsements, along with their sources:

» "In my view, Leopard is better and faster than Vista."—Walt Mossberg, *Wall Street Journal*
» "Leopard is powerful, polished, and carefully conceived." —David Pogue, *New York Times*
» "With Leopard, Apple's operating system widens its lead esthetically and technologically."—Ed Baig, *USA Today*
» "It's by far the best operating system ever written for the vast majority of consumers."—Ed Mendelson, *PC* magazine

The last quote drew laughs. The irony of *PC* magazine's favorably reviewing a Mac gave the audience a chuckle. Reading favorable reviews was a common technique in a Steve Jobs presentation. Although Americans rate journalists among the least trustworthy professionals (only one step above politicians), a favorable endorsement from a top-tier media outlet or blogger still carries weight, giving buyers confidence that they are making a wise choice.

Successful companies that launch a splashy new product usually have tested it with a group of partners who have agreed to endorse it publicly or distribute review copies to the media and influencers. This arrangement gives those companies instant references, endorsements, and testimonials. Your customers need a reason to believe in you, and they want to minimize the risk associated with a new product or service. Having experts, customers, or partners testify to the effectiveness of your product will help you overcome the psychological barrier to participation.

Give Credit Where Credit's Due

Employees also got top billing in a Steve Jobs presentation. At the conclusion of Macworld 2007, Jobs said, "I want to highlight the folks who worked on these products. Would all of the folks who worked on today's products please stand up? Let's give them a round of applause. Thank you so much. I also can't leave without thanking the families. They haven't seen a lot of us in the last six months. Without the support of our families, we couldn't do what we do. We get to do this amazing work. They understand when we're not home for dinner on time because we've got to be in the lab, working on something because the intro is coming up. You don't know how much we need you and appreciate you. So, thank you."[6]

It's very easy to make the presentation all about you and your product. Don't forget to credit the people who make it possible. It shows your customers that you are a person of integrity, and, by praising your employees or colleagues publicly, you inspire them to work harder for you.

Finally, Jobs shared the stage with his audience, his customers, often thanking them profusely. He kicked off Macworld 2008 by recapping the previous year. "I just want to take a moment to say thank you. We have had tremendous support from all of our customers, and we really, really appreciate it. So, thank you for an extraordinary 2007."[7] Jobs built a rapport with his audience by acknowledging the people who matter—the people who build the products and the people who buy them.

Jobs Even Shares the Stage . . . with Himself!

Steve Jobs was the only person who could invite another Steve Jobs onstage. In 1999, "ER" star Noah Wyle traded in his scrubs for blue jeans, playing Jobs in the TV movie *Pirates of Silicon Valley*. In a practical joke at the 1999 Macworld Expo in New York, Wyle appeared onstage to kick off the keynote. At first glance (and to people seated far away), he looked like Jobs—blue jeans, black mock, and running shoes. Wyle had the same mannerisms and even used some of Jobs's famous phrases. "This is going to be a great Macworld," he said. "There's something happening here. The resurgence of Apple. You're going to see great new products today. Some insanely great new products. Some really, totally, wildly, insanely great new products!" The audience went crazy when the real Jobs showed up.

Jobs had a ton of fun with Wyle, telling the actor that he was blowing the impression. Jobs showed Wyle how he should act, talk, and walk if he really wanted to nail the impersonation.

Jobs told the audience, "I invited Noah here to see how I really act and because he's a better me than me!"

"Thank you. I'm just glad you're not mad about the movie," said Wyle.

"What? Me upset? It's just a movie," said Jobs. "But if you do want to make things right, you could get me a part on *ER*."[8]

The exchange generated a h-uge laugh and the bit showed that Jobs could poke some fun at himself. I still haven't seen any other presenter who could share the stage with himself!

DIRECTOR'S NOTES

» Upon release of a new product or service, make sure you have customers who tested the product and are available to back your claims. Media reviews are also helpful, especially from highly reputable publications or popular blogs.

» Incorporate testimonials into your presentation. The easiest way is to videotape your customer talking about your product, edit the tape to no more than two minutes in length, and insert it into your presentation.

» Publicly thank employees, partners, and customers. And do it often.

SCENE 12

Stage Your Presentation with Props

Jobs has turned his keynote speeches at Macworld into massive media events. They are marketing theater, staged for the world's press.

—LEANDER KAHNEY

ndustry observers credit Apple for redefining notebook computer design with its MacBook family of computers unveiled on October 14, 2008. As described in the preceding chapter, Jobs had solicited Apple designer Jony Ive to explain the process of making the computer. The new MacBooks were built with a frame (unibody enclosure) crafted from a single block of aluminum. It doesn't sound impressive, but it represented a feat of engineering that produced thinner, lighter, more rugged notebooks that looked a lot cooler than their predecessors. About twenty-five minutes into the October presentation, Jobs discussed the new aluminum frame. He could have talked about it and perhaps shown a photograph or two, but Jobs being Jobs, he went above and beyond. He turned the presentation into a kinesthetic experience, letting the audience of analysts and reporters see and touch the frame for themselves.

"This is what the unibody looks like. It's especially beautiful," Jobs said as he held up a sample frame.

"It's a much more rigid, stronger construction. It's so cool, I'd like you to see it. If we can get the lights up, I'd actually like to pass one of these around so you can see how beautiful and high-tech this is."

At this point, Apple representatives who had been positioned at the end of each row handed audience members samples of the aluminum frames to pass around. As people touched and examined the frames for themselves, Jobs joked, "We need them back," eliciting a laugh from the audience. For the next sixty seconds, Jobs did not say a word. He let the product speak for itself.

Jobs then channeled his inner John Madden and provided color commentary as the audience members continued to examine the frames: "Teams of hundreds of people have worked on this for many, many months to figure out how to design these things and manufacture them economically. This is a tour de force of engineering."

Jobs remained silent for the next thirty seconds until everyone had a chance to handle the frames. "OK. A precision unibody enclosure. You're the first to get your hands on one," Jobs said as he closed the section and moved on to another feature of the new notebooks.[1] Using props, Jobs had transformed what could have been a boring explanation into an interesting, multisensory experience.

Kawasaki Method

Jobs introduced stage props in every presentation, usually during demonstrations. In *The Macintosh Way*, Guy Kawasaki writes that master communicators give good demo. "The right demo doesn't cost much," he points out, "but it can counteract your competitors' marketing and advertising. A great demo informs the audience about your product, communicates the benefits of owning your product, and inspires the audience to take action."[2] Kawasaki describes the five qualities of an outstanding demonstration. According to Kawasaki, good demos are as follows:

» **Short.** A good demo does not suck the wind out of your audience.
» **Simple.** A good demo is simple and easy to follow. "It should communicate no more than one or two key messages. The goal is to show the audience enough to get them tantalized but not so much that they get bewildered."[3]
» **Sweet.** A good demo "shows the hottest features and differentiates your product from the competition's." There's more: "You have to show real functionality, though. Imagine that every time you show a feature someone shouts, 'So what?'"[4]
» **Swift.** A good demo is fast paced. "Never do anything in a demo that lasts more than fifteen seconds."[5]
» **Substantial.** A good demo clearly demonstrates how your product offers a solution to a real-world problem your audience is experiencing. "Customers want to do things with your product, so they want to know how the product works."[6]

As noted in Scene 9, Jobs nailed all of Kawasaki's conditions for a good demo when he launched the iPhone 3G at the WWDC in October 2008. The phone ran on the faster, 3G cellular networks, an upgrade to the second-generation (2G) wireless data networks. Jobs's words from the presentation are listed in the left column of Table 12.1, and the right column describes the corresponding slides.[7]

In a brief demo, Jobs had met Kawasaki's criteria for a great demo.

» **It's short.** The EDGE-versus-3G demo lasted less than two minutes.
» **It's simple.** What could be more simple than showing two websites loading on a smartphone? That was as complicated as it got.
» **It's sweet.** Jobs placed the 3G network in a head-to-head face-off with its primary competitor, the EDGE network.
» **It's swift.** Jobs kept the demo moving but remained silent at critical points to build the drama.
» **It's substantial.** The demo resolved a real-world problem: waiting an excruciatingly long time for graphically rich sites to load.

TABLE 12.1 JOBS'S GREAT DEMO AT THE 2008 WWDC

STEVE'S WORDS	STEVE'S SLIDES
"Why do you want 3G? Well, you want it for faster data downloads. And there's nowhere you want faster data downloads than the browser and downloading e-mail attachments."	Photographs of two icons: one represents the Internet, and the second represents e-mail
"So, let's take a look at the browser. We've taken an iPhone 3G and, at the same place and same location, we've downloaded a website on the EDGE network and one using 3G."	Animated image of two iPhones loading a website simultaneously: the same National Geographic website begins loading on each; the left iPhone is on the EDGE network, and the one on the right is using the new iPhone 3G network
"Let's see how we do." [Jobs remains silent as both images continue to load on the screen; it's a site with a lot of images and a complex layout]	Website loading on both iPhone images
"Twenty-one seconds on 3G; [waits silently for an additional thirty seconds, crossing his hands in front of his body, smiling, watching the audience— elicits laughs] fifty-nine seconds on EDGE. Same phone, same location: 3G is 2.8 times faster. It's approaching Wi-Fi speeds. It's amazingly zippy!"	3G site has completely loaded, while EDGE phone is still loading

History-Making Demo

Demonstrations and props played a role in every Steve Jobs presentation, some of which were more history-making than others. "We're going to make some history today," Steve Jobs said as he kicked off Macworld 2007. The history-making event was the introduction of the iPhone:

"We want to reinvent the phone," Jobs said. "I want to show you four things: the phone app, photos, calendar, and SMS text messaging [texting between two cell phones]—the kind of things you would find on a typical phone—in a very untypical way. So, let's go ahead and take a look." As he always does, Jobs walked to stage right (the audience's left) to sit down and conduct the demo, giving the audience a clear view of the screen.

"You see that icon in the lower-left corner of the phone? I just push it, and boom, I have the phone. Now I'm in Contacts. How do I move around Contacts? I just scroll through them. Let's say I want to place a call to Jony Ive. I just push here, and I see Jony Ive's contact with all his information. If I want to call Jony, all I do is push his number. I'll call his mobile number right now." The phone rings, and Ive picks up to say hello.

Jobs continued, "It's been two and a half years, and I can't tell you how thrilled I am to make the first public phone call with iPhone." At this point in the demo, Apple's SVP of corporate marketing, Phil Schiller, calls in. Jobs places Ive on hold and conferences in the two callers to demonstrate one-click conferencing. Jobs proceeds to demonstrate the SMS texting function, followed by the photo package that came standard in the iPhone. "We have the coolest photo management app ever—certainly on a mobile device, but I think maybe ever." Jobs then shows off the capabilities of the photo gallery, using his fingers to widen, pinch, and manipulate the images. "Pretty cool," he says. "Isn't this awesome?"[8] Jobs appeared genuinely thrilled with the new features and, as he often did when demonstrating new products, looked like a kid in a candy store.

Having Fun with Demos

Don't forget to have fun with demos. Jobs certainly did. He concluded the iPhone demonstration by showing how to put Google Maps to work on the device. He searched for a Starbucks in San Francisco near Moscone West, the site of the conference. A list of Starbucks stores appeared on the phone, and Jobs said, "Let's give them a call." A Starbucks employee picked up and said, "Good morning. Starbucks. How can I help you?"

"Yes," said Jobs. "I'd like to order four thousand lattes to go, please. No, just kidding. Wrong number. Good-bye."[9] This

Props Galore for an Italian TV Host

I'm always looking for communicators who push the envelope and create exciting ways to engage an audience, just like Jobs did. I've rarely seen anyone use more props than a young Italian entrepreneur and television host, Marco Montemagno.

Montemagno frequently speaks on the topic of Internet culture, showing Italians why the Internet should be embraced and not feared. He presents to groups as large as three thousand people in places such as Rome, Milan, and Venice. Since the majority of people in his audience are Web novices, he uses language that everyone can understand (well, assuming you know Italian). His slides are very simple and visual; he often employs just photographs, animation, and video. But what truly differentiates Montemagno from the majority of presenters is his unbelievable number of props and demonstrations. Here are three guidelines he follows to create dynamic moments:

1. **Give your audience something to do.** Montemagno's audience members get a pen and paper before taking their seats. During the presentation, he asks them to turn to the person next to them and, in thirty seconds, sketch the person's portrait. After that, he asks them to write the title of their favorite song, movie, and so forth. They then pass the paper around, continuing until each paper has changed hands up to five times. Everyone eventually takes home a piece of paper that once belonged to someone else. The exercise is intended to demonstrate how information is shared among individuals across networks.

2. **Ask someone to share the stage.** In other parts of his presentation, Montemagno will ask for volunteers to join him onstage. In one exercise, he asks them to fold a T-shirt. Most people will take about twenty seconds and fold the shirt in a conventional way. When they're done, he shows a popular YouTube video of someone demonstrating how to fold a shirt in five seconds. Montemagno then duplicates the feat as the audience cheers. His point is that the

Internet can instruct on a deep, intellectual level, but it can also make the most mundane tasks easier.

3. **Make use of your skills onstage.** Montemagno is a former world-ranked table tennis player and works that unique skill into his presentations. He invites another professional player onstage, and the two hit the ball back and forth quickly and effortlessly. As they do, Montemagno, speaking into a wireless headset, compares table tennis to the Internet.

Steve Jobs has elevated presentations to an art form, but few of us will ever introduce a product as world-changing as a revolutionary new computer. This fact is all the more reason to find new, exciting ways to engage your audience. To see video clips of Montemagno in action, visit his site: YouTube site: youtube.com/user/montymonty.

exchange elicited a huge laugh. Jobs had literally crank-called a Starbucks as part of the demo. Jobs had so much fun showing off new products that his enthusiasm lept off the stage and rubbed off on everyone in attendance. It was precisely because he had fun that people enjoyed watching him.

In another prime example of having fun with demos, Jobs took some quirky photographs of himself while introducing a feature called Photo Booth on October 12, 2005. Photo Booth is a software application for using a Web camera to take photographs and video.

"Now I want to show you Photo Booth," said Jobs. "This is an incredible way to have some fun. I can just go ahead and take my picture." Jobs looked into the built-in Web camera on the computer and smiled for a few seconds as his photograph was snapped and appeared on-screen. He said, "Isn't that great? Let me show you some pretty cool effects." Jobs proceeded to snap comical photographs of himself using features such as Thermal, X-Ray, and Andy Warhol. "But it gets even better," Jobs said as he smiled and rubbed his hand together. "We decided to put in the teenage effects."[10] Jobs snapped more photographs of himself as the software distorted his face into funny shapes—squeezing it, widening it, and otherwise contorting the images. The audience roared as Jobs relished the moment.

Focus on the One Thing

Each new Apple product or application contains numerous benefits and features, but Jobs would often highlight just one. Think of it like a movie trailer that teases the audience by revealing only the best parts. If people want the full experience, they'll have to watch the movie.

At WWDC in October 2007, Jobs spent most of the keynote presentation discussing OS X Leopard, but, as he often did, he had "one more thing" for the audience. Jobs introduced Safari for Windows, the "most innovative browser in the world and now the fastest browser on Windows." After telling the audience that he would like to show them the new browser, he walked to stage right, took his seat behind a computer, and started the demo. He told the audience that what he really wanted to show off was Safari's speed compared with Internet Explorer (IE 7).

Add Pizzazz to Online Meetings

Today popular online "webinar" and collaboration tools, including WebEx, Citrix GoToMeeting, Adobe Connect, and Microsoft Office Live Meeting, allow you to add some high-tech pizzazz to demos. For example, you can create polls and receive instant feedback. Sales professionals can conduct a live demonstration of a product from a computer—drawing, highlighting, and pointing to areas right on the screen. Better yet, those same sales professionals can turn over mouse control to the client or prospect, letting the customer on the other end see, touch, and "feel" the product. Demonstrations are important elements in any presentation, offline or online.

The demo screen showed both browsers side by side. Jobs loaded a series of websites simultaneously on both. Safari accomplished the task in 6.64 seconds, while IE 7 took 13.56 seconds to accomplish the same task. "Safari is the fastest browser on Windows," Jobs concluded.[11] The entire demo took less than three minutes. It could have lasted much longer, but Jobs chose to focus on one feature and one feature only. Jobs didn't overwhelm his audience. Just as he eliminated clutter on slides, his demos were likewise free of extraneous messages.

In 2006, Apple added a podcast studio to GarageBand, a tool bundled into the iLife suite of applications intended to make it easy for users to create and distribute multimedia content. "We've added a lot of great stuff to GarageBand," said Jobs, "but I'm going to focus on *one thing* to demo today, and that is we have added a podcast studio to GarageBand. We think GarageBand is now going to be the best tool in the world to create podcasts. It's pretty great. Let me go ahead and give you a demo."

Jobs walked to stage right, sat down, and created a short podcast in four steps. First, Jobs recorded the audio track and had loads of fun with it. He even stopped the first recording and started over because the audience caused him to laugh so hard. Jobs recorded the following: "Hi, I'm Steve. Welcome to my weekly podcast, 'Supersecret Apple Rumors,' featuring the hottest rumors about our favorite company. I have some pretty good sources inside Apple, and this is what I'm hearing: the next iPod will be *huge*, an eight-pounder with a ten-inch screen! Well, that's all for today. See you next week."

After making the playful recording, Jobs walked through the next three steps, showing the audience how to add artwork and background music. Once done, he played the podcast and said, "Pretty cool, huh? That is the podcast studio, which is now built into GarageBand."[12]

Although Jobs did a nice demonstration of the podcast studio, it could not compete with the first release of GarageBand in 2005: "Today we're announcing something so cool: a fifth app that will be part of the iLife family. It's name is GarageBand. What is GarageBand? GarageBand is a major new pro music tool. But it's for everyone. I'm not a musician, so to help me demo GarageBand, we asked a friend, John Mayer, to help us."[13] Jobs took a seat behind a computer, and Mayer sat down at a mini keyboard hooked to the Mac. As Mayer played, Jobs manipulated the sound to make the piano resemble a bass, a choir, a guitar, and other instruments. Jobs then laid down multiple tracks, creating a bandlike sound. He took care to explain what he was doing at every step, to show the audience just how easy it was to create a studio-like experience.

Jobs must have rehearsed the demo for hours, because he looked like an expert musician. Nevertheless, Jobs knew what he didn't know, and sometimes, as in the case of GarageBand, it makes more sense to bring in an outsider who speaks directly to the intended audience.

Element of Surprise

Jobs stunned developers when he announced a transition that had been rumored but largely dismissed—the transition from IBM/Motorola PowerPC chips to Intel processors. During the 2005 WWDC, where he made the announcement, Jobs acknowledged that one of the major challenges would be to make sure

The Next-Best Thing to John Mayer

Of course, you're not going to persuade John Mayer to perform at your next event, but do think about creative ways to reach your target audience. I watched an entrepreneur pitching his new Web service to venture capitalists in San Francisco. The service was geared to the teenage market, so it didn't make sense for a forty-something entrepreneur to demonstrate it. Instead, the founder introduced the company and then passed the demo off to two teens (a boy and a girl), who talked about their experience with the site and what they especially loved about it. The demo was different, engaging, and ultimately successful.

OS X would run efficiently on Intel chips. Having some fun with the audience, he said that the OS X had been "living a double life" for five years, secretly being developed to run on both PowerPC and Intel processors "just in case." The result, said Jobs, was that Mac OS X is "singing on Intel processors."

He then hit the audience with the unexpected: "As a matter of fact, this system I've been using . . ." His voice trails off, he flashes a knowing smile, and the audience laughs when it sinks in that the system is running on new Intel processors. "Let's

Connect with Three Types of Learners

Demonstrations help speakers make an emotional connection with every type of learner in the audience: visual, auditory, and kinesthetic.

» **Visual learners.** About 40 percent of us are visual learners, people who learn through seeing. This group retains information that is highly visual. To reach visual learners, avoid cramming too much text onto the screen. Build slides that have few words and plenty of pictures. Remember: individuals are more likely to act on information they have a connection with, but they cannot connect with anything that they have not internalized. Visual learners connect through seeing.

» **Auditory learners.** These people learn through listening. Auditory learners represent about 20 to 30 percent of your audience. Individuals who learn through listening benefit from verbal and rhetorical techniques that are featured in Act 3. Tell personal stories or use vivid examples to support your key messages.

» **Kinesthetic learners.** These people learn by doing, moving, and touching. In short, they are "hands-on." They get bored listening for long periods. So, include activities in your presentation to keep kinesthetic learners engaged: pass around objects as Jobs did with the aluminum frame, conduct writing exercises, or have them participate in demonstrations.

have a look," Jobs says as he walks to the side of the stage. He sits down and begins exploring many of the conventional computer tasks, such as calendar functions, e-mail, photographs, browsing, and movies, loading and working quickly and effortlessly. He concluded the two-minute demo by saying, "This is Mac OS X running on Intel."[14]

The launch of the iPhone in 2007 also provided Jobs with a memorable prop. He showed the audience how they could listen to their favorite music by playing one of his favorite songs from

The CEO Sidekick

Cisco's Jim Grubb played the sidekick to executive chairman and former CEO John Chambers. Grubb's title is, literally, VP, Emerging Technologies and Chief Demonstration Officer. Nearly every Chambers presentation involves a demonstration, and Grubb was Chambers's go-to guy for some sixty events a year. The demonstrations were unique and truly remarkable. Cisco replicated a scenario onstage complete with furniture and props: it could be an office, a retail store, or rooms of a house. In a demonstration at the 2009 Consumer Electronics Show in Las Vegas, Chambers and Grubb called a doctor in a remote location thousands of miles away and, using Cisco's TelePresence technology, which lets you see a person as though he or she is right in front of you, held a medical evaluation over the network.

Chambers enjoyed needling Grubb with lines such as "Are you nervous, Jim? You seem a little tense," or "It's OK if you mess up. I'll just fire you." Most of the jokes between the two men were scripted but were still funny as Grubb just smiled, laughd it off, and continued with the demonstration—the perfect straight man. Grubb studied music and theater in college. His polished performance reflects his training. Although it appears effortless, he and his staff spend countless hours in the lab testing and practicing, not only to simplify complicated networking technology so it's easy to understand in a fifteen-minute demonstration but also to make sure it works, so his boss doesn't get mad!

the Red Hot Chili Peppers. A phone call interrupted the music and a photo of Apple's SVP of Marketing, Phil Schiller, appeared on the phone. Jobs answered it and talked to Schiller who was standing in the audience on another phone. Schiller requested a photograph; Jobs retrieved it and e-mailed it, and went back to listening to his song. Jobs was a showman, incorporating just the right amount of theater to make features came alive.

DIRECTOR'S NOTES

» Build in a product demo during the planning phase of your presentation. Keep the demo short, sweet, and substantial. If you can introduce another person on your team to participate in the demonstration, do so.

» Commit to the demo. Comedians say a joke works only if you commit to it. In the same way, commit to your demo, especially if your product has any entertainment value at all. Have fun with it.

» Provide something for every type of learner in your audience: visual, auditory, and kinesthetic.

SCENE 13

Reveal a "Holy Shit" Moment

People will forget what you said, people will forget what you did, but people will never forget how you made them feel.

—MAYA ANGELOU

Every office worker has seen a manila envelope. But where most people see a manila envelope as a means of distributing documents, Steve Jobs saw a memorable moment that would leave his audience in awe.

"This is the MacBook Air," he said in January 2008, "so thin it even fits inside one of those envelopes you see floating around the office." With that, Jobs walked to the side of the stage, picked up one such envelope, and pulled out a notebook computer. The audience went wild as the sound of hundreds of cameras clicking and flashing filled the auditorium. Like a proud parent showing off a newborn, Jobs held the computer head-high for all to see. "You can get a feel for how thin it is. It has a full-size keyboard and full-size display. Isn't it amazing? It's the world's thinnest notebook," said Jobs.[1]

The photo of Jobs pulling the computer from the envelope proved to be the most popular of the event and was carried by major newspapers, magazines, and websites. The dramatic introduction even sparked an entrepreneur to build a carrying sleeve for the MacBook Air that looked like, you guessed it, a manila envelope. See Figure 13.1.

Figure 13.1 Jobs holding up the MacBook Air after dramatically removing it from an office-sized manila envelope.

TONY AVELAR/AFP/Getty Images

When Jobs slipped the computer out of the envelope, you could hear the gasps in the room. You knew most people in the audience that day were thinking, "Holy shit. That's thin!" ABC News declared, "The MacBook Air has the potential to reshape the laptop industry. The laptop fits inside a standard office manila envelope, which is how Jobs presented it as the showstopper of this year's conference of all things Apple."[2] The "showstopper" had been planned all along. Well before Jobs enacted the stunt in front of an audience, press releases had been written, images created for the website, and ads developed showing a hand pulling the notebook from a manila envelope. The "holy shit" moment had been scripted to elicit an emotional response; the presentation as theater.

Raising a Product Launch to an Art Form

On January 24, 2009, Macintosh celebrated its twenty-fifth anniversary. Apple's Macintosh had reinvented the personal computer industry in the eighties. A computer with a mouse and graphical user interface was a major transformation from the old command-line interfaces prevalent then. The Mac was much easier to use than anything IBM had at the time. The Mac's introduction was also one of the most spellbinding product launches of its day. The unveiling took place a quarter-century earlier during the Apple shareholders meeting, held at the Flint Center at De Anza College, near the Apple campus. All 2,571 seats were filled as employees, analysts, shareholders, and media representatives buzzed with anticipation.

Jobs (dressed in gray slacks, a double-breasted jacket, and bow tie) kicked off the presentation with a quote by his favorite musician, Bob Dylan. After describing the features of the new computer, Jobs said, "All of this power fits into a box that is one-third the size and weight of an IBM PC. You've just seen pictures of Macintosh. Now I'd like to show you Macintosh in person. All of the images you are about to see on the large screen are being generated by what's in that bag." He pointed to a canvas bag in the center of the stage. After a pause, he walked to center stage and pulled the Macintosh computer out of the bag. He plugged it in, inserted a floppy disk, and stood aside. The lights darkened, the Vangelis theme from *Chariots of Fire* began to play, and a series of images scrolled across the screen (MacWrite and MacPaint, which came free with the Mac). As the music faded, Jobs said, "Now, we've done a lot of talking about Macintosh recently, but today for the first time ever, I'd like to let Macintosh speak for itself." On that cue, Macintosh spoke in a digitized voice:

"Hello, I am Macintosh. It sure is great to get out of that bag. Unaccustomed as I am to public speaking, I'd like to share with you a maxim I thought of the first time I met an IBM mainframe: Never trust a computer you can't lift. Obviously, I can talk right now, but I'd like to sit back and listen. So, it is with considerable pride that I introduce a man who has been like a father to me: Steve Jobs."[3] The crowd went wild, standing, cheering, hollering.

Letting Macintosh speak for itself was a brilliant technique to garner the most buzz and publicity. Thirty years later, the

YouTube video clip from that portion of the announcement has been viewed millions of times. Jobs had created a memorable moment that people would talk about for decades. A genuine showstopper.

One Theme

The secret to creating a memorable moment is to identify the one thing—the one theme—that you want your audience to remember after leaving the room. Your listeners should not need to review notes, slides, or transcripts of the presentation to recall the *one thing*. They will forget many of the details, but they will remember 100 percent of what they *feel*. Think about the one thing Apple wanted you to know about MacBook Air: it's the world's thinnest notebook. That's it. A customer could learn more by visiting the website or an Apple store; the presentation was meant to create an experience and to bring the headline to life. It struck an emotional connection with the listener.

Jobs had one key message that he wanted to deliver about the first iPod: it fits one thousand songs in your pocket. The

The Mental Post-it Note

"The brain doesn't pay attention to boring things," writes scientist John Medina. It does pay attention to an "emotionally charged event," as Medina explains: "The amygdala is chock-full of the neurotransmitter dopamine . . . When the brain detects an emotionally charged event, the amygdala releases dopamine into the system. Because dopamine greatly aids memory and information processing, you could say the Post-it note reads 'Remember this!' "[4]

According to Medina, if you can get the brain to put what amounts to a chemical Post-it note on an idea or a piece of information, the item will be more "robustly processed" and easily remembered. As you could imagine, this concept applies to business professionals as well as teachers and parents!

message was simple and consistent in presentations, press releases, and the Apple website. However, it remained a tagline until Jobs brought it to life in October 2001.

Just as a playwright sets the stage early and reveals the plot over time, Jobs never gave away the big moment right out of the gate. He built the drama. Jobs took the stage to introduce the iPod and, slowly, added layers to the message until he hit the big note.

"The biggest thing about iPod is that it holds a thousand songs," Jobs said.

"To have your whole music library with you at all times is a quantum leap in listening to music." (A device that carried a thousand songs wasn't unique at the time; what came next was the big news.) "But the coolest thing about iPod is your entire music library fits in your pocket. It's ultraportable. iPod is the size of a deck of cards." Jobs's slide showed a photograph of a card deck. "It is 2.4 inches wide. It is four inches tall. And barely three-quarters of an inch thick. This is tiny. It also only weighs 6.5 ounces, lighter than most of the cell phones you have in your pockets right now. This is what's so remarkable about iPod. It is ultraportable. This is what it looks like." Jobs showed a series of photographs. He still hadn't shown the actual device. "In fact, I happen to have one right here in my pocket!" Jobs then took a device out of his pocket and held it up high, as the audience cheered. He had his photo opp. He concluded, "This amazing little device holds a thousand songs and goes right in my pocket."[5]

The headline in the *New York Times* read: "1,000 Songs in Your Pocket." Jobs could not have written a better headline. Actually, he did write it! He also created an emotionally charged event that planted the headline into the dopamine-dumping frontal cortex of his listeners' brains.

Dropping a Welcome Bombshell

Jobs returned to Apple as the interim CEO in 1997. He dropped the "interim" from his title two and half years later. Instead of

Deliver Memorable Stories

A memorable moment need not be a major new product announcement. (After all, few of us will announce breakthrough products like iPod.) Something as simple as a personal story can be memorable.

I once worked with a major grower of organic produce. The executives were preparing a presentation and filled it with mind-numbing statistics to prove that organic was better than conventionally grown fruits and vegetables. The statistics provided supporting points, but there was no emotionally charged event, until a farmer turned to me and told me the following story: "Carmine, when I worked for a conventional farm, I would come home and my kids would want to hug me, but they couldn't. Daddy had to take a shower first, and my clothes had to be washed and disinfected. Today I can walk right off the lettuce field and into the waiting arms of my kids, because there is nothing toxic on my body to harm them." Several years later, I cannot recall any of the statistics this company presented, but I remember the story. The story became the emotionally charged highlight of the presentation.

simply announcing that news via a press release as most CEOs would do, Jobs created an experience out of it.

At the end of a two-hour presentation on January 5, 2000, Jobs said, almost as an aside, "There is one more thing." But he did not break the news immediately. He built the anticipation. Jobs first acknowledged the people at Apple who had been working on the Internet strategy he had just described in the presentation, asking them to stand for applause. He publicly thanked his graphics and advertising agencies as well. Then he dropped the news.

"Everyone at Apple has been working extra hard these two and a half years. And during this time, I've been the interim CEO. I have another job at Pixar as the CEO, which I love. I hope that after two and a half years, we've been able to prove to our shareholders at Pixar that maybe we can pull this interim CEO thing off. So, I'm not changing any of my duties at either Pixar or Apple, but I'm pleased to announce today that I'm dropping the 'interim' title." The audience went nuts; people leaped from their seats, yelling, hollering, and cheering. Jobs was humbled and made it clear that he did not deserve all the credit for Apple's resurgence. "You're making me feel funny, because I get to come to work every day and work with the most talented people on the planet. I accept your thanks on the part of everyone at Apple," Jobs concluded.[6]

Revolutionary Product That Changes Everything

Twenty-six minutes into his Macworld 2007 keynote presentation, Jobs had just finished a discussion of Apple TV. He took a swig of water and slowly walked to the center of the stage, not saying a word for twelve seconds. He then told a story that would lead to one of the greatest product announcements in corporate history. We've discussed several elements of this presentation, including Jobs's use of headlines and the rule of three. For this discussion, let's examine a longer section of the segment. As you can see from the excerpt in Table 13.1, Jobs took his time to reveal the news that would rattle the industry and change the way millions of people access the Internet on the go.[7]

Once the laughter subsided, Jobs spent the rest of the presentation explaining the current limitations of existing smartphones, unveiling the actual iPhone, and reviewing its key features. Anyone who saw the entire presentation will most likely tell you that the three-minute introduction described in the table was *the* most memorable part of the entire keynote.

Take note of how Jobs heightened anticipation to create the experience. He could easily have said: "The next product we would like to introduce is called iPhone. It's Apple's first entry into the smartphone market. Here's what it looks like. Now

TABLE 13.1 EXCERPT FROM JOBS'S MACWORLD 2007 PRESENTATION

STEVE'S WORDS	STEVE'S SLIDES
"This is a day I've been looking forward to for two and a half years. Every once in a while, a revolutionary product comes along that changes everything. One is very fortunate if you get to work on just one of these in your career. Apple has been very fortunate. It's been able to introduce a few of these into the world."	Image of Apple logo
"In 1984, we introduced the Macintosh. It didn't just change Apple; it changed the whole computer industry."	Full-screen photo of Macintosh; the date "1984" appears at the upper left next to the image
"In 2001, we introduced the first iPod. It didn't just change the way we all listen to music; it changed the entire music industry."	Full-screen photo of the original iPod; the date "2001" appears at the upper left
"Well, today we are introducing three revolutionary products of this class."	Back to image of Apple logo
"The first one is a wide-screen iPod with touch controls."	Only image on slide is an artistic rendering of iPod; words beneath the image: "Widescreen iPod with touch controls"
"The second is a revolutionary mobile phone."	Single artistic rendering of a phone, with the words "Revolutionary mobile phone"
"And the third is a breakthrough Internet communications device."	Single rendering of a compass, with the words "Breakthrough Internet communicator"

STEVE'S WORDS	STEVE'S SLIDES
"So, three things: a wide-screen iPod with touch controls, a revolutionary mobile phone, and a breakthrough Internet communications device."	The three images appear on the same slide, with the words "iPod, Phone, Internet"
"An iPod, a phone, and an Internet communicator. An iPod, a phone— are you getting it? These are not three separate devices."	Three images rotate
"This is one device, and we are calling it iPhone."	Text only, centered on slide: "iPhone"
"Today Apple is going to reinvent the phone!"	Text only: "Apple reinvents the phone"
"And here it is." [laughter]	A gag image appears: it's a photo of iPod, but instead of a scroll wheel, an artist had put an old-fashioned rotary dial on the MP3 player

let me tell you more about it." Not very memorable, is it? By contrast, the actual introduction whetted the audience's appetite with every sentence. After Jobs outlined the revolutionary products of the past, a listener could be thinking, "I wonder what this third revolutionary product will be. Oh, I see: Jobs is going to announce three new products of this class. Cool. Wait. Is it three? Oh my gosh, he's talking about one product! All of those features in one product. This I've got to see!"

Every Steve Jobs presentation—major product announcements and minor ones—was scripted to have one moment that would leave everyone talking. The product took center stage, but Jobs played the role of director. Jobs was the Steven Spielberg of corporate presentations. What do you remember most from Spielberg's movies? Spielberg always has one scene that sticks in your memory for years: Indiana Jones pulling a pistol to kill the swordsman in *Raiders of the Lost Ark*, the opening scene of *Jaws*, or E.T. asking to phone home. In the same way, Jobs created one moment that would define the experience.

Jobs changed many things about his presentation style over his career, including his wardrobe, slides, and style. Through it all, one thing remained consistent—his love of drama.

DIRECTOR'S NOTES

» Plan a "holy shit" moment. It need not be a breakthrough announcement. Something as simple as telling a personal story, revealing some new and unexpected information, or delivering a demonstration can help create a memorable moment for your audience. Movie directors such as Steven Spielberg look for those emotions that uplift people, make them laugh, or make them think. People crave beautiful, memorable moments. Build them into your presentation. The more unexpected, the better.

» Script the moment. Build up to the big moment before laying it on your audience. Just as a great novel doesn't give away the entire plot on the first page, the drama should build in your presentation. Did you see the movie *The Sixth Sense*, with Bruce Willis? The key scene was at the end of the movie—one twist that the majority of viewers didn't see coming. Think about ways to add the element of surprise to your presentations. Create at least one memorable moment that will amaze your audience and have them talking well after your presentation is over.

» Rehearse the big moment. Do not make the mistake of creating a memorable experience and having it bomb because you failed to practice. It must come off crisp, polished, and effortless. Make sure demos work and slides appear when they're supposed to.

Schiller Learns from the Best

P hil Schiller had some mighty big shoes to fill on January 6, 2009. Schiller, Apple's senior vice president of worldwide product marketing, replaced Steve Jobs as the keynote presenter at Macworld. (Apple had earlier announced that this would be the company's last year of participation in the event.) Schiller had the unfortunate role of being compared with his boss, who had more than thirty years of experience on the big stage. Schiller was smart, however, and delivered a product launch that contained the best elements of a typical Steve Jobs presentation. Following are seven of Schiller's techniques that Jobs himself would surely have used had he given the keynote:[1]

» **Create Twitter-like headlines.** Schiller set the theme of the day right up front. "Today is all about the Mac," he told the audience. This opening is reminiscent of how Jobs opened the two preceding Macworld shows. Jobs told the 2008 audience that something was in the air, foreshadowing the MacBook Air announcement, and in 2007, Jobs said that Apple was going to make history that day. It sure did when Jobs later introduced the iPhone.

» **Draw a road map.** Schiller verbally outlined a simple agenda at the beginning of his presentation and provided verbal reminders along the way. Just as Jobs used the rule of three to describe products, Schiller also introduced the presentation as three separate categories. "I have three new things to tell you about today," he said (accompanying slide read: "3 New Things"). The first was a new version of iLife. The second product he discussed was a new version of iWork. Finally, the third was a new MacBook seventeen-inch Pro notebook computer.

» **Dress up numbers.** As his boss did, Schiller added meaning to numbers. He told the audience that 3.4 million customers visit an Apple store every week. To give his audience a relevant perspective, Schiller said, "That's one hundred Macworlds each and every week."

» **Stage the presentation with props.** Demonstrations played a prominent role in every Steve Jobs presentation. Schiller also used the technique smoothly and effectively. As Jobs likely would have done had he given the presentation, Schiller sat down at a computer on the stage and demonstrated several new features that come standard in '09 versions of iLife and iWork. My favorite demo was the new Keynote '09, which comes closer than ever to letting everyday users create Jobs-like slides without an expertise in graphic design.

» **Share the stage.** Schiller did not hog the spotlight. He shared the stage with employees who had more experience in areas that were relevant to the new products he introduced. For a demo of iMovie '09, a new version of the video-editing software, Schiller deferred to an Apple engineer who actually created the tool. When Schiller revealed the new seventeen-inch MacBook Pro, he said the battery was the most innovative feature of the notebook computer. To explain further, Schiller showed a video that featured three Apple employees describing how they were able to build a battery that lasted eight hours on a single charge without adding to the notebook's size, weight, or price.

» **Create visual slides.** There were very few words on a Steve Jobs slide, and there were few on Schiller's slides as well. The first few slides had no words at all, simply photographs. Schiller started by giving the audience a tour of some of the new Apple stores that had opened around the world the past year. There were no bullet points on Schiller's slides. When Schiller did present a list of features, he used the fewest words possible and often paired the words with an image. You can view the slide set yourself by watching the actual keynote presentation on the Apple website or visiting Slideshare.net.[2]

» **Deliver a "holy shit" moment.** In true Steve Jobs fashion, Schiller surprised the audience by announcing "just one more thing" to close his presentation. He applied the rule of three as he had done earlier, but this time to iTunes. He said there were three new things for iTunes in 2009: a change to the pricing structure, the ability of iPhone customers to download and buy songs on their 3G cellular network, and the fact that all iTunes songs would be DRM free (i.e., without copy protection). Schiller received a big round of applause when he announced that eight million songs would be DRM free "starting today" and got an even bigger round of applause when he said that all ten million songs on iTunes would be DRM free by the end of the quarter. Schiller knew that DRM-free songs in iTunes would be the big headline of the day, and he saved it for last. The announcement did, indeed, dominate the news coverage that followed.

ACT 3

Refine and Rehearse

So far, we've learned how Steve Jobs planned his presentations. We've talked about how he supported the narrative through his words and slides. We've discussed how he assembled the cast, created demos, and wowed his audience with one dynamic moment that left everyone in awe. Finally, you'll learn how Jobs refined and rehearsed his presentation to make an emotional connection with the audience. This final step is essential for anyone who wants to talk, walk, and look like a leader. Let's preview the scenes in this act:

» **SCENE 14: "Master Stage Presence."** *How* you say something is as important as *what* you say, if not more so. Body language and verbal delivery account for 63 to 90 percent of the impression you leave on your audience, depending upon which study you cite. Steve Jobs's delivery matched the power of his words.

» **SCENE 15: "Make It *Look* Effortless."** Few speakers rehearse more than Steve Jobs did. His preparation time was legendary among the people closest to him. Researchers have discovered exactly how many hours of practice it takes to achieve mastery in a given skill. In this chapter, you'll learn how Jobs confirmed these theories and how you can apply them to improve your own presentation skills.

» **SCENE 16: "Wear the Appropriate Costume."** Jobs had the easiest wardrobe selection in the world: it was the same for all of his presentations. His attire was so well known that even "Saturday Night Live" and "30 Rock" poked some good-natured fun at him. Learn why it was OK for Jobs to dress the way he did but it could mean career suicide if you follow his lead.

» **SCENE 17: "Toss the Script."** Jobs talked to the audience, not to his slides. He made strong eye contact because he had practiced effectively. This chapter will teach you how to practice the right way so you, too, can toss the script.

» **SCENE 18: "Have Fun."** Despite the extensive preparation that went into a Steve Jobs presentation, things didn't always go according to plan. Nothing rattled Jobs, because his first goal was to have fun!

Master Stage Presence

I was hooked by Steve's energy and enthusiasm.

—GIL AMELIO

Steve Jobs had a commanding presence. His voice, gestures, and body language communicated authority, confidence, and energy. Jobs's enthusiasm was on full display at Macworld 2003. Table 14.1 shows his actual words as well as the gestures he used to introduce the Titanium PowerBook.[1] The words he verbally emphasized in his presentation are in italics.

The words Jobs used to describe a product were obviously important, but so was the *style* in which he delivered the words. He punched key words in every paragraph, adding extra emphasis to the most important words in the sentence. He made expansive gestures to complement his vocal delivery. We'll examine his body language and vocal delivery more closely later in the chapter, but for now, the best way to appreciate his skill is to call on a guest speaker who pales in comparison.

"Who's Mr. Note Card?"

During the iPhone introduction at Macworld 2007, Jobs invited Cingular/AT&T CEO Stan Sigman to join him onstage and to share a few words about the partnership. Sigman took the floor and sucked the energy right out of the room. He immediately

TABLE 14.1 JOBS'S MACWORLD 2003 PRESENTATION

STEVE'S WORDS	STEVE'S GESTURES
"Two years ago, we introduced a *landmark product* for Apple. The Titanium PowerBook *instantly* became the best notebook in the industry. The number *one lust object*."	Raises index finger
"Every review said so."	Pulls hands apart, palms up
"And you know what? Nobody has caught up with it in *two years*."	Holds up two fingers on right hand
"Almost every reviewer today *still* says it is the number one notebook in the industry. No one is even *close*."	Chops air with left hand
"This is important for Apple because we believe that someday *notebooks* are even going to outsell *desktops* . . . We want to replace even *more* desktops with notebooks."	Makes an expansive gesture with both hands
"So, how do we do this? What's next? Well, the Titanium PowerBook is a milestone product, and it's not going away. But we're going to step it up a notch to attract even *more* people from a desktop to a notebook."	Gestures, moving hand in a broad stroke from right to left
"And how do we do that? We do that with *this*."	Pauses
"The new *seventeen-inch PowerBook*. A seventeen-inch landscape screen."	Another expansive gesture, hands pulled apart, palms up
"It's *stunning*."	Pauses
"And when you close it, it is only *one inch* thick."	Makes thin gesture with left hand
"The *thinnest* PowerBook *ever*. Let me go ahead and show you one. I happen to have one right here."	Walks to stage right while maintaining eye contact with audience

STEVE'S WORDS	STEVE'S GESTURES
"It is the most incredible product we have ever made."	Picks up computer and opens it
"The new seventeen-inch PowerBook. It's amazing. Look at that screen."	Holds up computer to show screen
"Look at how *thin* it is. Isn't it incredible? It's beautiful, too."	Shuts computer and holds it up
"This is clearly the most advanced notebook computer ever made *on the planet*. Our competitors haven't even caught up with what we introduced two years ago; I don't know what they're going to do about *this*."	Smiles and looks directly at audience

put his hands into his pockets and proceeded to deliver his comments in a low-key monotone. Worst of all, he pulled note cards out of his jacket pocket and started reading from them word for word. As a result, Sigman's delivery became more halting, and he lost all eye contact with the audience. He continued for six long minutes that seemed like thirty. Observers were fidgeting, waiting for Jobs to return.

A post on CNN's international blog read: "Sigman . . . read stiffly from a script, pausing awkwardly to consult notes. By contrast, the silver-tongued Jobs wore his trademark black turtleneck and faded blue jeans . . . Jobs is one of the best showmen in corporate America, rarely glancing at scripts and quick with off-the-cuff jokes." Bloggers were relentless during Sigman's talk. Among the comments: "Who's Mr. Note Card?"; "Blah, blah, blah, and blah"; "Painfully bad"; and "A snoozer."

Sigman left AT&T that same year. Macworld.com wrote: "Sigman is perhaps best remembered by Apple fans as *completely negating* Jobs's Reality Distortion Field in an incident which left almost half of the entire keynote audience sound asleep. He has been sentenced to a cruel afterlife of being the butt of roughly 99 percent of Scott Bourne's jokes [Bourne is a Mac pundit and podcaster] . . . And what will Stan do in retirement? Word is he's thinking of giving public speaking workshops to underprivileged youth."[2]

Sigman spent forty-two years at AT&T, rising from the lowest rungs in the company to running its wireless division. Yet, to many people unfamiliar with his leadership, Sigman's appearance at Macworld will be his lasting legacy. It wasn't Sigman's fault. He had to follow the master. And, unfortunately, this book wasn't out yet to help him prepare!

Three Techniques to Improve Body Language

Steve Jobs resigned from Apple in 1985 after losing a boardroom battle for control of the company in a power struggle with then CEO John Sculley. He would remain away for eleven years, returning triumphantly when Gil Amelio, Apple's CEO in 1996, announced that Apple was going to buy Jobs's NeXT for $427 million. "I was hooked by Steve's energy and enthusiasm," Amelio wrote in *On the Firing Line: My Five Hundred Days at Apple*. "I do remember how animated he is on his feet, how his full mental abilities materialize when he's up and moving, how he becomes more expressive."[3]

Jobs came alive when he was up and moving onstage. He was seemingly boundless energy. When he was at his best, Jobs did three things anyone can, and should, do to enhance one's speaking and presentation skills: he made eye contact, maintained an open posture, and used frequent hand gestures.

EYE CONTACT

Great communicators like Jobs make appreciably more eye contact with the audience than average presenters. They rarely read from slides or notes. Jobs didn't eliminate notes entirely. He often had some notes tucked out of view during demonstrations. Apple's presentation software, Keynote, also makes it easy for speakers to see speaker's notes while the audience sees the slides displayed on the projector. If Jobs was reading, nobody could tell. He maintained eye contact with his audience nearly all the time. He glanced at a slide and immediately turned his attention back to where it belonged—on those watching.

Most presenters spend too much time reading every word of text on a slide. During demonstrations, mediocre presenters will break eye contact completely. Research has discovered that eye contact is associated with honesty, trustworthiness, sincerity, and confidence. Avoiding eye contact is most often associated with a lack of confidence and leadership ability. Breaking eye contact is a surefire way to lose your connection with your audience.

Jobs could make solid eye contact with his listeners because he practiced his presentations for weeks ahead of time (see Scene 15). He knew exactly what was on each slide and what he was going to say when the slide appeared. The more Jobs rehearsed, the more he had internalized the content, and the easier it was for him to connect with his listeners. The majority of presenters fail to practice, and it shows.

The second reason why Jobs could make solid eye contact was that his slides were highly visual. More often than not, there were no words at all on a slide—just photographs (see Scene 8 and Scene 17). When there were words, they were few—sometimes just one word on a slide. Visual slides force the speaker to deliver the information to those whom the message is intended to reach—the audience.

OPEN POSTURE

Jobs rarely crossed his arms or stood behind a lectern. His posture was "open." An open posture simply means he placed nothing between himself and his audience. During demos, Jobs sat parallel to the computer so nothing blocked his view of the audience or the audience's view of him. He performed a function on the computer and immediately turned to the audience to explain what he just did, rarely breaking eye contact for a long stretch of time. In Jobs's early presentations, most notably the 1984 Macintosh introduction, he stood behind a lectern. He abandoned the lectern soon after and has never used one since (with the exception of his 2005 Stanford commencement address). See Figure 14.1.

HAND GESTURES

Jobs emphasized nearly every sentence with a gesture that complemented his words. Some old-fashioned speaking coaches still instruct clients to keep their hands at their sides. I'm not sure where this started, but it's the kiss of death for any speaker hoping to captivate an audience. Keeping your hands at your sides will make you look stiff, formal, and, frankly, a little weird. Extraordinary communicators like Jobs use *more* gestures than the average speaker, not fewer. There's even research to back up this observation.

Dr. David McNeill, at the University of Chicago, is known for his exhaustive research in the area of hand gestures. He's made it his passion since 1980. His research has shown that gestures and language are intimately connected. In fact, the *use* of gestures can help presenters speak better by clearing up their thought process. Yes, he says, it actually takes concentrated

Figure 14.1 Steve Jobs engaged his audience with strong eye contact, hand gestures, and an open posture.

JOHN G. MABANGLO/AFP/Getty Images

effort *not* to use gestures. McNeill has found that very disciplined, rigorous, and confident thinkers use hand gestures that reflect the clarity of their thinking—it's like a window to their thought process.

Use hand gestures to emphasize your point. Be careful, however, that your hand gestures do not become robotic or overrehearsed. In other words, don't copy Jobs and his mannerisms. Be yourself. Be authentic.

Say It with Style

Steve Jobs used his voice as effectively as his gestures. His content, slides, and demos created excitement, but his delivery tied the package together. When he introduced the iPhone in January 2007, he told a magnificently woven story, and his vocal expression provided just the right amount of drama. We reviewed the announcement and its slides in previous chapters. Now let's focus on *how* Jobs said what he said. It is a package

Is That a CEO or a Preacher?

Few among us have the public-speaking confidence to rival Cisco executive chairman and former CEO John Chambers. People are often shocked the first time they watch him give a presentation. Like a preacher, Chambers roams among the audience. He spends only a minute or two onstage at the beginning of his presentation before stepping into the crowd. Chambers walks right up to people, looks them in the eye, calls some by name, even places his hand on someone's shoulder. Very few people have the confidence to pull this off.

I know as a fact that Chambers's confidence is the result of hours of relentless practice. He knows every word on each of his slides, and he knows exactly what he's going to say next. Observers have said watching a Chambers presentation is an "astonishing" experience. Be astonishing. Rehearse your presentation, and pay close attention to your body language and verbal delivery.

deal, after all. Great slides mean little without a great delivery. A great story will fall flat if delivered poorly.

Table 14.2 illustrates Jobs's vocal delivery. It's from the same iPhone presentation featured in Scene 13, with a focus on his actual delivery. The words Jobs chose to emphasize are italicized in the first column; the second column lists notes on his delivery, including the moments when he pauses right after a phrase or sentence.[4] Pay particular attention to pacing, pausing, and volume.

Jobs varied his delivery to create suspense, enthusiasm, and excitement. Nothing will do more to destroy all of the work you put into crafting a spectacular presentation than to deliver it in a boring monotone, which Jobs most certainly did not.

Jobs's voice complemented the drama of the plot. He used similar devices in every presentation. This section details four related techniques that Jobs used to keep his listeners engaged: inflection, pauses, volume, and rate.

INFLECTION

Jobs changed his inflection by raising or lowering the pitch of his voice. Think about how flat the iPhone launch would have sounded if all of his words had been delivered with exactly the same tone. Instead, Jobs raised his pitch when he said, "Are you getting it?" and "This is one device." Jobs had some favorite descriptors that found their way into many of his presentations: *unbelievable, awesome, cool,* and *huge.* These words would not carried the same impact if the tone in which they were delivered sounded exactly like the rest of the sentence. Jobs modified his tone frequently, keeping his listeners on the edge of their seats.

PAUSES

Nothing is more dramatic than a well-placed pause. "Today we're introducing a third kind of notebook," Jobs told the Macworld audience in January 2008. Then he paused a few beats before saying, "It's called the MacBook Air." He paused again before the delivering the headline: "It's the world's thinnest notebook."[5]

Jobs did not rush his presentation. He let it breathe. He would often remain quiet for several seconds as he let a key point sink

TABLE 14.2 JOBS'S 2007 iPHONE PRESENTATION

STEVE'S WORDS	STEVE'S DELIVERY
"This is a day I've been looking forward to for two and a half years."	Pause
"Every once in a while, a revolutionary product comes along that *changes everything*."	Pause
"Apple has been very fortunate. It's been able to introduce a few of these into the world. In 1984, we introduced *Macintosh*. It didn't just change Apple; it changed the whole computer industry."	Pause
"In 2001, we introduced the first *iPod*."	Pause
"It didn't just change the way we all listen to music; it changed the entire *music* industry."	Pause
"Well, today we're introducing *three* revolutionary products of this class. The *first* one"	Pause
"is a wide-screen iPod with touch controls. The *second*"	Pause
"is a *revolutionary mobile phone*."	Voice grows louder
"And the *third*"	Pause
"is a *breakthrough* Internet communications device. So, three things: a wide-screen iPod with touch controls, a revolutionary mobile phone, and a breakthrough Internet communications device."	Pause
"An iPod, a phone, and an Internet communciator."	Voice grows louder
"An iPod, a phone—are you getting it?"	Speaks faster, voice grows louder
"These are not three separate devices. This is *one* device,"	Voice grows louder still
"and we are calling it *iPhone*."	Voice gets even louder
"Today Apple is going to *reinvent* the *phone*!"	Loudest volume of the presentation

in. Most presenters sound as though they are trying to rush through the material. In many ways, they are, because they scripted more material than the time allows. Jobs never hurried. His presentation was carefully rehearsed to give him plenty of time to slow down, pause, and let his message take hold.

VOLUME

Jobs would lower and raise his voice to add drama. He typically did this when introducing a hot new product. He often lowered his voice as he built up to the announcement and then raised his volume to hit the big note. He would do the opposite as well. When he introduced the first iPod, he raised his voice and said, "To have your whole music library with you at all times is a *quantum leap* in listening to music." He then lowered his voice and delivered the knockout: "But the coolest thing about iPod is your entire music library fits in your pocket."[6] Just as inflections and pauses keep your audience riveted to your every word, so does the volume of your voice.

RATE

Jobs sped up the delivery of some sentences and slowed down for others. Demonstrations were typically delivered at his normal rate of speech, but he slowed down considerably when he delivered the headline or key message that he wanted everyone to remember. When Jobs introduced the iPod for the first time, he lowered his voice nearly to a whisper to emphasize the key takeaway. He also slowed the tempo of his sentences to build the drama. Table 14.3 offers highlights.[7]

Act Like the Leader You Want to Be

Do not make the mistake of believing body language and vocal delivery are unimportant, "soft skills." UCLA research scientist Albert Mehrabian studied expression and communication for his book *Silent Messages*.[8] He discovered that nonverbal cues carry the most impact in a conversation. Tone of voice—vocal expression—was the second most influential factor. The third, and least important, were the actual words spoken.

TABLE 14.3 EXCERPT FROM JOBS INTRODUCING THE iPOD, WITH DELIVERY NOTES

STEVE'S WORDS	STEVE'S DELIVERY
"Now, you might be saying, 'This is cool, but I've got a hard disk in my portable computer, my iBook. I'm running iTunes. I'm really happy. I don't get ten hours of battery life on my iBook, but iBook has better battery life than any other consumer portable.'"	Slows down rate of speech
"'So, what's so special about iPod here?'"	Pauses and lowers volume
"It's ultraportable. An iBook is portable, but this is *ultra*portable. Let me show you what I mean."	Speeds up rate of speech
"iPod is the size of a deck of cards. It is 2.4 inches wide. It is four inches tall. And barely three-quarters of an inch thick. This is tiny. It also only weighs 6.5 ounces, lighter than most of the cell phones you have in your pockets right now. This is what's so remarkable about iPod."	Slows down and lowers voice
"It is ultraportable."	Almost at a whisper

To a large extent, how Steve Jobs spoke and carried himself left his audience with a sense of awe and confidence in him as a leader. U.S. president Barack Obama once said the most valuable lesson he learned as he worked himself up from a community organizer to the most powerful person on the planet was to "always act confident."

People are making judgments about you all the time, but especially in the first ninety seconds of meeting you. How you deliver your words and what your body language says about you will leave your listeners disillusioned or inspired. Steve Jobs was an electrifying communicator because he was expressive in both voice and gesture.

Bueller? Bueller?

Ben Stein provides us with one of the best examples of a horribly dull, monotone vocal delivery. In the 1986 movie *Ferris Bueller's Day Off*, Ben Stein played a boring economics teacher. Stein's most famous line in the movie occurred when he was taking attendance and Bueller (the Matthew Broderick character) was nowhere to be found. In the driest monotone on film, Stein asked, "Bueller . . . ? Bueller . . . ? Bueller . . . ?" as the camera flashed to an empty chair. In another scene, Stein discussed the Hawley-Smoot Tariff Act and voodoo economics. The looks on the students' faces are hilarious. One kid has his head on the desk as drool is coming out of the side of his mouth. Stein's character is so boring, it's funny.

If Stein were to read a transcript of a Steve Jobs presentation in the same manner in which he played the teacher, it would surely be one of the longest, dullest presentations in the history of corporate America. This proves once again that words matter, but an effective delivery makes the difference.

DIRECTOR'S NOTES

» Pay attention to your body language. Maintain eye contact, have an open posture, and use hand gestures when appropriate. Don't be afraid of using your hands. Research has shown that gestures reflect complex thinking and give the listener confidence in the speaker.

» Vary your vocal delivery by adding inflection to your voice, raising or lowering your volume, as well as speeding up and slowing down. Also, let your content breathe. Pause. Nothing is as dramatic as a well-placed pause.

» Record yourself. Watch your body language, and listen to your vocal delivery. Watching yourself on video is the best way to improve your presentation skills.

Make It *Look* Effortless

**Practice isn't the thing you do once you're good.
It's the thing you do that makes you good.**

—MALCOLM GLADWELL

Steve Jobs was a master showman, working the stage with precision. Every move, demo, image, and slide was in sync. He appeared comfortable, confident, and remarkably effortless. At least, it *looked* effortless to the audience. Here's his presentation secret: Jobs rehearsed for hours. To be more precise: many, many hours over many, many days.

"Jobs unveils Apple's latest products as if he were a particularly hip and plugged-in friend showing off inventions in your living room. Truth is, the sense of informality comes only after grueling hours of practice," observed a *BusinessWeek* reporter. "One retail executive recalls going to a Macworld rehearsal at Jobs's behest and then waiting four hours before Jobs came off the stage to conduct an interview. Jobs considers his keynotes a competitive weapon. Marissa Mayer, a Google executive who plays a central role in launching the search giant's innovations, insists that up-and-coming product marketers attend Jobs's keynotes. 'Steve Jobs is the best at launching new products,' she says. 'They have to see how he does it.'"[1]

How did he do it? The *BusinessWeek* reporter provided the answer in the article: Steve Jobs put in *hours of grueling practice.* When was the last time you could say that you devoted hours of grueling practice to prepare for a presentation? The honest answer is probably "never." If you really want to talk the way Jobs did, plan on spending more time rehearsing every portion of your presentation.

Glimpse Behind the Magic Curtain

In an article published in the *Guardian* on January 5, 2006, former Apple employee Mike Evangelist wrote about his personal experience rehearsing a portion of a demonstration for a Jobs keynote: "To a casual observer these presentations appear to be just a guy in a black shirt and blue jeans talking about some new technology products. But they are in fact an incredibly complex and sophisticated blend of sales pitch, product demonstration, and corporate cheerleading, with a dash of religious revival thrown in for good measure. They represent weeks of work, precise orchestration, and intense pressure for scores of people who collectively make up the 'man behind the curtain.'"[2]

According to Evangelist's first-person account, Jobs began his preparation weeks in advance, reviewing products and technologies he was going to talk about. Evangelist had been tapped to demo the new iDVD, Apple's DVD-burning software, for Macworld 2001. Evangelist said his team spent hundreds of hours preparing for a segment that lasted five minutes. That's not a typo: *hundreds* of hours for a five-minute demo.

Evangelist said Jobs rehearsed for two full days before the presentation, asking for feedback from the product managers in the room. Jobs spent a lot of time on slides, personally writing and designing much of the content, along with some help from the design team. "On the day before show time, things get much more structured, with at least one and sometimes two complete dress rehearsals. Throughout it all Steve is extremely focused. While we were in that room, all his energy was directed at making this keynote the perfect embodiment of Apple's messages."[3]

In the weeks before the keynote, Evangelist saw the full range of Steve's emotions from disappointment to elation. "I believe it is one of the most important aspects of Steve Jobs's impact on Apple: he has little or no patience for anything but excellence from himself or others," Evangelist concluded.[4]

In October 1999, then *Time* magazine reporter Michael Krantz was interviewing Jobs one day before the introduction of a line of multicolored iMacs. Jobs was rehearsing the big moment when he would announce, "Say hello to the new iMacs." The computers were then supposed to glide out from behind a dark curtain, but according to Krantz, Jobs was unhappy with the lighting. He wanted the lights to be brighter and to come up sooner. "Let's keep doing it till we get it right, OK?" said Jobs.[5] The show's lighting folks practiced again and again as Jobs grew increasingly frustrated.

"Finally," Krantz reports, "they get it right, the five impeccably lighted iMacs gleaming as they glide forward smoothly on the giant screen. 'Oh! Right there! That's great!' Jobs yells, elated at the very notion of a universe capable of producing these insanely beautiful machines. 'That's perfect!' he bellows, his voice booming across the empty auditorium. 'Wooh!' And you know what? He's right. The iMacs do look better when the lights come on earlier."[6] The scene that Krantz described could be interpreted in one of two ways: either Jobs was a micromanager or, as one of Jobs's friends observed in the article, he was "single-minded, almost manic, in his pursuit of quality and excellence."

What Steve Jobs, Michael Jordan, and Winston Churchill Have in Common

Psychology professor Dr. K. Anders Ericsson has studied top athletes such as Michael Jordan as well as superachievers in other walks of life: chess players, golfers, doctors, even dart throwers! Ericsson discovered that star performers refine their skills through *deliberative practice*. In other words, they do not just do the same thing over and over, hoping to get better.

Instead, they set specific goals, ask for feedback, and continually strive to improve over the long run. From Ericsson's research, we have learned that star performers practice specific skills again and again over many, many years.

Ordinary speakers become extraordinary because they practice. Winston Churchill was one of the foremost communicators of the twentieth century. He was a master of persuasion, influence, and motivation. Churchill, too, deliberately practiced the skills required to inspire millions of British during the darkest days of World War II. "He would prepare in the days before a big parliamentary speech, practicing quips or parries against any number of possible interjections. Churchill practiced so thoroughly that he seemed to be speaking extemporaneously . . . he held his audience spellbound," wrote Churchill's granddaughter Celia Sandys and coauthor Jonathan Littman in *We Shall Not Fail*. "The lesson is simple but requires lots of hard work. Practice is essential, particularly if you want to sound spontaneous."[7] The world's greatest communicators have always known that "spontaneity" is the result of planned practice.

You *can* speak the way Jobs did, but it takes practice. Jobs made an elaborate presentation look easy because he put in the time. In *The Second Coming of Steve Jobs*, Paul Vais, a NeXT executive, was quoted as saying, "Every slide was written like a piece of poetry. We spent hours on what most people would consider low-level detail. Steve would labor over the presentation. We'd try to orchestrate and choreograph everything and make it more alive than it really is."[8] Making your presentation "more alive" takes practice. Once you accept this simple principle, your presentations will stand out in a sea of mediocrity.

Ten Thousand Hours to Mastery

There are no "naturals." Steve Jobs was an extraordinary presenter because he worked at it. According to Malcolm Gladwell in *Outliers*, "Research suggests that once a musician has enough ability to get into a top music school, the thing that distinguishes one performer from another is how hard he or she works. That's it. And what's more, the people at the very top don't work just harder or even much harder than everyone else. They work much, *much* harder."[9] Although the observation Gladwell makes in *Outliers* applies specifically to musicians, the vast amount of research on the subject of peak performance shows that practice is the common thread among all individuals who excel at a particular task. Neuroscientist and musician Daniel Levitin believes that the magic number is ten thousand.

"The emerging picture of such studies is that ten thousand hours of practice is required to achieve the level of mastery associated with being a world-class expert—in anything . . . In study after study, of composers, basketball players, fiction writers, ice-skaters, concert pianists, chess players, master criminals, and what have you, this number comes up again and again. Of course, this doesn't address why some people don't seem to get anywhere when they practice, and why some people seem to get more out of their practice sessions than others, but no one has yet found a case in which true world-class expertise was accomplished in less time. It seems that it takes the brain this long to assimilate all that it needs to know to achieve true mastery."[10]

The ten-thousand-hours theory is consistent with what we know about how the brain learns, according to Levitin and Gladwell. They say that learning requires consolidation in neural tissue; the more experiences we have with a particular action, the stronger those connections become.

Now let's do the math. Ten thousand hours is equivalent to roughly three hours a day, or twenty hours a week, over a period of ten years. To substantiate this theory, Gladwell tells the story of the Beatles, who performed together in Hamburg over a long period before they hit it big. According to Gladwell, before the Beatles enjoyed their first success in 1964, they had performed live together some twelve hundred times, sometimes for eight hours at a stretch. This is an extraordinary feat, because most groups don't perform that often in their entire careers. The band members became better and more confident the longer they played together. "Incidentally," writes Gladwell, "the time that elapsed between their founding and their arguably greatest artistic achievements—*Sgt. Pepper's Lonely Hearts Club Band* and *The Beatles* [White Album]—is ten years."[11]

With the ten-thousand-hours theory in mind, let's turn our attention once again to Jobs. Although Apple was founded in 1976, Jobs and friend-cofounder Steve Wozniak started attending meetings of the Homebrew Computer Club in 1974. Homebrew was an early computer-hobbyist club in Silicon Valley, California. It was at Homebrew that Jobs began tinkering and talking about how computers could change the world. Exactly ten years later, Jobs gave an outstanding presentation— the introduction of the Macintosh in 1984. Most people who saw that presentation consider it to be a magnificent achievement, packed with suspense, drama, and excitement. But remarkably, Jobs continued to practice, refine, and improve his presentation style.

A decade later, in 1997, Jobs had returned to Apple and was onstage at Boston's Macworld to discuss the steps he had taken to restore Apple to health. Everything about his performance that day was more polished and natural than it had been in previous years. He had lost the lectern, walking comfortably across the stage, and had started creating more visually engaging slides.

Flash forward another ten years to Macworld 2007, which, in my opinion, was Jobs's greatest presentation if you take into account every element of the keynote from start to finish. He hit home runs in every presentation, but he hit a bases-loaded homer in 2007. Everything clicked. Several sections of the presentation have been discussed throughout this book. The overall presentation was smooth and polished, with dramatic highs and lows, confident body language, captivating verbal delivery, and gorgeous slides. The iPhone announcement had even overshadowed every product at the vastly larger Consumer Electronics Show, held the same week in Las Vegas.

The chief misconception about Jobs is that he was a natural presenter, that he was born with the charisma that he exhibits onstage. Not true. As research has shown, nobody is a natural. You can achieve the same level of proficiency of the world's greatest communicators if you work at it much, *much* harder than everyone else.

Flushing Away $25,000

I once saw the executive of a major publicly traded company give a keynote presentation to a large audience of customers, press, and analysts. I later learned that the company had spent upwards of $25,000 for professional designers to create slick, animated slides. That figure did not account for the lighting, audio, and venue. The most creative slides will fail to impress your audience unless you practice your delivery; this guy did not practice, and it showed. Since he had not practiced coordinating his words to the animation, the slides were off, and he lost his place numerous times. He stumbled through most of the presentation and at one point threw up his hands in exasperation! If you spend money and time on a presentation—and time is money—you owe it to yourself to practice, practice, and practice some more!

Make Video Your Best Friend

Nearly every year, I'm asked to work with CEOs who give major presentations at the Consumer Electronics Show in Las Vegas. The conference is usually scheduled for the first full week in January, which means we're rehearsing over the holidays, often while the rest of the company's employees are off. Regardless, CEOs will show up for practice, because they know how important it is.

In one particular year, after several days of rehearsals, one of my CEO clients took the stage in Vegas but had trouble with the slides. The clicker had failed, and the slides were not advancing. Most amateur speakers who don't spend enough time practicing would have frozen, calling even more attention to the problem. Not this guy. He was so well prepared that he casually motioned to an assistant to advance the slides for him (we rehearse contingency plans). He didn't miss a step and kept talking. It didn't end there: something was wrong with the computer; it had locked and would have to be rebooted for the slide show to continue. The assistant simply shook his head, but the CEO stayed the course. He continued to deliver the rest of the presentation with no slides. He did so effortlessly and confidently.

He later told me that without practice (which I had urged him to do), he would have lost his confidence and floundered in front of employees, analysts, investors, customers, and the media. When I asked employees after the presentation what they had thought, none of them realized that anything had gone wrong.

VIDEO TRAINING TIPS

We had used a video camera during rehearsals. Very few presenters watch themselves on camera, even though perfectly appropriate camcorders are available for less than $300. I know that watching yourself on TV, especially a wide-screen, is not the most pleasant experience, but take my word for it: it's essential. Record your presentation and play it back. If possible, find objective friends and colleagues who will offer honest feedback. Use an external, clip-on microphone instead of the built-in microphone standard on all camcorders. Your voice will sound louder, clearer, and more resonant.

As you watch the video, pay close attention to these five areas:

> » **Eye contact.** Commit most of your presentation to memory to avoid reading from notes. Your slides should act as your cue. Public-speaking expert Andrew Carnegie observed that notes destroy the intimacy between speaker and audience and make the speaker appear less powerful and confident. Notice that I didn't tell you to give the presentation "completely" without notes. Steve Jobs kept notes out of his audience's sight. Only a careful observer would spot him glancing at them. He referred to notes during demonstrations, but since the audience's attention was on the demo itself, his notes did not detract from the presentation. The notes he did keep onstage were also unobtrusive and simple. He just needed to glance at them to find his place. Although it's easier in Keynote than PowerPoint to have a notes page for the speaker's view, you should still strive to deliver most of your presentation with no notes at all.

» **Body language.** Is your body language strong, confident, and commanding? Are your arms crossed or open? Are you keeping your hands in your pockets instead of keeping an open posture? Do you fidget, rock, or have other distracting habits? Are your gestures natural and purposeful or stiff and wooden? Remember that body language and verbal delivery account for the majority of the impression you leave on your listeners. Your body language should reflect the confidence of your words.

» **Filler words.** Are you constantly using "um," "ah," and "you know" to fill the space between thoughts? Just as text shouldn't fill every inch of your slide, your words shouldn't fill every pause between sentences. Reviewing your performance is the best way to eliminate these often distracting fillers. Once you catch yourself a few times, you will be more aware of the habit next time. Awareness is more than 90 percent of the solution!

» **Vocal delivery.** Vary the volume and inflection of your voice to keep the attention of your audience riveted on your words. Raise and lower your volume at different points in your presentation. Change your cadence. Varying the speed at which you talk will keep your presentation from sounding monotone. Speed up at certain points and then slow down. Pause for impact. Again, nothing is as dramatic as a well-placed pause. Don't sound rushed. Let the presentation breathe.

» **Energy.** Do you look as if you rolled out of bed on a Sunday morning, or do you appear vibrant, enthusiastic, and genuinely thrilled to be sharing your story with the audience? We all enjoy being around people with energy. They inspire us. They are stimulating, fun, and uplifting. An energetic person has passion in his voice, a bounce in his step, and a smile on his face. Energy makes a person likable, and likability is a key ingredient in persuasive communications. Many business professionals underestimate the energy level required to generate enthusiasm among their listeners. Electrifying speakers like Jobs bring it. Jobs always had more energy than most other speakers who shared the stage with him.

LEAVE YOUR COMFORT ZONE

Most business professionals could use an energy boost. But how do you project the right level of vigor without seeming over the top? By weighing yourself on an energy scale. And on this scale, more is better.

I often ask clients, "On a scale of one to ten—one being fast asleep and ten being wildly pumped up like motivational speaker Tony Robbins—tell me where you are right now."

"A three," most of my clients reply.

"OK," I say, "what would it feel like to be a seven, eight, or nine? Give it a try."

If they're being honest, most presenters place themselves at a three to six on the energy scale. That means there is plenty of room to raise their energy level.

Energy is hard to describe, but you know it when you see it. Television host Rachael Ray has it. President Barack Obama and Tony Robbins have it as well. These three individuals have different styles, but they speak with energy.

Try this exercise—practice leaving your comfort zone: record several minutes of your presentation as you would normally deliver it. Play it back, preferably with someone else watching. Ask yourself and the observer, "Where am I on the energy scale?" Now try it again. This time, break out of your comfort zone. Ham it up. Raise your voice. Use broad gestures. Put a big smile on your face. Get to a point where you would feel slightly awkward and uncomfortable if you actually delivered the presentation that way. Now watch it again. Odds are your energy will be just right. You see, most people underestimate how little energy they actually have during a presentation. When they are asked to go "over the top" and to leave their comfort zone, they hit the right note.

Five Steps to Rehearsing "Off-the-Cuff" Remarks

With the economy plunging deeper into a recession, 2009 was a tough year to introduce a new car, but automobile companies

Caroline Kennedy's, Ah, Um, You Know, Performance

Filler words such as "ah," "um," and "you know" should not disqualify someone from public office, nor should they limit a person's effectiveness as a business leader. All too often, though, fillers will diminish your influence in the eyes of others. In early 2009, Caroline Kennedy had expressed interest in the New York Senate seat vacated by Hillary Rodham Clinton, who became U.S. secretary of state. The media skewered Kennedy's performance because of her verbal tendency to pack her remarks with, um, you know, like, fillers. Kennedy said "you know" more than thirty times in a two-minute interview. Listening for her filler words became sport among bloggers and radio talk-show hosts. She soon withdrew her name from consideration.

Here are three ways to eliminate fillers from your remarks before they detract from your message:

» **Ask for feedback.** Most of your colleagues are afraid of offending you. When someone asks me for advice and I see some real areas for improvement, I will be tough. At the same time, as is true of most other people, I hesitate to offer unsolicited advice even when I'm dying to say something that can improve someone's presentation skills. Likewise, since most of your family, friends, and peers avoid critiques for fear of "insulting" you, they will not voluntarily tell you that your mannerisms are annoying! Perhaps if Kennedy had asked for honest feedback, someone may have said, "Caroline, before you pitch yourself to the governor as the next New York senator, we need to work on how you answer the inevitable questions. Your answers must be specific, inspiring, and free from the filler words you use in everyday conversation."

» **Tap the glass.** I came across this technique entirely by chance, and it worked out extremely well. I was helping a woman rehearse a presentation and noticed that every other word was "ah" or "um." It became very distracting, so I told her I would tap a water glass with a spoon every time she used a filler word. My tapping became frequent—and irritating—prompting her to eliminate the fillers almost immediately. I've used it a few times since with equal success. Of course, this technique requires a second person to watch you and to tap the glass during your presentation rehearsal.

» **Record yourself, and play it back in the presence of others.** If you are serious about improving your presentation skills, record yourself on video, and replay it with someone else in the room. You don't have to tape your entire presentation, just the first five minutes. That should give you all the information you need to make some adjustments. You might be floored to hear how many filler words you use. For most people, simply watching themselves on video is enough to overcome some issues. Video feedback is even more effective in the presence of others who can pick up on some verbal mannerisms you might overlook.

A few "um"s and "ah"s from time to time will not detract from your ability to persuade an audience, but a steady stream of fillers can damage your efforts. The good news is that once you are made aware of the problem, you can easily follow the suggestions here to reduce or eliminate them.

can't put the brakes on designs and plans set in motion years ago. In January, I spoke to a group of auto executives who were designated spokespeople for new car models arriving soon to showrooms in North America. They were looking for advice on how to answer tough questions from the media. The same day, U.S. secretary of state–designate Hillary Clinton was fielding questions from the Senate Foreign Relations Committee in a confirmation hearing. The Associated Press called her performance "smooth," and NBC's Tom Brokaw said Clinton is known for her "legendary" preparation. I told the auto execs to prepare for tough questions in the same way that Clinton had probably prepared for her five-hour appearance.

It's a technique I call the "bucket method," and it is used in one form or another by CEOs and politicians, and, yes, Steve Jobs, who seemd to have ready answers to any question, used it, too. You can use it to prepare for presentations, pitches, sales calls, or any other situation in which you anticipate difficult or sensitive questions.

1. Identify the most common questions likely to be raised. Clinton expected a question about her husband's international foundation and its list of donors. Critics had widely publicized the issue, saying her appointment would be a conflict of interest. She also knew that each of the world's hot spots at the time would be fair game: Gaza, Iran, Iraq, Pakistan, and others. For the car executives, the most common question would be along the lines, "How do you expect to sell cars in this economy?" Or, "Will 2009 only get worse for the auto industry?"

2. Place the questions into "buckets," or categories. There might be only one question in a bucket, as in the case of the Clinton Foundation, or there might be several, as in the case of the carmakers and the economy. The point is to reduce the number of questions for which you must prepare. It's uncanny, but in my experience training thousands of speakers, the majority of questions will fall into about seven categories.

3. Create the best answer you have for the category. And this is critical—the answer must make sense regardless of *how* the question is phrased. You must avoid getting pulled into a detailed discussion based on the wording of the question. For example, here is Clinton's answer about her husband's fund-raising efforts: "I am very proud to be the president-elect's nominee for secretary of state, and I am very proud of what my husband and the Clinton Foundation and the associated efforts he's undertaken have accomplished, as well."[12] She would have said exactly the same thing regardless of how pointed the question from Republican senators was.

4. Listen carefully to the question, and identify a key word—a trigger—that will help you isolate the correct bucket from which to pull to your answer.

5. Look the person in the eye and respond with confidence.

"Well-prepared" speakers do not memorize answers to hundreds of potential questions. Instead, they prepare answers to *categories* of questions. The *way* a question is phrased is secondary. Think about it this way: your goal is to launch a mini-presentation within a presentation.

You can use the bucket method to reframe the question in your favor. Let's assume that your company's product is more expensive than a similar offering by one of your competitors. Let's also assume that there is a good reason behind the higher price. The way the question is phrased is not as important as the answer you have created for the category, which is "price." A conversation might sound like this:

> **CUSTOMER:** Why are you charging 10 percent more for the same product that I can get from company X?
>
> **YOU:** You're asking about price. [Here, "charging more" is the trigger for the answer that you prepared on "price." Although the wording the customer chose is different from the term you chose, it triggers your prepared response on the subject.] We believe our product is priced competitively, especially for a product that improves the bottom line for our clients by 30 percent on average. It's important to remember that we have the best service team in the industry. That means when you need support, you'll get it. Our team is available to you 24-7. None of our competitors can say that.

I know the CEO of a large publicly traded company who uses this method very effectively. For example, during one tough meeting, an analyst asked him to respond to some unfavorable comments made by his largest competitor. "Competition" was his trigger word. This CEO smiled and confidently maintained the high road by saying, "Our view on competition is different from many others. Our view is that you play with class. We compete by giving our customers superior service and sharing our vision for where we see this industry going. As we get more successful, we see more competitors entering the market. It's part of the process of being a leader." With this one response, the CEO deflected his competitor's comments and reframed the issue to focus on his company's leadership.

When former secretary of state Henry Kissinger was asked how he handled media questions, he said, "What questions do you have for my answers?" He had his answers already prepared. The media is a tough audience, and these days so are your customers. Don't let uncomfortable questions throw you off your game.

Best Antidote to Nerves

Relentless preparation is the single best way to overcome stage fright: know what you're going to say, when you're going to say it, and how you're going to say it. Too many people focus inward during their presentations, creating even more anxiety for themselves. They'll ask themselves, "Is my shirt wrinkled? What is that person in the third row thinking?" In other words, it's all about you. Instead, go from "me" to "we." Shift the focus to what your product or service means to the lives of your listeners, and be confident in your preparation. I have worked with several executives who are worth millions (in some cases, billions) of dollars. Guess what? They get nervous speaking in front of groups. Funny thing about nerves, though—the more you practice, the less nervous you will be.

I know a world-famous business leader who gets very nervous before major presentations. He gets over it by preparing to the extreme. He knows the content on every slide and exactly what he is going to say. He arrives early to the venue so that he can test the audio and projector and advance through his slides. This particular executive even knows where the lights are in the room, so he is never in shadow. That's preparation! He might get nervous, but his routine makes him feel much more confident, and he is considered one of the best speakers in corporate America.

Golfer Vijay Singh hits thousands of balls a day to prepare for a tournament. Olympic gold-medal winner Michael Phelps swims fifty miles a week to prepare for a competition, and Steve Jobs spent hours of grueling practice before a keynote presentation. Superstar performers in all fields leave nothing to chance. If you want to thrill any audience, steal a page from the Jobs playbook and start practicing!

DIRECTOR'S NOTES

» Practice, practice, and practice some more. Don't take anything for granted. Review every slide, every demo, and every key message. You should know exactly what you're going to say, when you're going to say it, and how you're going to say it.

» Record your presentation. You don't need to record the entire presentation. The first five minutes should give you plenty of information. Look for distracting body language and verbal tics, or fillers. When possible, review the video with someone else.

» Use the bucket method to prepare for tough questions. You will find that most lines of questions will fall into one of seven categories.

Wear the Appropriate Costume

It is hard to think that a $2 billion company with 4,300-plus people couldn't compete with six people in blue jeans.

—STEVE JOBS, RESPONDING TO AN APPLE LAWSUIT AGAINST HIM
AFTER HE RESIGNED TO FORM NeXT

Steve Jobs was the anti-Cher. In her Vegas concert, Cher and her dancers had 140 costume changes; Jobs had one costume for every performance. For presentations, Jobs *always* wore a black mock turtleneck, faded blue jeans, and white sneakers. If you want to get more specific, he wore a *St. Croix* sweater, *Levi's 501* blue jeans, and *New Balance* running shoes. Not that it matters much, because you're not going to dress like he did. He could get away with it because he was Steve Jobs and you're not. Seriously. When you're a business legend who is credited with reinventing the entire computer industry, you can show up in pretty much anything you want.

Although most people are familiar with Jobs's black shirt and blue jeans attire (even "The Simpsons" cartoon creators dressed the Jobs character in jeans and a black mock for an episode in 2008), Jobs did not always dress this way. When Jobs was a young man trying to be taken seriously by investors and the public, he dressed much more conservatively. The Jobs of 1984 looked a lot different from the Jobs of 2009. The first cover of *Macworld* magazine in January 1984 showed Jobs standing behind a desk with three of the original Macintosh computers. He was wearing a brown pin-striped suit, brown tie, and white shirt. Yes, Jobs once donned pinstripes. He wore an even more conservative outfit for the actual presentation when he unveiled the Macintosh, appearing in a white shirt, gray slacks, a dark blue double-breasted blazer, and a green bow tie. Imagine, Jobs in a bow tie! It's true.

Jobs was smart. His wardrobe always reflected the leader he wanted to become. He was well aware of the impression clothes could leave on people. While Jobs was away from Apple, he pitched his new company, NeXT, to Bank of America. Dan'l Lewin, NeXT's marketing executive, showed up at Jobs's house in blue jeans to accompany him to the meeting. Jobs walked out wearing an expensive Brioni suit from Wilkes Bashford. "Hey," Jobs said, "we're going to the bank today."[1] For Jobs, jeans were appropriate for the office, but not the bank. Now you might be confused. Jobs wore a suit to the bank and jeans in the office. What lesson does this hold for the rest of us? A true military hero, former U.S. Army ranger Matt Eversmann, once gave me the best piece of wardrobe advice I'd ever heard. Eversmann led troops in a fierce battle in Mogadishu, Somalia, in October 1993. The battle was turned into a movie called *Black Hawk Down*. I met Eversmann at a business conference and asked him for some leadership advice I could share with my readers. Eversmann told me that great leaders dress a little better than everyone else. He said that when he would meet a subordinate for the first time, his shoes were shinier, his whites were whiter, and his pants were better pressed.

I never forgot that piece of advice. I later interviewed George Zimmer, the founder of the Men's Wearhouse clothing chain. Zimmer agreed with Eversmann but added, "appropriate for the culture." It makes sense: you wouldn't show up for the company picnic in the same attire that you wear to the office. Also, different companies have different cultures. Apple is rebellious, creative, and committed to "think different." It's OK for an

Apple employee to wear more informal attire than a Wall Street executive.

Once you invent a product that changes the world, we can talk about dressing down. For now, here's the best wardrobe advice you'll ever hear: always dress a little better than everyone else, but appropriate for the culture.

DIRECTOR'S NOTES

» Dress like the leader you want to become, not for the position you currently have. Great leaders dress a little better than everyone else in the room. Remember, when Jobs was looking for funding at the bank, he dressed in an expensive suit.

» Wear clothes that are appropriate for the culture. Steve Jobs could get away with a black mock, blue jeans, and running shoes because everything about his brand was built on the concept of disrupting the status quo.

» If you're going to dress like a rebel, dress like a well-off rebel. Jobs wore St. Croix sweaters. It might have looked like a black T-shirt—but at least he spent money on it.

Toss the Script

Be a yardstick of quality. Some people aren't used to an environment where excellence is expected.

—STEVE JOBS

Steve Jobs was the consummate presenter for twenty-first-century audiences who wanted to engage in conversations, not lectures. Jobs had a casual speaking style, an informality that, as discussed in the preceding chapter, came from hours of practice. Practice allowed him to work largely without a script. During demonstrations, Jobs concealed notes discreetly from the audience but never read them word for word. The notes served only as cue cards for the next step in the demonstration. Jobs performed largely without notes for the majority of his presentation.

As suggested in Scene 8, most presenters create "slideuments": documents masking as slides. Slideuments act as a crutch for mediocre presenters who read every word on the slide, often turning their backs to the audience to do so. Jobs did have a script—largely in his head. His slides, which were highly visual, acted as a prompter. Each slide had one key idea and one idea only.

After Jobs pulled the new MacBook Air from a manila envelope in the "holy shit" moment at Macworld 2008, he explored the new computer in more detail. As you can see in Table 17.1, his slides contained very few words but contained just enough information to act as a prompter for one idea—one theme per slide.[1]

Jobs went on to explain that MacBook Air had the same processor used in all of Apple's other notebooks and iMacs. He

TABLE 17.1 ONE THEME PER SLIDE AT JOBS'S MACWORLD
2008 PRESENTATION

STEVE'S WORDS	STEVE'S SLIDES
"It's the world's thinnest notebook."	Text only: "World's thinnest notebook"
"Open it up and it has a magnetic latch; no hooks to catch on your clothing."	Photo of computer with the words "Magnetic latch" on left side of screen
"It's a got a full-size, 13.3-inch wide-screen display."	Photo of computer with the words "13.3 inch widescreen" in the middle of a black display
"The display is gorgeous. It has an LED-backlit display. It saves power, it's bright, and it's instant on the minute you open it."	Photo of computer with the words "LED backlight " on left side of screen
"On top of the display is a built-in iSight camera for videoconferencing right out of the box."	Photo of computer fades, revealing iSight camera on top of display
"Flip it down and there is a full-size keyboard. This is perhaps the best notebook keyboard we've ever shipped. It's a phenomenal keyboard."	Photo of keyboard with the words "Full size keyboard" on left side of screen
"We've got a very generous track pad, which is great. We've also built in multi-touch gesture support."	Photo of computer's track pad with the words "Multi-touch gestures" on left side of screen
"Again, you can see how beautiful and thin this product is. Now, how did we fit a Mac in here? I'm still stunned that our engineering team could pull this off."	Photo of computer from its side with the words "How did we fit a Mac in here?"
"The real magic is in the electronics. This is a complete Mac on a board. What's so special about that? This is how big the board is [does not mention pencil; let's the visual speak for itself]. It's really tiny. To fit an entire Mac on this thing was an amazing feat of engineering."	Photo of motherboard with image of a pencil alongside it—the board is smaller than the length of the pencil

STEVE'S WORDS	STEVE'S SLIDES
"We didn't compromise on performance. MacBook Air has the Intel Core 2 Duo. This is a really speedy processor . . . a 'screamer.'"	Photo of Intel Core 2 Duo microprocessor

marveled at the fact that Intel could step up to the challenge, creating a chip with the same power but in a package that was 60 percent smaller. Jobs then introduced Intel CEO Paul Otellini, who gave Jobs a sample processor. The chip was barely visible to anyone sitting past the front row, but Jobs lit up the auditorium with his smile. "This is awesome technology," he said, making no attempt to conceal his enthusiasm. See Figure 17.1.

Figure 17.1 Jobs shows genuine enthusiasm as he holds up the tiny Intel processor from the MacBook Air.

TONY AVELAR/AFP/Getty Images

Five Steps to Tossing the Script

Great actors rehearse for months before opening night. The audience would walk out if an actor appeared onstage with a script in hand. We expect actors to speak naturally, not as though they had memorized lines, even though that is exactly what they did. Your audience expects the same—a conversational speaker who, instead of rambling, hits each mark precisely. Following are five steps that will help you memorize your script while making you appear as natural as a gifted actor or a gifted presenter like Steve Jobs:

1. **Write your script in full sentences in the "notes" section of PowerPoint.** This is not the time for extensive editing. Simply write your ideas in complete sentences. Do try, however, to keep your ideas to no more than four or five sentences.

2. **Highlight or underline the key word from each sentence, and practice your presentation.** Run through your script without worrying about stumbling or forgetting a point. Glance at the key words to jog your memory.

3. **Delete extraneous words from your scripted sentences, leaving only the key words.** Practice your presentation again, this time using only the key words as reminders.

4. **Memorize the *one* key idea per slide.** Ask yourself, "What is the one thing I want my audience to take away from the slide?" The visual on the slide should complement the one theme. In this case, the visual becomes your prompter. For example, when Jobs talked about the Intel Core 2 Duo as the standard processor built into the MacBook Air, his slide showed only a photo of the processor. The "one thing" he wanted the audience to know was that Apple had built an ultrathin computer with no compromise in performance.

5. **Practice the entire presentation without notes, simply using the slides as your prompter.** By the time you execute these five steps, you will have rehearsed each slide four times, which is much more time than the average speaker commits to practicing a presentation.

Now let's put the five-step method into practice. I came across an ad for Vanguard no-load mutual funds.[2] It showed two glasses of water; the glass on the left contained a small amount of water, and the glass on the right was completely full. The headline read: "The lower the cost, the more you keep." Ads such as this one provide excellent examples of how to create compelling visual slides. Assume the ad is one slide: Table 17.2 shows what a hypothetical script written with the five steps in

TABLE 17.2 APPLYING THE FIVE-STEP METHOD TO TOSSING THE SCRIPT

STEP	PRESENTATION SCRIPT
1	How much your investment costs is very important and could have an impact on how much money you make over the long run. In general, the lower the cost, the more you keep. Many investment firms say they are low cost, but the fact is they charge six times more than we do. This can cost you thousands of dollars. For example, if you invest $10,000 for twenty years at an 8 percent return, you would keep $58,000 more with our fund versus the industry average.
2	Your *investment costs* are very *important* and could have an impact on how much money you make over the long run. In general, *the lower the cost, the more you keep.* Many investment firms say they are low cost, but the fact is they charge *six times more* than we do. This can cost you thousands of dollars. For example, if you invest $10,000 for twenty years at an 8 percent return, you would *keep $58,000 more* with our fund versus the industry average.
3	Investment costs important Lower the cost, the more you keep Six times more Keep $58,000 more
4	The lower the cost, the more you keep.
5	Rehearse presentation with no notes. The slide of two water glasses—one empty, one full—should be enough to prompt you to deliver the information: the four bullets in step 3.

mind might look like. (I created the content based on information in Vanguard's marketing material.)

When you're actually delivering the final presentation, if the notes give you peace of mind, by all means, keep them available. A major benefit of Apple's Keynote presentation software is that it allows the speaker to see notes on the computer screen while the audience sees the slide on the projector. This is harder, but not impossible, to do with PowerPoint. However, regardless of the software you use, if you practice enough, you will find that you don't need to rely on your notes at all.

How to Use Notes When Notes Are a Must

Notes are not inherently bad. In a rare glimpse at how Jobs actually did use notes, a blogger took a photograph of Jobs's demo

How Joel Osteen Inspires Millions

Joel Osteen is the hugely popular pastor of Houston's Lakewood Church. He preaches to some forty-seven thousand people a week who show up to see him in person and to millions of others on television. Osteen speaks in a natural, conversational style and rarely misses a beat, despite creating thirty minutes of content every week. How does he do it? First, he commits. Osteen begins working on sermons on the Wednesday prior to his appearance and spends the better part of four days practicing. Second, he uses notes but glances at them very discreetly. He places notes on a lectern but never stands behind the lectern. This approach lets him keep eye contact with the audience and maintain an open posture. He never reads a full sentence from his notes. Instead, he walks behind the lectern, glances at his notes, and keeps walking to the opposite side, delivering his messages directly to worshippers.

notes at Macworld 2007, famous for the release of the iPhone. The notes were neatly bound, and color-coded tabs separated the sections. The blogger's photo showed the booklet opened to the page where Jobs demonstrated the Internet capabilities of iPhone. Four categories were clearly marked in bold and a larger font: Mail, Safari, Widgets, and Maps.[3] Under each main category, there were two to five supporting points. Let's take one in particular, the Maps section. Here is exactly what was printed on the page:

MAPS

» Moscone West
» Starbucks order 4,000 lattes to go
» Washington Monument
» Show satellite
» Eiffel Tower, Colosseum

That's it. These notes were all the prompting Jobs needed to walk his audience through a particular section of the demo.

Jobs began by telling his audience that he wanted to show them something "truly remarkable"; Google Maps on iPhone. First, he opened up the application and zoomed in to a street-level view of San Francisco and Moscone West, the site of Macworld.

The second thing he did was to type "Starbucks" to search for a nearby coffee shop. He then called Starbucks on the iPhone and played the prank discussed in Scene 12, ordering four thousand lattes to go. (I had no idea that the lattes gag was scripted until I saw the photograph of Jobs's notes on the stage. He played it off as if it was a spontaneous moment, showing, once again, that Jobs took nothing for granted.)

The third thing he did was visit the Washington Monument, double-tapping the screen to bring the map closer. Fourth, he selected the option to replace the map with satellite photographs. He brought up a live image of the Washington Monument. "Isn't that incredible, right on my phone?" he said. Finally, he visited the Eiffel Tower and Roman Colosseum and showed both in the satellite view. He concluded by saying, "Satellite imagery right on our phone. Unbelievable. Isn't that incredible?"[4] Jobs did rely on his script for the demo, but it had been written and rehearsed extensively so that only a few key words were all he needed to prompt him.

Yes, Steve Jobs appeared conversational, but by now you should know that being "conversational" requires a lot of practice. And *how* you practice makes all the difference. Use the slides as your teleprompter, sticking to one theme per slide and several supporting points. If you forget some of your supporting points, you will at least have hit the main theme. Above all, toss the script. Notes will interfere with the emotional connection you need to establish with your audience, detracting from the presentation experience. Theatrics can turn an average presentation into an extraordinary event. A script gets in the way.

DIRECTOR'S NOTES

» Don't read from notes except in special circumstances in which you must follow a step-by-step process, such as a demonstration.

» When you must read from notes, create no more than three or four large-font bullet points on one note card or sheet of paper. Create one note card per slide. If you're using speaker's notes in Keynote or PowerPoint presentation software, keep your bullet points to no more than three or four. One is even better.

» Use the visuals on your slide to prompt you to deliver just one key theme—one main message—per slide. Think "one theme per slide."

Have Fun

**Everyone wants a MacBook Pro
because they are so bitchin'.**

—STEVE JOBS

n 2002, the Mac OS X was brand new, and Apple was striving to get customers and developers to embrace it. Jobs decided to put the issue to rest, literally, at the Worldwide Developers Conference.

As the presentation began, Jobs was not onstage. Instead, white smoke surrounded a casket. Gloomy pipe-organ music played in the background. Jobs finally emerged from behind a curtain, walked to the casket, lifted the lid, and pulled out a large-scale copy of OS 9, Apple's previous operating system. The audience got the joke immediately and started laughing and applauding.

Jobs was committed to the joke and took it further. With a copy of OS 9 lying in the casket, Jobs pulled out a sheet of paper and eulogized the software. "Mac OS 9 was a friend to us all," he started.

He worked tirelessly on our behalf, always posting our applications, never refusing a command, always at our beck and call, except occasionally when he forgot who he was and needed to be restarted. He came into this world in October of 1998 . . . We are here today to mourn the passing of OS 9. He is in the great bit bucket in the sky, no doubt looking down upon this with that same smile he displayed every time he booted. Mac OS 9 is survived by his next generation, Mac

OS X . . . Please join me in a moment of silence as we remember our old friend, Mac OS 9."[1]

Jobs walked back to the casket, put the box back in, closed the lid, and gently laid a rose on the top. The audience ate it up. Jobs made his point, and he had a lot of fun doing it.

Jobs had fun, and it showed. Despite relentless planning and preparation, hours and hours of rehearsal, and near-fanatical devotion to getting every slide and every demo just right, sometimes things go wrong, but Jobs didn't let the small stuff get to him. He was going to have fun, whether a demo worked or not.

"Let's take a look at how big this market is," said Jobs as he described the market opportunity for the iPhone at Macworld 2007. Suddenly, his slides failed to advance. "My clicker's not working," he said. As he walked to the right of the stage to check the computer, the slide seemed to advance. "Oh, maybe it is working. No, it's not." Jobs picked up another clicker but it, too, failed to work. He smiled and said, "The clicker is not working. They're scrambling backstage right now."[2] The audience laughed, and after a few more seconds of trying to fix the clicker, Jobs simply paused, smiled, and told the following story:

> You know, this reminds me, when I was in high school, Steve Wozniak and I—mostly Steve—made this little device called a TV jammer. It was this little oscillator that put out frequencies that would screw up the TV. Woz would have it in his pocket. We would go out to a dorm at Berkeley, where he was going to school, and a bunch of folks would be watching "Star Trek." He would screw up the TV, someone would go to fix it, and just as they had their foot off the ground, he'd turn it back on, and then he'd screw up the TV again. Within five minutes, he'd have someone like this [contorts his body; see Figure 18.1] . . . OK, it looks like it's working now.[3]

In this one-minute story, Jobs revealed a side of his personality that few people got to see. It made him more human, engaging, and natural. He also never got flustered. I have seen even some experienced presenters get derailed over smaller problems.

A YouTube user posted a five-minute clip showing dozens of Jobs "bloopers."[4] The number of things that went wrong is surprising given the level of extraordinarily detailed practice that went into a Steve Jobs keynote. This blooper reel proves that even the best-laid plans go awry from time to time: a slide may not advance, a wrong slide may come up, and a demo may not work. These things happen to even the best-prepared presenter, and they can, and probably will, happen to you at some point.

The difference between mediocre presenters and a true master such as Jobs is that when demonstrations did not turn out as planned, Jobs reacted with a cool confidence. The audience saw a showman in complete control of his material. If something failed to work, Jobs did not dwell on it or call undue attention

Figure 18.1 Jobs demonstrates a prank he and Apple cofounder Steve Wozniak would pull on unsuspecting college students.

David Paul Morris/Getty Images

to the issue. He smiled, had fun, explained to the audience what they should have seen, and moved on.

Don't Sweat the Small Stuff

During a demonstration of Apple TV at Macworld 2008, Jobs brought up a live connection to Flickr, a photo-sharing site. Jobs selected several categories to show the audience how photographs could be served from the site and displayed on a wide-screen television in a living room. Unfortunately, the screen went black. After about twenty seconds of trying to retrieve the images, Jobs simply turned to the audience, grinned, and said, "Well, I'm afraid Flickr isn't serving up photos on that one."[5]

Jobs didn't let anything ruffle him onstage. Instead, he acknowledged the problem, continued the presentation, summarized the material, and enjoyed himself. He concluded the Apple TV demonstration by saying, "All of this from your wide-screen: movies, TV shows, music, podcasts, photos from dot-Mac and—when they're serving up photos—Flickr! So, that's what I wanted to show you today. Isn't that incredible?"[6] Jobs never lost his enthusiasm. The demo might not have gone perfectly, but that didn't diminish the joy he had for the product.

No matter how much you prepare, something might, and probably will, go differently from how you had planned. Notice that I did not say something will go "wrong." It goes wrong only when you call attention to the issue or you let it ruin the rest of your presentation. People are there to hear you, to learn something new about a product, service, or initiative that could improve their lives.

When a demo failed to come off as smoothly as Jobs had rehearsed, he never lost his cool. He said something like, "Oops, that's not what I wanted" or "I need some help here, guys; this thing isn't working." He would take a few moments to get it working, and he would do so very calmly.

In one presentation, Jobs could not get a digital camera to work, so he had some fun with it, tossed it to an Apple employee in the front row, and said, "I need an expert to fix it. It's too technical for me. It's pretty awesome when it works."[7] That's it. *It's pretty awesome when it works.*

Think about watching an ice-skater perform an intricately choreographed routine. You know that the slightest mistake could land the skater on her butt. When it happens, you wince, but you hope the skater gets up to finish her routine on a high note. The same applies to your audience. Nobody expects perfection except you. Your audience will forgive a blooper as long as you get back on your feet.

During Jobs's leave of absence for a liver transplant, much had been written about what he revealed, how much he should have revealed, and whether he should have revealed it sooner. Jobs was clearly frustrated with the press, calling some reporters to chastise them about covering matters he wanted to keep private. While bloggers and reporters were scrambling to get the scoop on the exact nature of his illness, I was struck at how Jobs kept his trademark good humor.

In September 2008, Jobs walked onstage at the WWDC and said, "Good morning. Thank you for coming this morning. We have some really exciting stuff to share with you. Before we do, I just wanted to mention this." He pointed to the slide behind him, which had only one sentence: "The reports of my death are greatly exaggerated." "Enough said," Job told the audience, and he promptly continued with his presentation.[8] The audience laughed and cheered. The media and investors wanted more information, of course, but that's all that Jobs would give them at the moment, and he had fun with it at their expense.

Now, That's Infotainment!

Most business communicators lose sight of the fact that their audiences want to be informed *and* entertained. Jobs approached presentations as infotainment; he taught you something new and had fun doing it. It was the best of all worlds for his audience. Most business professionals do not smile nor relish the moment as much as they should. They get too caught up in "presentation mode" and lose the enthusiasm they really have about their company, product, or service. Jobs always walked onstage with a broad smile, an easy laugh, and a joke or two (often at Microsoft's expense).

On October 16, 2003, Jobs had finished the discussion of a new music alliance with AOL and an explanation of the new iTunes features. The audience thought he was done, but Jobs had "just one more feature" to talk about. He said it was a feature that "a lot of people thought we would never add till this happened." He pointed to the slide, which read: "Hell froze over." He said, "I'm here to report to you today that this has happened."[9] And with that introduction, Jobs announced iTunes for Windows. The audience laughed even harder when Jobs said, "iTunes for Windows is probably the best Windows app ever written!" The audience was thrilled, and Jobs himself was clearly enjoying the reaction.

Apple cofounder Steve Wozniak has said he and Jobs loved two things in common: electronics and pranks. From the early seventies when Jobs and "Woz" were building computers together in their parents' garages, Jobs had a passion for bringing personal computing to the masses. That "spirit" came across in every Steve Jobs presentation. A Steve Jobs presentation was passionate, exciting, informative, and, above all, fun. In many ways, it came naturally, because it was the way he had lived his life.

When Jobs took his leave of absence in 2009, Apple's shares plummeted on speculation over Jobs's health, a possible lack of new and exciting products, and potential management changes. Observers wondered, would Apple without Jobs be successful?

Richard the Fun-Hearted

I have no secret. There are no rules to follow in business. I just work hard and, as I always have done, believe I can do it. Most of all, though, I try to have fun.

—RICHARD BRANSON

One analyst, Shaw Wu, had a different take on all of it. Apple without Jobs would prosper, he argued, because his spirit had been "institutionalized." Wu said Apple had an uncanny ability to attract hardworking entrepreneurs who are looking to change the world.

PC World said that Jobs, a master showman, had raised new product presentations to an art form and wished him a "speedy return to health" so Jobs could head up the company again and take the stage once more.[10]

For more than three decades, Jobs cast his spell on the world. And whether you're a "Mac" or a "PC," we all owe Jobs a debt of gratitude for a chance to have joined him on his "magic swirling ship," to quote his favorite musician, Bob Dylan.[11] It's been a magnificent ride, and if you pay close enough attention, the lessons Jobs left behind can help you sell your ideas more successfully than you ever thought possible.

DIRECTOR'S NOTES

» Treat presentations as "infotainment." Your audience wants to be educated and entertained. Have fun. It'll show.

» Never apologize. You have little to gain from calling attention to a problem. If your presentation hits a glitch, acknowledge it, smile, and move on. If it was not obvious to anyone but you, do not call attention to it.

» Change your frame of reference. When something does not go exactly as planned, it did not "go wrong" unless you allow it to derail the rest of your presentation. Keep the big picture in mind, have fun, and let the small stuff roll off your back.

ENCORE

One More Thing

Stay hungry, stay foolish.

—STEVE JOBS

Steve Jobs kept his audience guessing. Frequently, but not always, he would leave the audience with "just one more thing" before he ended a presentation. For example, Jobs announced that he would return as Apple's full-time CEO (dropping the "interim" from his title) as the "one more thing" at the conclusion of his Macworld presentation on January 5, 2000. It is the element of surprise that audiences came to love and expect. Since his audience expected "one more thing," Jobs did not always deliver. A surprise would fail to surprise if everyone knows it's coming!

So, in true Steve Jobs fashion, I would like to add just "one more thing" to this discussion. On June 12, 2005, shortly after a bout with a rare, curable form of pancreatic cancer, Jobs gave the commencement address at Stanford University. It became an Internet sensation. It is one of the most popular commencement addresses on YouTube, far more popular than remarks of other famous commencement speakers such as Oprah; *The Last Lecture* author, Randy Pausch; or *Harry Potter*'s J. K. Rowling.

Jobs crafted the speech using many of the same techniques that make his presentations so electrifying. About the only thing absent that day were slides. The rest was classic Steve Jobs. I have excerpted sections to illustrate how he applied his extraordinary messaging and presentation skills to the now famous speech. I also urge you to watch the full speech on the Stanford website.[1]

> Today I want to tell you three stories from my life. That's it.
> No big deal. Just three stories.

We again see the rule of three (refer to Scene 5) playing a big role in Jobs's message. He drew a road map for his listeners by telling them to expect three stories—not one or four, but *three*. The structure of the speech itself is strikingly simple: opening, three stories, conclusion.

> The first story is about connecting the dots.

Here Jobs told the first of three personal anecdotes. This one was about his dropping out of Reed College after six months. Jobs said it was scary at first but ultimately worked out, because it allowed him to continue to take courses he was interested in, such as calligraphy. Ten years later, he incorporated calligraphy fonts into the Macintosh, "connecting the dots."

> It was beautiful, historical, artistically subtle in a way that
> science can't capture, and I found it fascinating.

Jobs found his passion for simplicity and design at an early age. He discovered his core purpose, a messianic zeal to change the world, and never looked back. Share your passion for your subject, and your enthusiasm will be contagious.

> My second story is about love and loss.

In this section, Jobs talked about falling in love with computers at the age of twenty and sharing that passion with his friend "Woz." He talked about building a $2 billion company in ten years and then, at the age of thirty, being fired by Apple's board of directors.

> I'm convinced that the only thing that kept me going was
> that I loved what I did. You've got to find what you love.

Again, passion was a central theme in Jobs's life. Jobs was convinced that he was successful because he followed his heart, his true passion. There's a lot of truth to it. Remember, none of his presentation techniques will work if you don't have genuine passion for your message. Find the one thing you love to do so much that you can't wait for the sun to rise to do it all over again. Once you do, you'll have found your true calling.

My third story is about death.

This sentence began the most poignant section of the speech. Jobs recalled the day doctors told him he had pancreatic cancer. He thought he had three to six months to live. The cancer turned out to be a very rare, curable form of the disease, but the experience left an indelible impression on Jobs.

No one wants to die. Even people who want to go to heaven don't want to die to get there.

Jobs always had fun. He found a way to inject humor into a morbid subject.

Your time is limited, so don't waste it living someone else's life. Don't be trapped by dogma—which is living with the results of other people's thinking. Don't let the noise of others' opinions drown out your own inner voice.

This paragraph is an example of a powerful rhetorical device called anaphora, repetition of the same word(s) in consecutive sentences. Think of Martin Luther King's "I have a dream that . . . I have a dream . . . I have a dream today." Great political speakers from Churchill to King, from Reagan to Obama, have all used anaphora to structure strong arguments. As Jobs demonstrated, this classic sentence structure need not be reserved for political leaders. It is available to any person who wants to command an audience.

And most important, have the courage to follow your heart and intuition. They somehow already know what you truly want to become . . . stay hungry, stay foolish.

Jobs ended the speech with his headline, his key theme and advice—stay hungry, stay foolish. As we've discussed, Jobs repeated his key theme several times in a presentation. In this case, he repeated "stay hungry, stay foolish" three times in the concluding paragraph.

Jobs's speech reveals the secret to his success as a business leader and communicator: do what you love, view setbacks as opportunities, and dedicate yourself to the passionate pursuit of excellence. Whether it's designing a new computer, introducing new gadgets, running Apple, overseeing Pixar, or giving a presentation, Jobs believed in his life's work. This is the last and most important lesson Jobs can teach—the power of believing in yourself and your story. Jobs followed his heart his whole life. Follow yours to captivate your audience. You'll be one step closer to delivering insanely great presentations.

e Jobs
e Book

**married with liberal arts
kes our hearts sing.**

—STEVE JOBS

ternet search for the Apple iPad using
cal and *revolutionary* in 2010 yielded
million links to articles containing
an interesting choice of words when
10:00 A.M. on January 27, 2010, many
hat consumers needed another elec-
nd. By 11:00 A.M. they were converts.
, Steve Jobs would unveil more new
esentations, including the iPhone 4,
ot a device exactly, but a new service
f 2011. Each presentation was classic
wowed his audience in each presenta-
se these techniques to sell your ideas
bs way.

*e than a laptop and so much more
ne.*

—STEVE JOBS

The iPad: January 27, 2010

A "Fox Business News" producer had asked m———
the morning show to preview the big annou r———
day Steve Jobs introduced the iPad at San F ———
Buena Events Center. Prior to the launch there ———
of speculation about Apple's new "tablet," ———
announcement. The best I could do was go b ———
discuss *how* Steve Jobs would introduce the ———
category of device. Sure enough, Jobs did stick t ———
chapter by chapter. Jobs used every single pri ———
have just read. The presentation itself was a ga ———
Apple, the technology industry, and corporate ———
in every field.

CREATE A TWITTER-FRIENDLY HEADLINE

Steve Jobs's first slide delivered the headline———
his presentation and previewed the iPad's tagli n———
kick off 2010 by introducing a truly magical an———
product today,"[1] said Jobs. At the conclusion of t———
Jobs summed up the iPad in one sentence:

> Our most advanced technology in a magical an———
> ary device.

Since Twitter allows 140 characters, Jobs cou———
this description on Twitter and still be left with ———
for people to retweet the post and add their com———
Your brain craves meaning before detail. ———
picture before filling in the details. If you can't ———
product or service in 140 characters or less, g———
drawing board.

INTRODUCE AN ANTAGONIST

Every great book or movie has a hero and a vil———
a presentation in the same way—a theatrical e———
with a protagonist and antagonist. The role of ———
in the iPad presentation was played by a categ———

Steve Jobs by the Book

It's technology married with liberal arts that makes our hearts sing.

—STEVE JOBS

Conducting an Internet search for the Apple iPad using the words *magical* and *revolutionary* in 2010 yielded more than two million links to articles containing the phrase. It's an interesting choice of words when you consider that before 10:00 A.M. on January 27, 2010, many observers were skeptical that consumers needed another electronic device to carry around. By 11:00 A.M. they were converts.

After the iPad launch, Steve Jobs would unveil more new devices in subsequent presentations, including the iPhone 4, the iPad2, and iCloud—not a device exactly, but a new service first introduced in June of 2011. Each presentation was classic Steve Jobs. Here's how he wowed his audience in each presentation and how you can use these techniques to sell your ideas and products the Steve Jobs way.

Introducing the iPad

It's so much more intimate than a laptop and so much more capable than a smartphone.

—STEVE JOBS

The iPad: January 27, 2010

A "Fox Business News" producer had asked me to appear on the morning show to preview the big announcement on the day Steve Jobs introduced the iPad at San Francisco's Yerba Buena Events Center. Prior to the launch there had been plenty of speculation about Apple's new "tablet," but no official announcement. The best I could do was go by the book and discuss *how* Steve Jobs would introduce the world to a new category of device. Sure enough, Jobs did stick to the playbook, chapter by chapter. Jobs used every single principle that you have just read. The presentation itself was a game changer for Apple, the technology industry, and corporate communicators in every field.

CREATE A TWITTER-FRIENDLY HEADLINE

Steve Jobs's first slide delivered the headline—or theme—of his presentation and previewed the iPad's tagline. "We want to kick off 2010 by introducing a truly magical and revolutionary product today,"[1] said Jobs. At the conclusion of the presentation Jobs summed up the iPad in one sentence:

> Our most advanced technology in a magical and revolutionary device.

Since Twitter allows 140 characters, Jobs could have posted this description on Twitter and still be left with plenty of room for people to retweet the post and add their comments.

Your brain craves meaning before detail. Deliver the big picture before filling in the details. If you can't describe your product or service in 140 characters or less, go back to the drawing board.

INTRODUCE AN ANTAGONIST

Every great book or movie has a hero and a villain. Consider a presentation in the same way—a theatrical event complete with a protagonist and antagonist. The role of the antagonist in the iPad presentation was played by a category of devices called Netbooks, which were growing in popularity at the time. Before unveiling the iPad—the hero—Jobs spent two minutes discussing the role of the villain in his narrative:

> All of us use laptops and smartphones. And the question has arisen lately, is there room for a third category of device in the middle? Something that is in between a laptop and a smartphone? In order to create a new category of devices, those devices have to be far better at doing some key tasks. Better than a laptop. Better than a smartphone. What kind of tasks? Things like browsing the Web. That's a tall order. Something that's better at browsing the Web than a laptop? Doing e-mail. Enjoying and sharing photographs. Watching videos. Enjoying your music collection. Watching games. Reading e-books. If there's going to be a third category of device it has to be better at these types of tasks than either a laptop or a smartphone, otherwise it has no reason for being. Now, some people have thought that's a Netbook. The problem is that Netbooks aren't better at anything. They're slow. They have low quality displays and they run clunky old PC software. They're not better than a laptop at anything. They're just cheaper. They're just cheap laptops and we don't think they're a third category of device. But we think we've got something that is and we'd like to show it to you today for the first time, and we call it the iPad.[2]

By introducing an antagonist—a problem in need of a solution—Jobs answered the question that most people had on their mind: Why do I need a third device? Jobs tackled the question head-on and even used the rhetorical device of raising a question and providing the answer. Your audience is asking, "What's in it for me?" Don't leave them guessing. A villain can be a competitor, a category of competitors, or in many cases, a problem in need of a solution.

STICK TO THE RULE OF THREE

The human mind can only consume three points of information in short-term memory. Steve Jobs understood this and often presented his content as three chunks of information. Here are some examples in the iPad presentation.

» Steve Jobs kicked off the presentation with "three updates": iPod sales, retail store growth, and App Store popularity.
» When he talked about the fact that 250 million iPods had been sold to date, Jobs said that iPods had changed the way consumers "discover, purchase, and enjoy music."
» Jobs said Netbooks had three failings: slow, low-quality displays, "clunky" old PC software.
» When Jobs picked up the iPad and demonstrated its functionality he chose three features to focus on: Web browsing, e-mail, and photographs.
» Jobs introduced the new iBooks Store as rounding out the three areas where Apple now sells digital content: iTunes Store, App Store, and the iBooks Store.
» The iPad would be made available in three options: 16GB, 32GB, and 64GB models.

UNLEASH YOUR INNER ZEN

Steve Jobs's "inner zen" was on full display during the iPad presentation. The slides were impactful because they contained very few words and plenty of compelling visuals. The first three minutes' worth of slides contained fewer words than most presenters put on one slide (fourteen words, five photographs, and five numbers). Take a look at Table 1.

USE "AMAZINGLY ZIPPY" WORDS

Jobs avoided the jargon and dense language that is so common among business professionals. Instead he wore his passion on his sleeve. If Jobs thought something was "cool," he'd tell you so. Here are some examples from the iPad launch:

» "It's pretty amazing."
» "It feels great."
» "It's an incredible phenomenon."

TABLE 1 VISUAL DISPLAY ACCOMPANYING STEVE'S WORDS
IN THE iPAD PRESENTATION, JANUARY 27, 2010[3]

STEVE'S WORDS	STEVE'S SLIDES
"We want to kick off 2010 by introducing a truly magical and revolutionary product. But before we do that I have a few updates."	Apple logo
"The first is an update on iPods."	Photo of iPods
"A few weeks ago we sold our 250-millionth iPod. iPods have changed the way we purchase, discover, and enjoy music."	250,000,000
"The second update is about our retail stores."	Photo of Apple Store
"We now have 284 retail stores."	284 Apple Retail Stores
"And last quarter, the holiday quarter, we had over fifty million visitors to our stores."	50,000,000 visitors last quarter
"One of our newest stores is our fourth store in New York City. It's really beautiful. This is a shot of it before it opened. It won't look this good again. It is so wonderful to be putting these stores with their phenomenal buying experience right in the neighborhoods of our customers. It feels great."	Photos of Apple Store in New York City
"Next update, a store of another kind. The App Store."	Image of Apple "App" logo
"We now have over 140,000 applications in the App Store."	140,000 applications in the App Store
"And a few weeks ago we announced that a user downloaded the three-billionth application from the App Store."	3 billion applications downloaded

» "It's unbelievably great."
» "It's awesome."
» "It's a dream to type on."
» "It has a gorgeous display."
» "It screams."

I'm not asking you to copy these phrases, but if you are genuinely excited about your product, let your audience know it. They are giving you permission to express your passion.

STAGE YOUR PRESENTATION WITH PROPS

Steve Jobs staged the iPad presentation beautifully. Instead of simply showing slides and demonstrating the device, Jobs walked to the center of the stage where a comfy leather chair and small coffee table had been set up. He picked up the iPad from the table, settled into the chair and said, "It's so much more intimate than a laptop and so much more capable than a smartphone."

Don't always think about "props" as a physical set. A prop can be something as simple as reading from a letter (some people still write them), writing on a flip chart, or demonstrating a physical product. Think of a prop as almost anything that takes the attention away from the presentation deck. Give the audience a break from the slides. They will appreciate the diversion.

DON'T FORGET TO PRACTICE

The iPad presentation lasted about ninety minutes and included seven speakers. Each of the speakers had been given a set time to speak and had been asked to practice on stage in front of the folks at Apple to make sure their demonstrations worked well and that they stuck to their time, not a second more. It's not uncommon for one hundred hours of work and practice to go into preparing for a five-minute demo in an Apple presentation. How many hours did you practice for your last presentation? If it didn't go as smoothly as you would have liked, you might benefit from more rehearsal time.

HAVE FUN AND INSPIRE

Steve Jobs ended the iPad presentation by reinforcing his Twitter-friendly headline. "To sum it up," he said as his delivery slowed considerably, "The iPad is our most advanced technology in a magical and revolutionary device at an unbelievable price." He also gave his audience some insight into what makes

Apple well, *Apple*. "The reason why Apple can create products like the iPad is because we've always tried to be at the intersection of technology and liberal arts. When you feel this much power and this much fun in your hands, you never want to go back. We hope you love the iPad as much as we do."[4]

When is the last time you heard the words "love" and "fun" in a presentation? That was the difference between Steve Jobs and average presenters—Jobs had the courage to express how he truly felt about the brand.

The iPhone 4: June 7, 2010

Steve Jobs introduced the iPhone 4 at Apple's Worldwide Developers Conference. The presentation itself made news because of a glitch in the demo—a rare event for an Apple launch. The way Jobs handled it, however, was a case study in preparation. The glitch and other notable moments are discussed here.

CREATE A TWITTER-FRIENDLY HEADLINE

According to Steve Jobs, the iPhone 4 would mark "The biggest leap since the original iPhone."[5] You could say this is more of a boast than a headline but if you conduct an Internet search for the phrase "biggest leap iPhone 4," it will show up in almost a million links. Whether or not you agree with Jobs's description is beyond the point. This was the way Apple and Jobs *chose* to frame it. Jobs crafted the narrative for press, bloggers, and customers.

Launching the iPhone 4

This is beyond a doubt one of the most beautiful things we've ever made.

—STEVE JOBS

Jobs also spent time building up the story before introducing his headline. He could have simply said, "It's been three years since our original iPhone and we thought it was time for an update. Here it is." Instead Jobs spent a few minutes reviewing the history of the iPhone. Jobs said that in 2007 Apple reinvented the phone with the iPhone. He explained that in 2008 Apple added 3G networking and the hugely popular App Store. In 2009 the iPhone 3Gs was "twice as fast with cool features like video recording." And finally, in 2010, "We're going to take the biggest leap since the original iPhone." Where most presenters would simply deliver information about a new product, Jobs told a story.

STICK TO THE RULE OF THREE

As in every presentation, Steve Jobs chose to focus the audience's attention on three chunks of information instead of overwhelming them with too much content. For example, Jobs divided the presentation into three parts. He told the audience that he had "three updates" to deliver: iPad, App Store, and iPhone (the update would be the release of iPhone 4). When he discussed the App Store, Jobs chose to demonstrate three new apps that would be made available on the App Store (Netflix, Farmville, and Guitar Hero).

Most presenters have more information than they can easily convey in a short amount of time. Don't try to squeeze in everything. Simplify your communications. Three pieces of information are easier to digest than thirteen, eighteen, or twenty-two. If you want to deliver a "Jobs-worthy" presentation, avoid content overload.

DRESS UP YOUR NUMBERS

In several instances Steve Jobs put large numbers into perspective. Here are some examples from the iPhone 4 presentation.[6]

» "We have sold over two million iPads in the first fifty-nine days. That's one every three seconds."
» "There are 8,500 native apps on the iPad and these apps have been downloaded thirty-five million times. If you divide that

by those two million iPads, that's seventeen apps per iPad that have already been downloaded. That's a great number for us."

» "Users have downloaded over five million books on the iPad Bookstore. That's in the first sixty-five days. That's two-and-a-half books per iPad."

» "The iPhone 4 is nine millimeters thick. That's 24 percent thinner than the iPhone3Gs. A quarter thinner just when you didn't think it could get any thinner. It's the thinnest smartphone on the planet."

FOLLOW THE TEN-MINUTE RULE

The ten-minute rule simply states that your audience will lose attention after approximately ten minutes. Jobs understood this instinctively. He would rarely speak longer than ten minutes without introducing an alternative stimulus (e.g., video, another presenter, or a demo). Approximately four minutes into his iPhone 4 presentation—before he introduced the new phone—he showed the audience a video clip of the international coverage the iPad had generated in the first few months of sale. Exactly ten minutes after the video clip ended, Steve Jobs introduced another speaker—Netflix CEO Reed Hastings, who took the stage for a few minutes to discuss his company's new mobile app.

Try to avoid presenting for more than ten minutes at a time. At the ten-minute mark introduce a break in the action: video, stories, another speaker, or a demo.

MAKE IT LOOK EFFORTLESS WITH PRACTICE

Now let's talk about "the glitch." Apple presentations are so finely tuned that when something goes wrong it makes news. Several news outlets called me immediately to get my reaction. Some reporters called it a "meltdown." Not quite. A true meltdown is what would have happened to most presenters. Steve Jobs wasn't pleased, by any means. But he recovered.

While attempting to demonstrate some of the new features of the iPhone 4, Jobs ran into a Wi-Fi problem. As he was attempting to download the *New York Times* website, it failed to load. "Our networks in here are always unpredictable,"[7] Jobs said. "You can help me out. If you're on Wi-Fi, if you can just get off I'd appreciate it," Jobs remarked with a smile. The smile quickly evaporated as it became clear the demo would not work. "We're having a problem here. I don't know what's wrong with our networks. I'm afraid there is a problem and I won't be able to show you much here today."

Most presenters would have completely frozen. Not Jobs. He knew where he wanted to go next and effortlessly showed the audience what he had intended to show later in the presentation, such as new photography capability on the phone. A few minutes later Jobs took control—not of the presentation, but the audience. "We figured out why my demo crashed," he said.

> There are 570 Wi-Fi base stations in this room and hundreds of those Mi-Fi bay stations. We can't deal with that. We have two choices. I have more demos that are really great that I'd really like to show you. Either you turn off all the stuff or we give up and I don't show you the demos. Would you like to see the demos? [Applause.] Here's the deal. Let's turn up the lights in the hall. All you bloggers turn off your bay stations, your Wi-Fi, put notebooks on the floor. Shut off laptops and these Mi-Fi bay stations. Police each other. I think bloggers have a right to blog but we're not going to see these demos unless we do this. . . . Go ahead, I've got time.

The glitch didn't hurt sales. AT&T temporarily suspended sales the next day because they were getting more orders than units available. Sales blew past the initial revenue for the original iPhone as consumers stood in line for hours to get their hands on the new device. Despite the technical snafu, Jobs had provided enough content to win over consumers.

Steve Jobs took nothing for granted. He practiced many, many hours over many, many weeks. Sometimes, despite the best plans, things can and do go wrong—they even did for Steve Jobs. The more you have internalized the content, the better prepared you'll be to handle the curve balls that come your way.

The iPad2: March 2, 2011

Steve Jobs shocked a packed audience at San Francisco's Yerba Buena Events Center on March 2, 2011, simply by showing up. Jobs had taken medical leave in January (his third health-related absence since 2004). Chief Operating Officer Tim Cook was running Apple in Jobs's absence and most observers expected Cook to give the presentation. The audience gave Jobs a standing ovation when he walked on stage. Jobs's passion was on full display when he said, "We've been working on this product for a while and I just didn't want to miss today."[8]

I found it remarkable that a leader who wasn't well enough to run his company day-to-day had the energy to carry a ninety-minute presentation. It spoke to his passion for the product and for the brand. Passion brings energy and Jobs wore his passion on his sleeve and the iPad2 presentation was no exception. The rest of the presentation was also vintage Steve Jobs.

ANSWER THE ONE QUESTION THAT MATTERS MOST

Remember, your customers are asking themselves one question: "Why should I care?" Steve Jobs used the "Rule of Three" and created a "Twitter-friendly headline" to explain the benefit of the iPad2. "First, it's dramatically faster. Second, it's dramatically thinner. And it's lighter as well,"[9] Jobs said. In a sentence, the iPad2 was "thinner, lighter, and faster" than the original.

If you only know three things about the new device— thinner, lighter, faster—it tells you a lot. It's a clever headline and it's memorable. A reporter for the *San Francisco Chronicle* began his review with "Apple CEO Steve Jobs took a break

Launching the iPad2

I just didn't want to miss today.

—STEVE JOBS

from his medical leave Wednesday to unveil a sequel to the company's best-selling iPad—one that is thinner, lighter, and faster." *Good Housekeeping* ran this headline: "iPad2. Thinner, lighter, faster." The *Wall Street Journal* said the new device was thinner, lighter, and came with a faster processor. Jobs had crafted the narrative and the press ran with it.

Apple's Twitter headline is remarkably consistent for each product. On the day that Jobs introduced the iPad2, millions of Apple customers received an e-mail with the subject line, "iPad: thinner, lighter, faster." The Apple website displayed a photo of the iPad2 with the words thinner, lighter, faster. Once you craft the story line—or the narrative—behind your product, service, or cause, make sure it is consistently communicated across all marketing channels.

INTRODUCE THE VILLAIN AND THE HERO

Steve Jobs took the opportunity to discuss Apple's vision for the future of computing: a post-PC world. "A lot of folks in the tablet market are rushing in and they look at this category as the next PC. They are talking about speeds and feeds just like they did with PCs. Every bone in our body says this is not the right approach. These are post-PC devices that need to be even easier to use than a PC. More intuitive than a PC. The software, hardware, and apps need to intertwine in a more seamless way than in a PC."[10]

Apple's hero, of course, would be the iPad2. "It's in Apple's DNA that technology is not enough," said Jobs. "It's technology married with liberal arts that makes our hearts sing." In two paragraphs, Jobs had introduced a villain—an entire category of devices that his competitors were launching—and a hero, a company that wants to make easy, fun, and simple-to-use devices.

CREATE VISUAL SLIDES

Apple presentations are always magnificent displays of visual storytelling, but the iPad2 presentation took visual display to the next level. The average presentation slide contains forty words. Steve Jobs's slides included a grand total of thirty-three words in the first *five minutes'* worth of slides. You owe it to yourself to watch the first five minutes of the iPad2 keynote presentation. You'll notice that Jobs does not clutter the slides with extraneous content. Every slide has one theme (see Table 2). In these seven slides, Jobs's presentation contained far fewer words than most presenters display on just one slide.

Since the average PowerPoint slide contains forty words and you couldn't find forty words in the first ten slides of a Steve Jobs presentation, I've come up with the Ten-Forty Rule: your first ten slides should contain forty words or less. It's very difficult to follow, but your presentations will be far more effective for doing so.

DRESS UP YOUR NUMBERS

When Jobs introduced the iPad2 he said that the previous year had turned out to be "the year of the iPad" with fifteen

TABLE 2 VISUAL DISPLAY ACCOMPANYING STEVE'S WORDS
IN THE iPAD2 PRESENTATION, MARCH 2, 2011[11]

STEVE'S WORDS	STEVE'S SLIDES
"We have some updates for you. The first is iBooks."	iBooks (with image of the iBook Store)
"We launched the iBooks Store under a year ago and users have downloaded a hundred million books in less than a year from the iBook Store."	100 million books downloaded
"Another milestone is in the App Store. Developers have earned over two billion dollars from selling their Apps on the App Store."	Image of check with the number 2,000,000,000
"Today we're here to talk about Apple's third post-PC blockbuster product."	Apple's third post-PC blockbuster
"We started off in 2001 with the iPod."	Photo of iPod
"In 2007 we added the iPhone."	Photo of iPhone
"And in 2010 we added the iPad."	Photo of iPad

million iPads sold in the first nine months of the product's release. Fifteen million sounds like a big number, but compared to what? Jobs put the statistic into context by adding, "That's more than every tablet PC ever sold."[12] He also mentioned that the iPad generated 9.5 billion dollars in revenue for Apple since its launch. "We've never had a product get off to such a fast start," he said. "Our competitors are flummoxed."

Again, don't let large numbers just hang out there. Put them into context.

OBEY THE TEN-MINUTE RULE

The iPad2 presentation proves, once again, that Steve Jobs didn't speak more than ten minutes without changing the action. Exactly nine minutes after he started speaking, Jobs showed a video that Apple had created called "The Year of the iPad." The video interspersed clips of Apple employees talking about the iPad along with video of customers using the devices in places around the world.

HAVE FUN

Sometimes Steve Jobs liked to have fun at the expense of his competitors. After the video ran about iPads' popularity in 2010, Jobs said, "So what about 2011? *Everybody's* got a tablet. Is 2011 going to be the year of the copycats? None of these tablets are even catching up with the first iPad. But we're not going to rest on our laurels because in less than one year we're introducing iPad2, the second generation iPad. We think 2011 is going to be the year of the iPad2."

iCloud: June 6, 2011

Steve Jobs returned from medical leave on June 6, 2011, for a brief introduction to Apple's new cloud-storage service called iCloud. In typical Jobs fashion he said he had three announcements. First, he offered a preview of OS X Lion, the new operating system for Macs. Second, he unveiled the iOS5, the mobile operating system for iPhones and iPads. Finally, Jobs described Apple's new service that fit in to his

Introducing iCloud

> *You like everything so far? Well, I'll try not to blow it.*
>
> —STEVE JOBS

vision of a "post-PC" world: a world in which people will create, share, and access content from a variety of devices. The idea behind iCloud is simple and powerful. Here's how Jobs unveiled it.

INTRODUCE AN ANTAGONIST

As we've discussed, in nearly every product launch, Steve Jobs outlined the problem before offering a solution. Before describing iCloud, Jobs took a couple of minutes to discuss the problem that the new service would solve—a problem many people could relate to.

> About ten years ago we had one of our most important insights. The PC would be the digital hub of our digital life. That's where you were going to put your digital photos, video, and music. It worked fine for the better part of ten years. But it's broken down in the last few years. Why? Because devices have changed. They now all have photos. They now all have music. They now all have video. If I acquire a song, I buy it on my iPhone, I want to get it to my other devices. I pick up my iPad and it doesn't have the other songs on it. So I have to sync my iPhone to my Mac to get those songs. Keeping these devices in sync is driving us crazy. We've got a great solution to this problem. We're going to demote the PC and the Mac to be a device. We're going to move the digital hub, the center of your digital life, to the cloud.[13]

CREATE A TWITTER-FRIENDLY HEADLINE

Steve Jobs followed up the problem statement with his one-sentence description that sold the benefit behind the service, made it simple for the audience to understand, and easily fit within a Twitter post: iCloud stores your content and wirelessly pushes it to all your devices (seventy-two characters).

Again, Apple kept the message consistent across all of its marketing, advertising, and communication channels. During the presentation, Steve Jobs displayed a slide that contained only the one-sentence headline. As soon as the presentation ended—not a minute later—the Apple website displayed the new iCloud icon along with the description: iCloud stores your content and wirelessly pushes it to all your devices. Sound familiar? The official Apple press release and in-store material all reflected the same headline. Make sure everyone on your team is speaking from the same playbook. Make the headline consistent across all communication channels.

DISPLAY VISUAL INFORMATION

The iCloud presentation is the most visual presentation of Steve Jobs's career. I can say that with confidence because just as I developed the Ten-Forty Rule, Jobs went one step further—no words in the first ten slides!

Each of the first ten slides in the iCloud presentation comprised device images and some subtle animation. No words. No bullet slides. No charts. No text. The first words appeared on slide eleven when Jobs introduced the Twitter-friendly headline. Steve Jobs was the storyteller. His slides *complemented* the story but the slides are not the story.

The four case studies in this Postscript prove that Steve Jobs—a man who was considered the world's greatest corporate storyteller—used the same techniques every time to deliver a presentation. The products might have changed, but the storytelling techniques remained the same.

You also have a story to tell. It might be the story behind a product, a company, a brand, a service, an initiative, or an idea. Is your presentation dull, confusing, and boring, or interesting, illuminating, and inspiring? Use this template to unleash your inner Steve Jobs. Your audience will love you for it.

Introduction

1. Jon Fortt, "Steve Jobs, Tech's Last Celebrity CEO," *Fortune*, December 19, 2008, http://archive.fortune.com/2008/12/19/technology/fortt_tech_ceos.fortune/index.htm (accessed January 30, 2009).
2. Wikipedia, "Charisma," includes Max Weber quote, http://en.wikipedia.org/wiki/charisma (accessed January 30, 2009).
3. Nancy Duarte, *Slide:ology* (Sebastopol, CA: O'Reilly Media, 2008), xviii.
4. Michael Hiltzik, "Apple's Condition Linked to Steve Jobs's Health," *Los Angeles Times*, January 5, 2009, latimes.com/business/la-fi-hiltzik5-2009jan05,0,7305482.story (accessed January 30, 2009).
5. Stephen Wilbers, "Good Writing for Good Results: A Brief Guide for Busy Administrators," *The College Board Review*, no. 154 (1989–90), via Wilbers, wilbers.com/cbr%20article.htm.
6. "The Big Idea with Donny Deutsch," first aired on July 28, 2008, property of CNBC.
7. Wikipedia, "Steve Jobs," includes Jobs's quote, http://en.wikiquote.org/wiki/steve_jobs (accessed January 30, 2009).
8. Alan Deutschman, *The Second Coming of Steve Jobs* (New York: Broadway Books, 2001), 127.

Scene 1: Plan in Analog

1. Garr Reynolds, *Presentation Zen* (Berkeley: New Riders, 2008), 45.
2. Nancy Duarte, *Slide:ology* (Sebastopol, CA: O'Reilly Media, 2008).
3. Cliff Atkinson, *Beyond Bullet Points* (Redmond, WA: Microsoft Press, 2005), 14.
4. Ibid., 15.
5. YouTube, "Macworld San Francisco 2007 Keynote Address," YouTube, youtube.com/watch?v=n7K3jCNxNGI (accessed January 30, 2009).
6. YouTube, "Steve Jobs, 'Computers Are Like a Bicycle for Our Minds,'" YouTube, youtube.com/watch?v=ob_GX50Za6c (accessed January 30, 2009).
7. John Paczkowski, "Apple CEO Steve Jobs," D5 Highlights from D: All Things Digital, May 30, 2007, http://d5.allthingsd.com/20070530/steve-jobs-ceo-of-apple (accessed January 30, 2009).
8. YouTube, "WWDC 2008 Keynote Address," YouTube, youtube.com/watch?v=aB2KGIlkwKw (accessed January 30, 2009).
9. Leander Kahney, *Inside Steve's Brain* (New York: Penguin Group, 2008), 29.

Scene 2: Answer the One Question That Matters Most

1. YouTube, "The First iMac Introduction," YouTube, youtube.com/watch?v=0BHPtoTctDy (accessed January 30, 2009).
2. YouTube, "Apple WWDC 2005—The Intel Switch Revealed," YouTube, youtube.com/watch?v=ghdTqnYnFyg (accessed January 30, 2009).
3. Wikipedia, "Virtual Private Server," http://en.wikipedia.org/wiki/server_virtualization (accessed January 30, 2009).
4. Ashlee Vance, "Cisco Plans Big Push into Server Market," *New York Times*, January 19, 2009, nytimes.com/2009/01/20/technology/companies/20cisco.html?scp=1&sq=cisco%20+virtualization&st=search (accessed January 30, 2009).

5. YouTube, "Macworld SF 2003 part I," YouTube, youtube.com/watch?v= Xac6NWT7EKY (accessed January 30, 2009).

6. Apple, "Apple Introduces the New iPod Nano: World's Most Popular Digital Music Player Features New Aluminum Design in Five Colors and Twenty-Four-Hour Battery Life," Apple press release, September 12, 2006, apple.com/pr/library/2006/sep/12nano.html (accessed January 30, 2009).

7. Apple, "Apple Announces Time Capsule: Wireless Backup for All Your Macs," Apple press release, January 15, 2008, apple.com/pr/library/2008/01/15timecapsule.html (accessed January 30, 2009).

8. Apple, "3G iPhone WWDC Keynote 6/9/08," Apple Keynotes, https://itunes.apple.com/us/podcast/apple-keynotes/id275834665?mt=2 (accessed January 30, 2009).

9. YouTube, "Steve Jobs Announces iTunes 8 with Genius," YouTube, September 9, 2008, youtube.com/watch?v=6XsgEH5HMvI (accessed January, 2009).

10. YouTube, "Steve Jobs CNBC Interview: Macworld 2007," YouTube, CNBC reporter Jim Goldman, youtube.com/watch?v=0mY4EIS82Jw (accessed January 30, 2009).

11. Guy Kawasaki, *The Macintosh Way* (New York: HarperCollins, 1990), 100.

Scene 3: Develop a Messianic Sense of Purpose

1. John Sculley, *Odyssey* (New York: Harper & Row, 1987), 90.

2. Alan Deutschman, *Inside Steve's Brain* (New York: Penguin Group, 2008), 168.

3. Stanford University, "'You've Got to Find What You Love,' Jobs Says," *Stanford Report*, June 14, 2005, Steve Jobs commencement address, delivered on June 12, 2005, http://news-service.stanford.edu/news/2005/june15/jobs-061505.html (accessed January 30, 2009).

4. YouTube, "Macworld Boston 1997—Full Version," YouTube, youtube.com/watch?v=PEHNrqPkefI (accessed January 30, 2009).

5. Carmine Gallo, "From Homeless to Multimillionaire," *BusinessWeek*, July 23, 2007, businessweek.com/smallbiz/content/jul2007/sb20070723_608918.htm (accessed January 30, 2009).

6. Jim Collins and Jerry Porras, *Built to Last: Successful Habits of Visionary Companies* (New York: HarperBusiness, 1994), 48.

7. *Triumph of the Nerds*, PBS documentary written and hosted by Robert X. Cringely (1996: New York).

8. Wikipedia, "Steve Jobs," includes Jobs's quote, http://en.wikiquote.org/wiki/steve_jobs (accessed January 30, 2009).

9. Malcolm Gladwell, *Outliers* (New York: Little, Brown and Company, 2008), 64.

10. John Markoff, "The Passion of Steve Jobs," *New York Times*, January 15, 2008, http://bits.blogs.nytimes.com/2008/01/15/the-passion-of-steve-jobs (accessed January 30, 2009).

11. John Paczkowski, "Bill Gates and Steve Jobs," D5 Highlights from D: All Things Digital, May 30, 2007, http://d5.allthingsd.com/20070530/d5-gates-jobs-interview (accessed January 30, 2009).

12. "Oprah," first aired on October 23, 2008, property of Harpo Productions.

13. Marcus Buckingham, *The One Thing You Need to Know* (New York: Free Press, 2005), 59.

14. Ibid., 61–62.

15. John Sculley, *Odyssey* (New York: Harper & Row, 1987), 65.

16. Smithsonian Institution, "Oral History Interview with Steve Jobs," Smithsonian Institution Oral and Video Histories—Steve Jobs, April 20, 1995, http://americanhistory.si.edu/comphist/sj1.html (accessed January 30, 2009).

17. *BusinessWeek*, "Steve Jobs: He Thinks Different," *BusinessWeek*, November 1, 2004, bloomberg.com/bw/stories/2004-10-31/steve-jobs-he-thinks-different (accessed January 30, 2009).
18. Jeff Goodell, "Steve Jobs: The *Rolling Stone* Interview," *Rolling Stone*, December 3, 2003, rollingstone.com/culture/news/steve-jobs-in-1994-the-rolling-stone-interview-20110117 (accessed January 30, 2009).
19. Jim Collins and Jerry Porras, *Built to Last: Successful Habits of Visionary Companies* (New York: HarperBusiness, 1994), 234.
20. *Triumph of the Nerds*, PBS documentary written and hosted by Robert X. Cringely (1996, New York).
21. Gary Wolf, "Steve Jobs: The Next Insanely Great Thing," *Wired*, 1996, via Wikipedia, wired.com/1996/02/jobs-2/ (accessed January 30, 2009).
22. Wikipedia, "Think Different," http://en.wikipedia.org/wiki/think_different (accessed January 30, 2009).
23. Alan Deutschman, *The Second Coming of Steve Jobs* (New York: Broadway Books, 2001), 242.
24. YouTube, "Macworld San Francisco 2007 Keynote Address," YouTube, youtube .com/watch?v=n7K3jCNxNGI (accessed January 30, 2009).

Scene 4: Create Twitter-Like Headlines

1. Vimeo, "Macworld San Francisco 2008 Keynote Address," Vimeo, vimeo.com/ 11328401 (accessed January 30, 2009).
2. Ibid.
3. Ibid.
4. CNBC, "Steve Jobs Shows off Sleek Laptop," CNBC interview after 2008 Macworld keynote, http://video.nytimes.com/video/2008/01/15/technology/1194817476407/ steve-jobs-shows-off-sleek-laptop.html (accessed January 30, 2009).
5. Ibid.
6. Apple, "Apple Introduces MacBook Air—The World's Thinnest Notebook," Apple press release, January 15, 2008, apple.com/pr/library/2008/01/15mbair.html (accessed January 30, 2009).
7. Ibid.
8. YouTube, "Macworld San Francisco 2007 Keynote Address," YouTube, youtube .com/watch?v=n7K3jCNxNGI (accessed January 30, 2009).
9. YouTube, "Steve Jobs Introduces GarageBand 1.0 (Assisted by John Mayer)," YouTube, youtube.com/watch?v=UT-rLy0CWc4 (accessed January 30, 2009).
10. YouTube, "The First iMac Introduction," YouTube, youtube.com/ watch?v=0BHPtoTctDY (accessed January 30, 2009).
11. YouTube, "Apple Music Event 2001—The First Ever iPod Introduction," YouTube, youtube.com/watch?v=kN0SVBCJqLs (accessed January 30, 2009).
12. Matthew Fordahl, "Apple's New iPod Player Puts '1,000 Songs in Your Pocket,'" Associated Press at seattlepi.com, November 1, 2001, http://seattlepi.nwsource .com/business/44900_ipod01.shtml (accessed January 30, 2009).
13. YouTube, "Macworld SF 2003 part 1," YouTube, youtube.com/watch?v= Xac6NWT7EKY (accessed January 30, 2009).
14. Apple, "Apple Unveils Keynote," Apple press release, January 7, 2003, apple.com/ pr/library/2003/jan/07keynote.html (accessed January 9, 2009).

Scene 5: Draw a Road Map

1. YouTube, "Macworld San Francisco 2007 Keynote Address," YouTube, youtube .com/watch?v=n7K3jCNxNGI (accessed January 30, 2009).

2. YouTube, "The Lost 1984 Video (The Original 1984 Macintosh Introduction)," YouTube, youtube.com/watch?v=2B-XwPjn9YY (accessed January 30, 2009).

3. YouTube, "Apple WWDC 2005—The Intel Switch Revealed," YouTube, youtube.com/watch?v=ghdTqnYnFyg (accessed January 30, 2009).

4. Michelle Kessler, "Intel vs. AMD: Better Computer Chips Raise Laptops' Abilities," *USA Today*, usatoday30.usatoday.com/tech/products/2008-07-14-intel-centrino-2-laptop-chips_N.htm (accessed January 30, 2009).

5. Edward Baig, "Windows 7 Gives Hope for Less-Bloated Operating System," *USA Today*, sec. 6B, January 22, 2009.

6. YouTube, "WWDC 2008 Keynote Address," YouTube, youtube.com/watch?v=aB2KGllkwKw (accessed January 30, 2009).

7. "Steve Ballmer and Robbie Bach Keynote: International Consumer Electronics Show 2009," remarks by Steve Ballmer and Robbie Bach at International CES 2009, January 7, 2009.

8. Vimeo, "Macworld 2008 Keynote Address," Vimeo, vimeo.com/11328401 (accessed January 30, 2009).

9. John F. Kennedy Presidential Library and Museum, "Special Message to the Congress on Urgent National Needs Page 4," President John F. Kennedy speech, May 25, 1961, jfklibrary.org/Asset-Viewer/xzw1gaeeTES6khED14P1Iw.aspx (accessed January 30, 2009).

10. American Rhetoric, "Barack Obama 2004 Democratic National Convention Keynote Address: The Audacity of Hope," July 27, 2004, americanrhetoric.com/speeches/convention2004/barackobama2004dnc.htm (accessed January 30, 2009).

11. American Rhetoric, "Barack Obama Presidential Inaugural Address: What Is Required: The Price and Promise of Citizenship," January 20, 2009, americanrhetoric.com/speeches/barackobama/barackobamainauguraladdress.htm (accessed January 30, 2009).

12. YouTube, "Apple Music Event 2001—The First Ever iPod Introduction," YouTube, youtube.com/watch?v=kN0SVBCJqLs (accessed January 30, 2009).

13. Stanford University, "'You've Got to Find What You Love,' Jobs Says," *Stanford Report*, June 14, 2005, Steve Jobs commencement address, delivered on June 12, 2005, http://news-service.stanford.edu/news/2005/june15/jobs-061505.html (accessed January 30, 2009).

14. American Rhetoric, "Jim Valvano Arthur Ashe Courage & Humanitarian Award Acceptance Address," March 4, 1993, americanrhetoric.com/speeches/jimvalvanoespyaward.htm (accessed January 30, 2009).

Scene 6: Introduce the Antagonist

1. Wikipedia, "1984 (Advertisement)," http://en.wikipedia.org/wiki/1984_ad (accessed January 30, 2009).

2. YouTube, "1983 Apple Keynote—The '1984' Ad Introduction," YouTube, youtube.com/watch?v=lSiQA6KKyJo (accessed January 30, 2009).

3. YouTube, "Macworld 2007—Steve Jobs Introduces iPhone—Part 1," YouTube, youtube.com/watch?v=Svo45oepsl0 (accessed January 30, 2009).

4. YouTube, "Steve Jobs CNBC Interview: Macworld 2007," YouTube, youtube.com/watch?v=0mY4EIS82Jw (accessed January 30, 2009).

5. Martin Lindstrom, *Buyology* (New York: Doubleday, 2008), 107.

6. Ibid.

7. John Medina, *Brain Rules* (Seattle: Pear Press, 2008), 84.
8. YouTube, "Macworld SF 2003 Part 1," YouTube, youtube.com/watch?v= Xac6NWT7EKY (accessed January 30, 2009).
9. YouTube, "TravelMuse @ DEMOfall '08 conference," YouTube, youtube .com/watch?v=L5ETATDkt0g (accessed January 30, 2009).
10. *An Inconvenient Truth*, DVD, directed by Davis Guggengeim (Hollywood: Paramount Pictures, 2006).

Scene 7: Reveal the Conquering Hero

1. YouTube, "1983 Apple Keynote," YouTube, youtube.com/watch?v= ISiQA6KKyJo (accessed January 30, 2009).
2. YouTube, "Apple Music Event 2001—The First Ever iPod Introduction," YouTube, youtube.com/watch?v=kN0SVBCJqLs (accessed January 30, 2009).
3. Mike Langberg, "Sweet & Low: Well-Designed iPod Upstarts Are Music for the Budget," *Seattle Times*, sec. C6, August 9, 2003.
4. YouTube, "Apple Get a Mac ad—Angel/Devil (2006)," YouTube, youtube .com/watch?v=zNME3SPi5vl (accessed January 30, 2009).
5. YouTube, "New iPhone Shazam Ad," YouTube, youtube.com/watch?v= P3NSsVKcrnY (accessed January 30, 2009).
6. Apple, "Why You'll Love a Mac," Get a Mac page, Apple website, apple .com (accessed January 30, 2009).
7. YouTube, "Macworld San Francisco 2006—The MacBook Pro Introduction," YouTube, youtube.com/watch?v=I6JWqllbhXE (accessed January 30, 2009).
8. Smithsonian Institution, "Oral History Interview with Steve Jobs," Smithsonian Institution Oral and Video Histories—Steve Jobs, April 20, 1995, http:// americanhistory.si.edu/comphist/sj1.html (accessed January 30, 2009).

Intermission 1: Obey the Ten-Minute Rule

1. John Medina, *Brain Rules* (Seattle: Pear Press, 2008), 74.
2. YouTube, "Macworld San Francisco 2007 Keynote Address," YouTube, youtube .com/watch?v=n7K3jGNxNGl (accessed January 30, 2009).

Scene 8: Channel Their Inner Zen

1. Rob Walker, "The Guts of a New Machine," *New York Times*, November 30, 2003, youtube.com/watch?v=n7K3jCNxNGl (accessed January 30, 2009).
2. Ibid.
3. Nancy Duarte, *Slide:ology* (Sebastopol, CA: O'Reilly Media, 2008), 93.
4. Gregory Berns, *Iconoclast* (Boston: Harvard Business Press, 2008), 36.
5. Garr Reynolds, *Presentation Zen* (Berkeley: New Riders, 2008), 68.
6. Ibid., 12.
7. Carrie Kirby and Matthew Yi, "Apple Turns Thirty: The Man Behind the Mac," SF Gate, March 26, 2006, sfgate.com/cgi-bin/article.cgi?file=/c/a/2006/03/26/ mng7ehueq51.dtl (accessed January 30, 2009).
8. Garr Reynolds, *Presentation Zen* (Berkeley: New Riders, 2008), 113.
9. Seth Godin's Blog, "Nine Steps to PowerPoint Magic," October 6, 2008, http:// sethgodin.typepad.com/seths_blog/2008/10/nine-steps-to-p.html (accessed January 30, 2008).
10. Leander Kahney, *Inside Steve's Brain* (New York: Penguin Group, 2008), 61.

11. Ibid., 60.
12. Ibid., 131.
13. Vimeo, "Macworld San Francisco 2008 Keynote Address," Vimeo, vimeo.com/ 11328401 (accessed January 30, 2009).
14. Vimeo, "Apple Special Event September 2008," Vimeo, vimeo.com/11588687 (accessed January 30, 2009).
15. Richard Mayer and Roxana Moreno, "A Cognitive Theory of Multimedia Learning: Implications for Design Principles," University of California, Santa Barbara, gustavus.edu/education/courses/edu241/mmtheory.pdf (accessed January 30, 2009).
16. *BusinessWeek*, "The Best Managers of 2008," BusinessWeek.com slide show, http:// images.businessweek.com/ss/09/01/0108_best_worst/14 .htm (accessed January 30, 2009).
17. Richard Mayer and Roxana Moreno, "A Cognitive Theory of Multimedia Learning: Implications for Design Principles," University of California, Santa Barbara, gustavus.edu/education/courses/edu241/mmtheory.pdf (accessed January 30, 2009).
18. Ibid.
19. Ibid.
20. Vimeo, "Apple Special Event September 2008," Vimeo, vimeo.com/ 11588687 (accessed January 30, 2009).
21. Garr Reynolds, *Presentation Zen* (Berkeley: New Riders, 2008), 105.
22. Nancy Duarte, *Slide:ology* (Sebastopol, CA: O'Reilly Media, 2008), 106.
23. Wikipedia, "Picture Superiority Effect," http://en.wikipedia.org/wiki/picture_ superiority_effect (accessed January 30, 2009).
24. John Medina, *Brain Rules* (Seattle: Pear Press, 2008), 234.
25. Ibid.
26. YouTube, "Apple WWDC 2008—iPhone 3G Introduction," YouTube, youtube.com/ watch?v=r7fVWjgxRwk (accessed January 30, 2009).
27. YouTube, "WWDC 2008 Keynote Address," YouTube, youtube.com/watch?v= aB2KGllkwKw (accessed January 30, 2009).
28. Plain English Campaign, "Before and After," section of site with before-and-after examples, http://s190934979.websitehome.co.uk/examples/before_and_after .html (accessed January 30, 2009).
29. Paul Arden, *It's Not How Good You Are, It's How Good You Want to Be* (London: Phaidon Press, 2003), 68.

Scene 9: Dress Up Your Numbers

1. YouTube, "Apple Music Event 2001—The First Ever iPod Introduction," YouTube, youtube.com/watch?v=kN0SVBCJqLs (accessed January 30, 2009).
2. Jeff Goodell, "Steve Jobs: The *Rolling Stone* Interview," *Rolling Stone*, December 3, 2003, rollingstone.com/culture/news/steve-jobs-in-1994-the-rolling-stone-interview-20110117 (accessed January 30, 2009).
3. YouTube, "WWDC 2008 Keynote Address," YouTube, youtube.com/watch?v= aB2KGllkwKw (accessed January 30, 2009).
4. Vimeo, "Macworld 2008 Keynote Address," Vimeo, vimeo.com/11328401 (accessed January 30, 2009).
5. John Markoff, "Burned Once, Intel Prepares New Chip Fortified by Constant Tests," *New York Times*, November 16, 2008, nytimes.com/ 2008/11/17/technology/ companies/17chip.html?_r=1&scp=1&sq= barton%20+%20intel%20&st=cse (accessed January 30, 2009).

6. IBM, "Fact Sheet and Background: Roadrunner Smashes the Petaflop Barrier," IBM press release, June 9, 2008, -03.ibm.com/press/us/en/pressrelease/24405.wss (accessed January 30, 2009).

7. Scott Duke Harris, "What Could You Buy for $700 Billion?" *San Jose Mercury News*, sec. E, October 5, 2008.

8. Cornelia Dean, "Emissions Cut Won't Bring Quick Relief," *New York Times*, sec. A21, January 27, 2009.

Scene 10: Use "Amazingly Zippy" Words

1. YouTube, "WWDC 2008 Keynote Address," YouTube, youtube.com/watch?v=aB2KGllkwKw (accessed January 30, 2009).

2. Brent Schlender and Christine Chen, "Steve Jobs's Apple Gets Way Cooler," *Fortune*, January 24, 2000, http://money.cnn.com/magazines/fortune/fortune_archive/2000/01/24/272281/index.htm (accessed January 30, 2009).

3. UsingEnglish.com, "Text Content Analysis Tool," usingenglish.com/resources/text-statistics.php (accessed January 30, 2009).

4. Todd Bishop, "Bill Gates and Steve Jobs: Keynote Text Analysis," The Microsoft Blog, January 14, 2007, http://blog.seattlepi.nwsource.com/microsoft/archives/110473.asp (accessed January 30, 2009).

5. Microsoft, "Bill Gates, Robbie Bach: 2007 International Consumer Electronics Show (CES)," Microsoft Corporation, CES, Las Vegas, January 7, 2007, news .microsoft.com/speeches/bill-gates-robbie-bach-2007-international-consumer-electronics-show-ces/ (accessed January 30, 2009).

6. YouTube, "Macworld San Francisco 2007 Keynote Address," YouTube, youtube .com/watch?v=n7K3jCNxNGI (accessed January 30, 2009).

7. Apple, "What Is Apple's Mission Statement?" Apple website: Investor Relations: FAQs: Apple Corporate Information, apple.com/investor (accessed January 30, 2009).

8. Carmine Gallo, *Ten Simple Secrets of the World's Greatest Business Communicators* (Naperville, IL: Sourcebooks, 2005), 116.

9. Ibid., 116–117.

10. Vimeo, "Macworld 2008 Keynote Address," Vimeo, vimeo.com/11328401 (accessed January 30, 2009).

11. Jack Welch, *Jack: Straight from the Gut* (New York: Warner Books, 2001), 70.

12. YouTube, "Apple Music Event 2001—The First Ever iPod Introduction," YouTube, youtube.com/watch?v=kN0SVBCJqLs (accessed January 30, 2009).

13. YouTube, "Macworld San Francisco 2003—PowerBook 17" + 12" Intro (Pt. 1)," YouTube, youtube.com/watch?v=3iGTDE9XqJU (accessed January 30, 2009).

14. Ibid.

15. YouTube, "Macworld SF 2003 Part 1," YouTube, youtube.com/watch?v= Xac6NWT7EKY (accessed January 30, 2009).

16. *Triumph of the Nerds*, PBS documentary written and hosted by Robert X. Cringely (1996, New York).

17. Peter Burrows, "Steve Jobs: The Wilderness, 1985–1997," Bloomberg, October 6, 2011, bloomberg.com/news/articles/2011-10-06/steve-jobs-the-wilderness-1985-1997 (accessed March 10, 2016).

18. Apple, "Apple Introduces New iPod Touch," Apple press release, September 9, 2008, apple.com/pr/library/2008/09/09touch.html (accessed January 30, 2009).

19. YouTube, "Macworld San Francisco 2003—PowerBook 17" + 12" Intro (Pt. 1)," YouTube, youtube.com/watch?v=3iGTDE9XqJU (accessed January 30, 2009).

20. Gregory Berns, *Iconoclast* (Boston: Harvard Business Press, 2008), 36.

Scene 11: Share the Stage

1. YouTube, "Macworld San Francisco 2006—The MacBook Pro Introduction," YouTube, youtube.com/watch?v=I6JWqllbhXE (accessed January 30, 2009).
2. YouTube, "Macworld Boston 1997—The Microsoft Deal," YouTube, youtube.com/watch?v=WxOp5mBY9IY (accessed January 30, 2009).
3. YouTube, "Steve Jobs introduces unibody MacBook Pro & MacBook—Apple Special Event," YouTube, youtube.com/watch?v=-rJRMafcRUU (accessed January 30, 2009).
4. Vimeo, "Macworld 2008 Keynote Address," Vimeo, vimeo.com/11328401 (accessed January 30, 2009).
5. Ibid.
6. YouTube, "Macworld San Francisco 2007 Keynote Address," YouTube, youtube.com/watch?v=n7K3jCNxNGI (accessed January 30, 2009).
7. Vimeo, "Macworld 2008 Keynote Address," Vimeo, vimeo.com/11328401 (accessed January 30, 2009).
8. YouTube, "Noah Wyle as Steve—EpicEmpire.com," YouTube, youtube.com/watch?v=_KRO5Hxv_No (accessed January 30, 2009).

Scene 12: Stage Your Presentation with Props

1. YouTube, "Steve Jobs introduces unibody MacBook Pro & MacBook—Apple Special Event (2008)," YouTube, youtube.com/watch?v=-rJRMafcRUU (accessed January 30, 2009).
2. Guy Kawasaki, *The Macintosh Way* (New York: HarperCollins, 1990), 149.
3. Ibid.
4. Ibid.
5. Ibid.
6. Ibid.
7. YouTube, "WWDC 2008 Keynote Address," YouTube, youtube.com/watch?v=aB2KGllkwKw (accessed January 30, 2009).
8. YouTube, "Macworld 2007—Part 4—Steve Jobs Demos the iPhone (Video)," YouTube, https://www.youtube.com/watch?v=IFmDSUIts40 (accessed January 30, 2009).
9. YouTube, "Macworld San Francisco 2007 Keynote Address," YouTube, youtube.com/watch?v=n7K3jCNxNGI (accessed January 30, 2009).
10. YouTube, "Demo of PhotoBooth (From All About Steve)," YouTube, https://www.youtube.com/watch?v=1rFV3BJqilk (accessed January 30, 2009).
11. YouTube, "Safari on Windows (WWDC 2007)," YouTube, youtube.com/watch?v=46DHMaCbdxc (accessed January 30, 2009).
12. YouTube, "Steve Jobs Keynote Macworld 2006 SF," YouTube, youtube.com/watch?v=iMDTOBsFens (accessed January 30, 2009).
13. YouTube, "Steve Jobs Introduces GarageBand 1.0 (Assisted by John Mayer)," YouTube, youtube.com/watch?v=UT-rLy0CWc4 (accessed January 30, 2009).
14. YouTube, "Apple WWDC—The Intel Switch Revealed," YouTube, youtube.com/watch?v=ghdTqnYnFyg (accessed January 30, 2009).

Scene 13: Reveal a "Holy Shit" Moment

1. Vimeo, "Macworld 2008 Keynote Address," Vimeo, vimeo.com/11328401 (accessed January 30, 2009).
2. Sasha Cavender, "Thinnest Laptop: Fits into Manila Envelope," ABC News, January 15, 2008, http://abcnews.go.com/print?id=4138633 (accessed January 30, 2009).

3. YouTube, "Steve Jobs Showcases Macintosh 24-Jan-1984," YouTube, youtube.com/watch?v=4KkENSYkMgs (accessed January 30, 2009).
4. John Medina, *Brain Rules* (Seattle: Pear Press, 2008), 81.
5. YouTube, "Apple Music Event 2001—The First Ever iPod Introduction," YouTube, youtube.com/watch?v=kN0SVBCJqLs (accessed January 30, 2009).
6. YouTube, "Macworld San Francisco 2000, Steve Jobs Become iCEO of Apple," YouTube, January 5, 2000, youtube.com/watch?v=JgHtKFuY3bE (accessed January 30, 2009).
7. YouTube, "Macworld San Francisco 2007 Keynote AddressYouTube, youtube.com/watch?v=n7K3jCNxNGI (accessed January 30, 2009).

Intermission 2: Schiller Learns from the Best

1. YouTube, "Macworld 2009 Keynote Address," YouTube, youtube.com/watch?v=DR3stDLEqxE (accessed January 30, 2009).
2. Slideshare, "Phil Schiller's Mac World 2009 Keynote Address," Slideshare, slideshare.net/kangaro10a/phil-schillers-mac-world-2009-keynote-presentation (accessed January 30, 2009).

Scene 14: Master Stage Presence

1. YouTube, "Macworld SF 2003 Part 1," YouTube, youtube.com/watch?v=Xac6NWT7EKY (accessed January 30, 2009).
2. Dan Moren, "Stan Sigman Says Sayonara," Macworld.com, October 12, 2007.
3. Gil Amelio, *On the Firing Line: My Five Hundred Days at Apple* (New York: Collins Business, 1999), 199.
4. YouTube, "Macworld San Francisco 2007 Keynote Address," YouTube, youtube.com/watch?v=n7K3jCNxNGI (accessed January 30, 2009).
5. Vimeo, "Macworld 2008 Keynote Address," Vimeo, vimeo.com/11328401 (accessed January 30, 2009).
6. YouTube, "Apple Music Event 2001—The First Ever iPod Introduction," YouTube, youtube.com/watch?v=kN0SVBCJqLs (accessed January 30, 2009).
7. Ibid.
8. Albert Mehrabian, *Silent Messages* (Stamford, CT: Wadsworth, 1980).

Scene 15: Make It *Look* Effortless

1. *BusinessWeek*, "Steve Jobs's Magic Kingdom," *BusinessWeek* cover story, February 6, 2006, bloomberg.com/news/articles/2006-02-05/steve-jobs-magic-kingdom (accessed January 30, 2009).
2. Mike Evangelist, "Behind the Magic Curtain," *Guardian*, for Guardian.co.uk, January 5, 2006, guardian.co.uk/technology/2006/jan/05/newmedia.media1 (accessed January 30, 2009).
3. Ibid.
4. Ibid.
5. Michael Krantz, "Apple and Pixar: Steve's Two Jobs," *Time*, October 18, 1999, content.time.com/time/magazine/article/0,9171,992258,00.html (accessed January 30, 2009).
6. Ibid.
7. Celia Sandys and Jonathan Littman, *We Shall Not Fail* (New York: Penguin Group, 2003), 55.
8. Alan Deutschman, *The Second Coming of Steve Jobs* (New York: Broadway Books, 2001), 82.

9. Malcolm Gladwell, *Outliers* (New York: Little, Brown and Company, 2008), 39.

10. Daniel Levitin, *This Is Your Brain on Music* (New York: Plume-Penguin, 2007), 97.

11. Malcolm Gladwell, *Outliers* (New York: Little, Brown and Company, 2008), 48.

12. *New York Times*, "Senate Confirmation Hearing: Hillary Clinton," January 13, 2009, *New York Times* transcript, nytimes.com/2009/01/13/us/politics/13text-clinton .html?pagewanted=all (accessed January 30, 2009).

Scene 16: Wear the Appropriate Costume

1. Alan Deutschman, *The Second Coming of Steve Jobs* (New York: Broadway Books, 2001), 22.

Scene 17: Toss the Script

1. Vimeo, "Macworld 2008 Keynote Address," Vimeo, vimeo.com/11328401 (accessed January 30, 2009).

2. Vanguard, ad on website, vanguard.com (accessed January 30, 2009).

3. Spymac, "Steve's Notes Closeup—Four Thousand Lattes to Go," Spymac, January 11, 2007.

4. YouTube, "Macworld San Francisco 2007 Keynote Address," Youtube, youtube .com/watch?v=n7K3jCNxNGI (accessed January 30, 2009).

Scene 18: Have Fun

1. YouTube, "Apple WWDC 2002—The Death of Mac OS 9," YouTube, youtube.com/ watch?v=Cl7xQ8i3fc0&feature=playlist&p= 72CF29777B67F776&playnext=1&index=9 (accessed January 30, 2009).

2. YouTube, "Steve Jobs, TV Jammer Story," YouTube, youtube.com/ watch?v=xiSBSXrQ8D0 (accessed January 30, 2009).

3. Ibid.

4. YouTube, "Apple Bloopers," YouTube, youtube.com/watch?v= AnVUvW42CUA (accessed January 30, 2009).

5. Vimeo, "Macworld 2008 Keynote Address," Vimeo, vimeo.com/11328401 (accessed January 30, 2009).

6. Ibid.

7. YouTube, "Apple Keynote Bloopers!!" YouTube, youtube.com/watch?v= vzDDO3Xb_QU (accessed January 30, 2009).

8. YouTube, "WWDC 2008 Keynote Address," YouTube, youtube.com/watch?v= aB2KGIlkwKw (accessed January 30, 2009).

9. YouTube, "iTunes for Windows," YouTube, October 16, 2003, youtube.com/ watch?v=iwxnWuG_Ruw (accessed January 30, 2009).

10. Nick Mediati, "Jobs Has Been an Extraordinary Spokesman," *PC World*, January 14, 2009, pcworld.com/article/157114/jobs_has_been_an _extraordinary_spokesman.html (accessed January 30, 2009).

11. Bob Dylan, "Mr. Tambourine Man," *Bringing It All Back Home*, Sony, 1965.

Encore: One More Thing

1. Stanford University, "'You've Got to Find What You Love,' Jobs Says," *Stanford Report*, June 14, 2005, Steve Jobs commencement address, delivered on June 12, 2005, http://news-service.stanford.edu/news/2005/june15/jobs-061505.html (accessed January 30, 2009).

Postscript: Steve Jobs by the Book

1. YouTube, "Apple iPad Event Part 2 of 10 (HD)," YouTube, http://www.you tube.com/watch?v=LK_VunL9rjY&feature=related (accessed June 6, 2011).
2. Ibid.
3. Ibid.
4. Ibid.
5. YouTube, "Apple WWDC 2010 Keynote Address," YouTube, youtube.com/watch?v=AmXc1Mjr5J4 (accessed June 6, 2011).
6. Ibid.
7. Ibid.
8. YouTube, "Apple iPad 2 Keynote, Special Event, March 2011," YouTube, youtube.com/watch?v=TGxEQhdi1AQ (accessed June 6, 2011).
9. Ibid.
10. Ibid.
11. Ibid.
12. Ibid.
13. Apple, "Apple-Special Event," Apple Events, June 6, 2011, http://events.apple.com.edgesuite.net/11piubpwiqubf06/event/ (accessed June 6, 2011).

INDEX

Revealing the Other Secrets of Steve Jobs

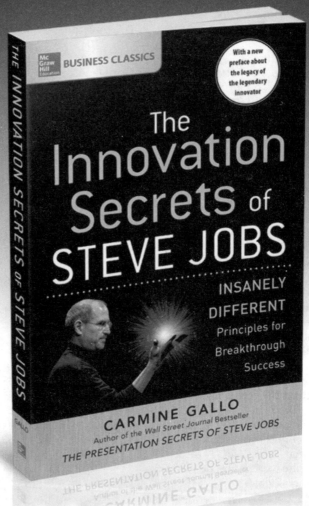

Bestselling author Carmine Gallo shares effective strategies for sparking true creativity—and real innovation—in any workplace. Pick up your copy of *The Innovation Secrets of Steve Jobs* for the simple, meaningful, and attainable principles that drive us all to "Think Different."